D1221683

CHICAGO STUDIES IN THE
HISTORY OF AMERICAN RELIGION

Editors

JERALD C. BRAUER

AND MARTIN E. MARTY

A CARLSON PUBLISHING SERIES

For a complete listing of the titles in this series,
please see the back of this book.

In America the Men Milk the Cows

FACTORS OF GENDER, ETHNICITY, AND RELIGION IN THE AMERICANIZATION OF NORWEGIAN-AMERICAN WOMEN

L. DeAne Lagerquist

PREFACE BY MARTIN E. MARTY

CARLSON
Publishing Inc

BROOKLYN, NEW YORK, 1991

Please see the end of this volume for a listing of all the titles in the Carlson Publishing Series *Chicago Studies in the History of American Religion*, edited by Jerald C. Brauer and Martin E. Marty, of which this is Volume 12.

Library of Congress Cataloging-in-Publication Data

Lagerquist, L. DeAne.
    In America the men milk the cows : factors of gender, ethnicity, and religion in the Americanization of Norwegian-American women / L. DeAne Lagerquist ; preface by Martin E. Marty.
        p.   cm. — (Chicago studies in the history of American religion ; 12)
        Includes bibliographical references and index.
        ISBN 0-926019-49-X
        1. Norwegian American women—Middle West—Social conditions.
        2. Norwegian American women—Middle West—Religious life.
        3. Americanization. I. Title. II. Series.
        F358.2.S2L34 1991
        305.48'83982—dc20   91-26844

Typographic design: Julian Waters

Typeface: Bitstream ITC Galliard

Case design: Alison Lew

Index prepared by Scholars Editorial Services, Inc., Madison, Wisconsin, using NL Cindex, a scholarly indexing program from the Newberry Library.

Printed on acid-free, 250-year-life paper.

Manufactured in the United States of America.

Contents

An Introduction to the Series

The *Chicago Studies in the History of American Religion* is a series of books that deal with topics ranging from the time of Jonathan Edwards to the 1970s. Three or four deal with colonial topics and three or four treat the very recent past. About half of them focus on the decades just before and after 1900. One deals with blacks; two concentrate on women. Revivalists, fundamentalists, theologians, life in the suburbs and life in heaven and hell, the Beecher family of old and a monk of new times, Catholics adapting to America and Protestants fighting one another—all these subjects assure that the series has scope. People of every kind of taste and curiosity about American religion will find some books to suit them. Does anything serve to characterize the series as a whole? What does the stamp of "Chicago studies" mean?

Yale historian Sydney Ahlstrom in *A Religious History of the American People*, as influential as any twentieth-century work in its field, pays respect to the "Chicago School" of American religious historians. William Warren Sweet, the pioneer in such studies (beginning in 1927) at Chicago and, in many ways, in America at large represented the culmination of "the Protestant synthesis" in this field. Ahlstrom went on to name two later generations of Chicagoans, including the seminal Sidney E. Mead and major figures like Robert T. Handy and Winthrop Hudson and ending with the two editors of this series. He saw them as often "openly rebellious" in respect to Sweet and his synthesis.

If, as Ahlstrom says, "a disproportionate number" of historians have some connection with the Chicago School, it must be said that the new generation represented in these twenty-one books carries on both the lineage of Sweet and something of the "openly rebellious" character that scholars at Chicago are encouraged to pursue. This means, for one thing, that the "Protestant synthesis" does not characterize their work. These historians question the canon of historical writing produced in the Protestant era even as many of them continue to pursue themes shaped in a Protestant culture. Few of them concentrate on the old "frontier thesis" that marked the early years of the school. The shift for most has been toward the urban and pluralist scene. They call into question, not in devastating rage but in steady patterns of inquiry, the received wisdom about who matters, and why, in American religion.

So it is that this series of books focuses on blacks, women, dispensationalists, suburbanites, members of "marginal" denominations, "ethnics" and immigrants as readily as it does on white men of progressive urban bent in mainstream denominations and of long standing in America. The authors relish religious diversity and enjoy discovering the power of people once considered weak, the centrality to the American plot of those once regarded as peripheral, and the potency of losers who were once disdained by winners. Thus this series enhances an understanding of an America overlooked by the people of Sweet's era two-thirds of a century ago when it all, or most of it, began.

Rebellion for its own sake would not long hold interest; it might tell more about the psychology of rebels and revisers than about their subject matter. Revision, better than rebellion, characterizes the scholars. Re+vision: that's it. There was an original vision that characterized the Chicago School. This was the contention that in secular America and its universities religion mattered, as a theme in the national past and as a presence in the present. Second, it argued that the study of religious history belonged not only in the seminaries and archives of denominations, but also in the rough-and-tumble of the secular university, where no religious meanings were privileged and where each historian had to make a case for the value of his or her story.

Other assumptions from the earliest days pervade the books in this series. They are uncommonly alert to the environment in which expressions of faith occur. That is, they do not take for granted that religion comes protected in self-evidently important and hermetically sealed packages. Churches and denominations are porous, even when they would be sealed off; they cannot be understood apart from the ways the social environs effect them, but their power to effect change in the environment demands equal and truly unapologetic treatment. These writers do not shuffle and mumble and make excuses for their existence or for the choice of apparently arcane subject matter. They try to present their narrative in such ways that they compel attention.

A fourth characteristic that colors these works is a refusal in most cases to be typed in a fashionable slot labeled, variously, "intellectual" or "institutional" history, "cultural" or "social" history, or whatever. While those which concentrate on magisterial thinkers such as Jonathan Edwards are necessarily busy with and devoted to his intellectual achievement, most of the books deal with figures who cannot be understood only as exemplars in a sequence of studies of "the life of the mind." Instead, their biographies and circumstances come very much into play. On the other hand, none of these writers is a reductionist who sees religion as "nothing but" this or that—"nothing but" the working out of believers' Oedipal urges or expressing the economic and class interests of the subjects. Social history becomes in its way intellectual history, even if the intellects are focused on something other than the theologians in the traditions might like to see.

Some years ago *Look* magazine interviewed leaders in various denominations. One was asked if his fellow believers considered that theirs was the only true faith. Yes, he said, but they did not believe that they were the only ones who held it. The editors of this series of studies and the contributors to it do not believe that the "Chicago School," whenever and whatever it was, is the only true approach to American religious history. And, if they did, they would not hold that Chicagoans alone held it. To do so would imply a strange solipsistic or narcissistic impulse that would be the death of collegiality in the historical field. They have welcomed the chance to be in a climate where their inquiries are given such encouragement, where they find a company of fellow scholars in the Divinity School, the History Department, and the Committee on the History of Culture, whence these studies first emerged, and elsewhere in a university that provides a congenial home for massed and massive concentration of a special sort on American religious history.

While the undersigned have been consistently involved, most often together, in all twenty-one books, we want to single out a third person mentioned in so many acknowledgment sections, historian Arthur Mann. He has been a partner in two or three dozen religious history dissertation projects through the years and has been an influential and decisive contributor to the results. We stand in his debt.

Jerald C. Brauer
Martin E. Marty

Editor's Preface

New England men have histories; Minnesota women do not. Southern generals deserve notice, northern homemakers and schoolteachers do not. Congregationalist religion matters, Lutheran piety does not. To mention such contrasts so boldly is to expose instincts that become prejudices. Of course, most people when challenged would be reluctant to make such contrasts, at least not so starkly. In theory we are democrats who believe in the value of lives of ordinary people. But ordinary people do not characteristically have the instruments or outlets for self-expression to make themselves interesting to others. One has to go digging.

L. DeAne Lagerquist has done some digging among upper Midwest Lutheran women, homemakers and schoolteachers, spouses and singles, and found them to be, or made them, "interesting." Along the way she gives some clues as to why certain people have histories, deserve notice, or matter, and others do not. Historians depend on records, and New England men left them in abundance. They were articulate, established, well-positioned. Their sermons and laws are leather-bound, available to anyone who gets a grant to a research library. Southern generals left enough dead bodies and occasioned enough myths that one knows right off that they made a difference and have to be studied. Congregationalist theologians in earlier America gave definitions to New England life off which novelists and lawmakers lived into the present.

The challenge to bring to view the lives of people in *local* institutions, *ordinary people*, whose *personal lives* make up *social history* in *feminist history* contexts and *ethnic* orbits—I am borrowing the italics from Lagerquist—is enormous. At first glance the life of a local congregation, an apparently nondescript invention that matters only to locals, seems beside the point. Ordinary people leave few traces or marks; they often bore us while alive. Why bother with them later? Personal lives attract us if they belong to television or rock stars, automakers, cheaters, and presidents, not diarists in parsonages and woebegone places. Social history is popular these years, but also more popular with producers than readers; it can bore one. Feminism can be a cause of an elite of women, ignored by other women who find its advocates strident or by men who would rather you did not bring up the subject. Ethnicity? It certainly leaves a stamp on American communities, but it can be overdone.

All those dismissals are likely to cross the mind of busy people who have to make choices in their reading. If by doing so they pass up *In America the Men Milk the Cows*, however, they are going to miss a revealing set of pieces in the American mosaic. One need not make the case that the women of Lagerquist's study are more important than southern women, Hawaiian mothers, or Pentecostals to make a case for this careful book. With great patience she has worked through archives of people whose voices were *almost* lost to history. With discernment she has found significances in the traces they often casually left for their descendants. Without ideology—feminist or religious or ethnic —she has paid attention to their ideas and practical existences.

What is especially appealing is the fact that she was able to bring coherence to her disparate materials by finding that the women she studied did make a contribution in the form of a distinctive practical piety that characterizes and challenges the lives of so many who, in later generations, would not find it easy to empathize with them. These women at the turn of the century lived such constrained, one is tempted to say "cooped up," lives that they hardly seem to be exemplars of anything except what one would escape. Not so, says Lagerquist, who deals with them as intrinsically valuable persons and lets their integrity make its own case. The reader is likely to become more patient with and curious about the quiet lives of any number of other people of the past after meeting the unambitious and unsuspecting heroines Lagerquist has discovered and here presents.

Martin E. Marty

Acknowledgments

Anyone remotely connected with the Divinity School at the University of Chicago is acutely aware that the road to a Ph.D. is well punctuated. Often these markers are described as "hoops" to be jumped; occasionally they are identified more neutrally as steps or landmarks. What is less frequently articulated and perhaps more significant is that the path is also populated by other travelers. Without these people, no one would ever reach the end, nor would the journey be as pleasant. As I near the end of the path to my Ph.D. I am all the more grateful for the company I have enjoyed along the way.

One's teachers are, of course, primary among those one meets. Marty E. Marty, my adviser, has given me his confidence and the benefits of his vast knowledge from the day that I met him. Jerald Brauer and Kathleen Neils Conzen, the other members of my dissertation committee, have each given their support and have stimulated my interests. Two other members of the University of Chicago faculty must also be mentioned. Anne Carr has given me (and many other students) encouragement and a model of a teacher who is kind, knowledgeable, and a companion in learning. Arthur Mann, truly a gentleman and a scholar, inspired me to strive for both human courtesy and academic integrity in my scholarship.

Among students it is more difficult to select whom to mention. Those named here, both individuals and groups, know what they contributed: Jim Brandt and Heidi Peterson, Janet Summers, Charlie Headington, Ed Queen, and the other members of our dissertation support group, the Divinity School Women's Caucus and its Ladies' Auxiliary, the "Lutheran Women's Mafia," Mary Ingeborg, Jane Strohl, and the men's intramural basketball team and its fans.

Beyond the boundaries of Hyde Park there are many people to be thanked. Perhaps my family and friends who are not engaged in this sort of work are most to be thanked for their willingness to listen and for taking it all seriously. My parents accepted my decision to keep studying as a matter of course and thereby made it seem possible. My brothers remind me that there is more to life than books and more ways to see life than mine. Joel gave me a Compaq, an indispensable tool, as a "helping you to finish" present. It worked.

Connections with friends and colleagues in other places have been important: among them are Brit Berggreen, Gracia Grindal, Carol Thysell, Nan Knutsen, and Joan Gunderson. I have been fortunate to find very gracious librarians and archivists everywhere I worked. The staff at Luther Northwestern Library is always accommodating. Paul Daniels, American Lutheran Church archivist, has been consistently helpful and interested.

In the final months of putting this dissertation together I have had the joy of being a part of Valparaiso University. My colleagues in the Department of Theology and throughout the university have shown me what lies beyond the degree. They confirm that the journey is worthwhile. Gail McGrew Eifrig has been kindness and wisdom itself. By inviting me into the university and into her own life she has helped me to make this a home. Mike Gee has cheerfully and competently assisted in getting the words off the disks and on paper. Richard Dunning has brought calmness, companionship, and much happiness to my life.

In America the Men Milk the Cows

Introduction

> Now, Marie, you see how we live in a Norwegian parsonage, but do not try to
> pattern your parsonage after this one. We are used to it in Norway and could
> not change, but it is not practical here in America.
>
> Cathinka Otteson

This advice was given by *Fru* Cathinka Tank Doderlein Otteson, mistress
of the Koshkonong parsonage in the 1870s, to a young woman soon to be
a pastor's wife. *Fru* Otteson's comment expressed the inevitability of changes
in women's lives when they moved from Norway to the United States. Much
more was involved than geography; it changed their notions of who they
were. Both intentional and unconscious adaptations were made in home life
and in religion. Personal relationships and contacts beyond the home and
church were also altered.

This transition, however, was far smoother than I anticipated. In their own
accounts, Norwegian women who belonged to Lutheran churches in the
United States gave very few hints that their transition to American ways
caused them any unusual or remarkable pain. *In America Men Milk the Cows*
is about Norwegian-American Lutheran women as they encounter new
situations in the United States and discover what is "practical here in America."

I consider them as a subgroup within three larger groups: Norwegian-
Americans, Christians (specifically, Lutherans who were associated with
congregations), and women. In doing this I am mindful of an aphorism
Martin Marty once dropped into a seminar discussion: If the people you are
writing about don't recognize themselves, you've probably missed them. In
this project I listen to the women's voices and watch their actions so that I
may portray them in a way that they would recognize as individuals and as a
group. The image I present is better compared with one made by a genre
painter, such as Harriet Backer, than with the one made by a mirror. Backer
was judged to be one of Norway's greatest colorists. Among her subjects were
women's daily activities from bleaching woolen cloth in the sun to an infant's

1

baptism. The artist's representation is true to her subject; she enriches the subject rather than merely reflecting it.

In my investigation into the identities of these women I ask questions posed by three sorts of history: religious, feminist, and ethnic. This triple lens is not accidental; it is the result of my conviction that because people, about whom historians write, are members of more than one group, the historian must observe them from as many angles and perspectives as possible. A true image, one the people being studied would recognize, requires this multiple-lens approach. The lenses are focused on four aspects of the women's identity: ethnicity, nationality, religion, and gender. Of these, nationality receives the least direct attention despite the underlying assumption that the process of becoming American entails much more than taking out citizenship papers. It is this process that provides the occasion for everything else this study is about. I am not only asking the questions of religious, feminist, and ethnic history, I am engaged in the "doing" of them.

My "doing" of religious history is directed by an additional conviction that religious history is enriched by attention to elements of the church that have until recently been neglected. Three such aspects of the church and its history are highlighted in this study. The first is the church's character as a *local* institution. Despite the conventional focus of scholars on doctrinal and large-scale institutional religious history, it is the local unit, the congregation, that is the setting for much of the church's life and that is the form most familiar to multitudes of Christians from the days of the apostles to the present. Throughout the changing fortunes of Christianity the congregation remains a basic unit of the church. Although it is certainly true that the church has been expanded by action from the top, that expansion takes place in the formation of new congregations. In the specific case of Norwegian-American Lutheranism, the church was first organized in local congregations, which were later united into larger units—synods, conferences, etc.

The *ordinary people* who are the church's membership are the second aspect highlighted here. The church's history is the history of these "people in the pews" as much as it is the history of the hierarchies. The laypeople are the very ones for whom the local church *is the church*. Their intercongregational contacts are exceptional, not daily or even regular, events. While this is true for a sizable portion of the laity, it has been particularly so for the female laity, who were ineligible to serve as delegates to meetings and conferences. Their own organizations were formed at the local level and were not joined beyond the parish boundaries until the turn of the century. Their experience of the church was firmly set in the context of their lives in their local community and families.

The third aspect is the church's involvement in the *personal lives* of its members. To understand the church requires attention to how it is intertwined with the lives of its people beyond the walls of the church building and outside the hours of worship. How does the church contribute to its members' self- and group identity? How does it shape their worldview? Does it give meaning to their activities and the events of their lives?

To ask these questions and to take account of the localness of the church, of the ordinary people who belong to it, and of the personal lives of those members is to take up the *social history* of the church. Scholars have only recently turned their research to this aspect of religious history. Lutheran historians have hardly glanced at the social elements of Lutheranism; the little that is published is more in the genre of family storytelling than of critical scholarship. The history of the laity and of the congregations is almost untold. The history of women is missing from denominational volumes.[1]

The approach of social history does not imply either skepticism about the members' faith or disdain for doctrinal and institutional history. Rather, it is an effort to expand and enrich those stories with the personal stories of ordinary people who are part of the local manifestations of the church. Indeed, in this study I use doctrine as a key to interpreting the social factors of church history. This action does not require that the people have articulated their experience in these terms; it does assume that there is continuity between the formal doctrines of a community and the lived faith of its members even if it is not expressed by the believers.

Feminist history is the second sort that informs and is being "done" in *In America the Men Milk the Cows*. It has developed in the past two decades from the dual impulse of twentieth-century feminism and a more general interest in people's history. Two historiographic issues are of central concern to feminist historians.[2] On what basis is a topic (event, person, group, etc.) judged to be "historically significant" or "interesting" and thus worthy of investigation? What role have women played in the past and how is that role to be interpreted?

The contemporary slogan, "The personal is political," has a historical application: the activities of women are worthy of scholarly investigation regardless of their impact on the "public" world. In the case of religious history, women's activities and experiences are worthy of investigation regardless of their influence on doctrine or polity, either in the arena of the

3

congregation or that of the larger church. The fact that women have had limited opportunities to make extralocal contacts in the church and limited opportunities to assume leadership roles beyond women's groups means that my decision to study women reinforces my desire to consider the local and personal aspects of religious history.

In determining the role women have played, feminist historians are also concerned with providing the formerly unheard actors of history with opportunities to speak. Women's roles cannot be adequately considered on the sole basis of reports by men and institutional statements that prescribe for women. Only after hearing both what women have done (rather than what they have been told to do) and how they (rather than those observing them) have assessed their experiences can a historian discuss what women's role was and interpret it.

Religious historians have provided women with very few opportunities to speak about their vigorous participation in the church's life or about how the church has enhanced or limited their lives.[3] The standard histories of American Lutheranism devote a very small number of their sentences to women and fewer paragraphs or pages. The published diaries of the wives of two patriarchs of Norwegian-American Lutheranism have insured that they and their sister-colleagues in pioneer parsonages have not been entirely neglected, but they have not led to a full consideration of their activities or those of women in lay families.[4]

Congregational historians, some of them women, have been more attentive to the role women have played in their churches' histories. Given that the arena of women's church life was local, this ought not be surprising. Anniversary histories usually include a section on the "Ladies' Aid," which praises their devotion to the church and their hard work on its behalf. The women's societies seldom kept detailed minutes; their histories were recorded instead in the memories of the members. In the early decades of the twentieth century many local groups preserved those memories in handwritten or typescript histories, which are now housed in the Region III, Evangelical Lutheran Church of America archive in St. Paul, Minnesota.

By combining the perspectives of feminist history and religious history I am able to provide a more richly textured account of both the churches and the women. The contributions women have made to their congregations and to the denominations come into higher relief. Listening to the women's own accounts prevents any easy conclusions about how "good" or how "bad" religion was for women. Perhaps those women who found this religion constricting of their femaleness or of their desire to move fully into their American environment left Norwegian Lutheranism. Those who remained, and who are the subject of this study, assessed the value of their beliefs and their involvement in congregations and women's groups in a generally positive way. This witness from the women themselves cannot be ignored by contemporary historians who find Christianity less attractive and might prefer to portray it as a web of exclusion and confinement. The contributions that Norwegian Lutheranism made to the women are a part of the story, as are the limitations it imposed on them.

The third sort of history done here is *ethnic*: the history of Norwegian-Americans. Norwegian-Americans have been careful stewards of their heritage. They were one of the first ethnic groups to form a historical society. The archive of the Norwegian-American Historical Association and its publications are highly esteemed. Their work has been supported by professional scholars and skilled amateurs. Consequently, Norwegian-American history has its own rich historiography and fine studies of language, settlement, and other aspects of immigration and adaptation. The close ties between Norwegian-Americans and Lutheranism have been carefully recorded.[5] Unfortunately, Norwegian-American ethnic history (and that of other Scandinavian-American groups to some degree) has been "the victim of its early success."[6] Its own richness, its own publications, its own academic home in Scandinavian studies programs isolated its students from conversation with other ethnic and social historians.

It should also be noted that historians of Italian-Americans, Irish-Americans, and Jewish-Americans (for example) seldom thought of initiating such a conversation. Their lack of initiative was, conceivably, the result of their preoccupation with urban settings and with "less assimilated" groups. Scandinavians were perceived to be rural and, from the nineteenth century forward, as having an outstanding ability to assimilate. The first assumption is true. Norwegians in particular were one of the most rural of all immigrant groups despite significant communities in Minneapolis, Chicago, Brooklyn, and Seattle. However, the second assumption is false. Norwegian-Americans provide an excellent opportunity to study ethnic retention.

Norwegian-American historians have also been relatively isolated from interaction with women's historians. Articles in *Norwegian-American Studies and Records* that consider women have been primarily reminiscences.[7] "Scandinavians and Other Immigrants in Urban America," a major conference at St. Olaf College in 1984, had no papers addressed to women's topics, nor did most of the papers reflect familiarity with the issues raised by feminist

5

historians who study other ethnic groups or native, white women.[8] The critical work that has been done on women within the Norwegian-American community is almost entirely unpublished.[9]

Norwegian-Americans' tenacious hold on their ethnic heritage cannot be attributed to any one factor. The timing of immigration, which coincided with Norwegian nationalism related to the end of the Kalmar Union and progress toward complete independence in the early 1900s, sharpened ethnic self-awareness. Settlement in relatively dense clusters allowed immigrants and their children to maintain their dialects, to marry within the ethnic community, and otherwise to reinforce their identity as Norwegians. The close association of nationality with the state Lutheran church in Norway was imported to the United States, where it was transformed into a similar association of Norwegian-American ethnicity with Lutheranism. The part played by the numerous Norwegian-Lutheran institutions—congregations, synods, publications, schools—must be given a large share of the responsibility.

The close association of Norwegian ethnicity with Lutheranism requires that any student of Norwegian-American women will also become a student of religion, even if the scholar is not initially interested in religious history. Similarly, any study of Lutheran women in the United States, as of Lutheranism, must take account of ethnicity. Here those women who are members of both groups—Norwegian-Americans and Lutherans—are the focus.

The triple lenses of religious history, feminist history, and ethnic history provide perspectives that are sensitive to religion, gender, and ethnicity. All three factors contribute to the identities of the women I study. Returning to the figure of the historian as artist, I then paint the women in three settings: their homes, their local congregations and women's societies, and the educational institutions and ministry of their churches. In each arena their experiences and responses were filtered through the expectations of each group to which they belonged. The process of becoming Norwegian-Americans took place in each of these settings as women learned to combine familiar housekeeping techniques with new materials, as they formed women's societies within voluntary congregations, and as they took an active part in the educational system that was closely affiliated with their religious and ethnic community.

In this book I draw upon several types of materials: published journals, letters, and reminiscences written by first-generation immigrant women or by their children; personal and institutional papers held by archives; local congregational anniversary histories and records; and records of congregational and federated women's societies. In all but the first category, the sources I use are only samples of the large quantity available. As this is in some sense a groundbreaking study, I have attempted to place materials together in a way that is illuminating for the topic under consideration and suggestive of topics for further investigation. Although these materials do not yield data that are readily quantified, other sources are available. Thus, this should be seen as a mere beginning, which can draw others to a field open for homesteading.

This is not a complete study of all women who have shared Norwegian-American Lutheran identity. Geographically, I focus on the rural, upper Midwest, which includes the three major areas of Norwegian settlement. While I concentrate on Wisconsin and Minnesota, I include some women who lived in Iowa and the Dakotas. A complete study would include women who lived in other regions of the United States such as the Norwegian settlements in Texas and in urban areas such as Minneapolis, Chicago, Brooklyn, and Seattle. My decision to use literary and primarily "churchly" sources rather than quantitative or secular sources further defines which women are included. These sorts of materials are particularly rich for clerical families, especially from those in the old Norwegian Synod. Church-related activities are more fully reported than any others. For example, only the most minimal references are made to reform work, while a great deal is made of missions. A study using other types of sources and methods of investigation would include other women and reveal aspects of their lives and types of activities which do not emerge here.

I observe the process of adaptation to the United States over the period of three-quarters of a century, beginning with the arrival of the Preuses, the Korens, and the Munchs prior to the American Civil War and continuing into the first years after the Norwegian Lutheran Church in America formed in 1917. In this regard my study is comprehensive. It includes all three waves of Norwegian immigration (1866-1873, 1880-1893, and 1900-1910) and at least three generations of women.[10] This time span is important from the perspective of both women's and ethnic history.

The cycle of women's lives is significant to their experience and to their perceptions of their surroundings. In each phase of her life a woman's role changes—from that of a young girl, to that of an unmarried women, to that of a bride, to that of a mother, to that of a grandmother, to that of a widow.[11] To freeze the frame at one point in the film of a woman's life and observe that moment or year or phase is not to see the whole of her life.

7

Women's personal views changed over time. The response of a young, single woman to the frontier might have been quite different from her feeling about it years later when she was the mature mother of an established family. The time of life in which a woman encountered the New World and its many opportunities and challenges influenced her reactions. A young single woman of "good family," such as Karine Neuberg, had a distinctly different response from that of the middle-aged mother of several children, such as Thorild Oleson. Similarly, those women who were born in the United States experienced being an American and being Norwegian in a way that their mothers did not.[12] A daughter took for granted the wooden floor for which her mother longed, and she learned to speak English from her schooldays. Thus I attempt to consider women in several phases of life even when it is not possible to follow one woman through her entire life.

From the perspective of ethnic history, the duration of this study is significant for the changes that took place in both Norway and the United States and for the development of the Norwegian-American community. The conditions that promoted immigration continued to change on both sides of the Atlantic. Modernization was accelerating in Norway as well as in the United States. The length of the period I consider allows some small attention to the variations this brought about in women's initial responses to the New World. During those seventy-five years Norwegian immigrants to the United States became Norwegian-Americans. I give more attention to generational shifts among women while this process was underway than to the changes in initial responses.

While ethnicity continued to be a strong factor, it was fluid.[13] Its expressions changed, as did the value placed on it. Gradually immigrants came to think of themselves as Norwegians as well as in terms of their original region of origin, Throndheim or Hardanger, for example. Naming patterns and language use also indicated adaptation to their American home.[14] Their diet and clothing styles became increasingly like those of Yankees. Changes in social roles and material expectations that had begun in Norway were continued in the United States. The ties of biological families became tighter and the importance of affection, even romance, in marriages increased. Women and men continued to work hard for the benefit of their household, but the specific tasks assigned on the basis of gender shifted somewhat, as did the image of ideal female behavior. Writers of letters back to Norway remarked that in a reversal of the pattern they had known, "in America the men milk the cows." As the title of this volume, this observation stands for the many shifts in behavior and attitude that were part of becoming American.

Some of these changes were linked as much to modernization as to Americanization.[15] Similar dynamics were at work in Norway. There too choices multiplied in the late nineteenth and early twentieth centuries. Technology made great leaps forward. Agricultural and fishing methods were standardized and farm products were placed in the commercial marketplace. Political activity was opened to an expanding group of people. Thus those Norwegians who did not immigrate but who were confronted by the modernizing world in their homeland made adaptations that were not unlike those made by their countryfolk across the Atlantic.

The Lutheran church played a notable role in the process of adaptation for those who did immigrate. It provided a place in which familiar sorts of people engaged in familiar activities in a familiar language. The divisions within the Norwegian Lutheran church forced members to make choices and allowed them to do so without leaving their ethnic community. At the same time, the church institutions and their leaders provided a mediated contact with American culture and eased the members' transition. It delayed the inevitable turn to English. It provided an ethnoreligious education parallel or supplementary to that given by the American public schools. It gave explicit and implicit guidance as to appropriate responses to the issues of the day. The guidance was sometimes rejected, as in the case of the Norwegian Synod clergy's position on slavery. In other cases the churches' positions were more influential, if perhaps also more subtle. For example, the clergy-folk may have exposed their "peasant" parishioners to social standards that were compatible with those of Yankees and thereby have given permission for adoption of similar standards.

This brings me to my thesis: As these Norwegian immigrant women and their daughters and granddaughters became Americans they adopted notions of female behavior that were appropriate to modernizing America, but these ideas were mediated through their continued sense of ethnic distinctiveness, which was supported by membership in Norwegian Lutheran churches and participation in the activities and institutions of those churches. As I indicated at the outset, the transition appears to have been less difficult and dramatic than I had anticipated on the basis of standard portrayals of the internal disputes of Norwegian-American Lutheranism and the novelistic accounts of immigrant life given by Ole Rölvaag, Martha Ostenso, and others.

These sorts of sources suggested that I would find intense religious contentiousness and psychological distress; neither of these is characteristic of the people I have studied nor of the materials I have read. I found that the effects of America seem to have been more material and external than psychological and intense. If conflicts took place, women did not mull them over or record them in detail. Fragments of evidence suggest that there were problems; however, rather than probing the sources of their problems, women seem to have closed around them as a tree grows around a nail hammered into its trunk. These observations appear to confirm stereotypical assumptions about the Norwegian and Norwegian-American personality and behavior patterns.[16]

In the face of such evidence I must emphasize that I have considered primarily women who were active participants in congregations and who were often members of women's societies. Frequently these women were members of the leadership families of the national church bodies. The sources I have consulted were usually produced for a public audience, whether that was the woman's family and neighbors in Norway, the members of the organization whose history was being summarized, or the author's children and grandchildren. These are not the sorts of women who were likely to have articulated dissatisfaction nor the kinds of materials that are most likely to preserve "unpleasant" evidence.

I employ a descriptive style that provides a narrative account of the experiences of Norwegian women who immigrated to the United States and there joined Lutheran congregations and of the experiences of their American-born daughters and granddaughters. I begin with two background chapters. In the first I consider the Norwegian social and religious situation from which these women came; in the second I take up the process of immigration, settlement, and formation of religious institutions in a general way. In the following three chapters I focus more narrowly on women in various settings, which move out from the individual in concentric circles of increasing size. The setting of Chapter Three is the domestic realm encompassing the trip to America, household activities both on farms and in parsonages, and familial relationships. Women's religious experience—in congregations, personally, and in women's groups—comprise the setting of Chapter Four. In Chapter Five I expand the scale of the church beyond the local to include women's activities in church-operated postelementary schools and as professional church workers, specifically as teachers, deaconesses, and missionaries. In a concluding section I reflect upon the interaction of gender, ethnicity, and religion as these factors contribute to the process of adaptation to modernizing America and maintenance of a continued sense of ethnic distinctiveness.

From Luther's explanation to the third petition of the Lord's Prayer in the *Small Catechism* Lutherans learn that God's will is done with or without the prayers of Christians; they also learn that they pray that it might be done in their community. The divine will is done when faith is strengthened and the people stay firm in God's Word. As God provides the believers with daily bread, "everything needed for this life," forgives them, and protects them their faith is strengthened. The *Catechism* was an essential part of religious education in Norwegian-American Lutheran churches. Its words were familiar to the women I study here. Their lives are well understood as a prayer that God's will be done among them.

Since I completed this work my research has continued to explore topics and approaches that are part of *In America the Men Milk the Cows*. At the request of the American Lutheran Church Women I collaborated with several researchers to investigate that organization and its predecessor bodies. *From Our Mothers' Arms*, the resulting book, considers a larger group of women, including Danes, Germans, and women of color, over a longer time span, but in a more narrowly defined segment of their lives. It focused almost entirely on women's organizations and women's churchly ministries as missionaries, deaconesses, and pastors. As part of the Congregational History Project (sponsored by the Lilley Endowment, housed at the Divinity School of the University of Chicago), I pursued the study of local religious organizations, giving particular attention in my work to the ways congregations shape identity. Ethnicity and gender were both factors, but others—such as class, race, and sexuality—also appear in my essay. Third, I am currently at work on a history of American Lutheranism. It will be significantly influenced by my earlier beginning point: the personal lives of ordinary people in local institutions.

ONE

The Norwegian Situation

Some acquaintance with immigrants' background and with the situation from which they came is a necessary prerequisite to understanding an immigrant community. Knowledge of the sorts of conditions they left and their reasons for leaving as well as of the sorts of expectations and customs they brought with them enriches discussions of what immigrants found in their new setting and how they adapted to it.[1] The Norway of this book was an emerging nation just coming to political maturity. B. J. Hovde described the years 1720-1865 in Scandinavia as the age of transition. In 1814 Norway escaped from a centuries-long, unequal yoking with Denmark only to be thrust into another unsatisfactory linkage with Sweden. In 1905 national autonomy was achieved. In the years between these two events the Norwegian people's sense of their national identity expanded and they entered into the international community. Social and cultural shifts kept pace with the political. The religious situation and the relation between the sexes are of particular importance as background for this study.[2]

Social Life and Gender in Nineteenth-Century Norway

Life in nineteenth-century Norway was being transformed in nearly all its aspects.[3] In the early years and at midcentury, religious revivals swept the country. Growing political consciousness and national autonomy were echoed among the common people and supported by popular nationalism. Romantic fondness for all things Norwegian combined with a desire for modernization and participation in the European community as a mature country. The economy of the household shifted from subsistence to participation in the marketplace. Industrialization commenced with commensurate changes in transportation and residence. These changes took place in Norway slightly later than in other parts of Europe; consequently, an alliance of romanticism and early ethnology preserved rich documentation of the shifts.

Far to the north and isolated from France and England, Norway never developed a feudal system such as was present in those areas. Its topography was unsuited to large manors. In 1349 a plague decimated the population; the hereditary aristocracy was particularly hard hit. Half a century later a dynastic alliance—the Kalmar Union—was formed with Denmark and Sweden. Just before the Reformation, in 1523, Sweden seceded from the union; Denmark became the dominant partner. This situation allowed the development of the two-class society composed of *alume*, the common people, and *conditioneret*, people of quality.

Conditioneret replaced the aristocracy. This professional and intellectual elite composed of physicians, lawyers, architects, engineers, higher civil servants, military officers, government officials, and the clergy together with their families developed in the sixteenth to the eighteenth centuries. Danes filled many government and church posts in Norway; Germans were represented in the commercial community. Families of quality were united by their Danish or German origins, intermarriage, language, and education as well as by their professions. Not all of them were wealthy; rather their status depended on *dannelse*, a quality similar to culture or breeding. Education and travel exposed *conditioneret* to the growing European middle class with whom they were sympathetic. Unlike the continental or British middle class, these Norwegians were at the top of the social system. They had, consequently, somewhat more influence than a true "middle" class.

Alumen was composed of two groups: *bφnder* and *husmenn*. The former were sometimes a sort of rural nobility of freeholders who traced their origins to the days of Viking glory. They owned land, while *husmenn* did not. Frequently the two were related. Both groups usually made their living through a mixed economy. The localized nature of their culture was reflected in their regionally distinct dress and dialects.

In 1800 the Norwegian population was overwhelmingly rural; the majority (85%) were peasants of a sort peculiar to Norway due to its nonfeudal past and the harsh factors of climate and topography.[4] In most of Norway farming alone was inadequate to support a household. Thus a peasant could not be equated with a farmer. Rather, a peasant household was engaged in a multiplicity of occupations in seasonally varying patterns according to the resources available in the region. A bit of farming was combined with animal husbandry, fishing, lumbering, handicrafts, and dairying to make a living.

Lack of land did not dictate a low social standing. Nor was the specific occupation of the male "head" of the household a reliable guide to its status.

14

The skipper of a ship, for example, had a highly respected and responsible position based on skill; this did not always translate into social status. A more dependable indication, in the 1860s, was the title of address used when referring to the female "head" and the daughters of the family. Married women of the elite were addressed as *frue*, their daughters as *frøke(n)*; one step down, married women were *madam*, their daughters *jomfru*; women of the lowest standing were called by their first name or if married by *kone* or *mor* (mother) and if not by *pige* (girl).[5]

Settlements were scattered *tuns*, not clustered villages. Several small houses, each with its own function—a dwelling house, a storehouse, a bathhouse, etc.—were grouped around a yard to house the members of the household that likely included both kin and nonkin. The landholdings of any one household might have included a summer farm, *seter*, higher up the valley and a boathouse down on the fjord as well as some fields around the central yard.

The household was the primary unit of production, consumption, and social life. It required an adult man and an adult woman to function; a marriage was an economic relationship as much as, if not more than, a romantic one. Additional labor was provided by children, siblings, or other relatives of the "couple," unrelated persons from the community, or the parents of the "couple." Together these individuals formed a social and economic unit. Such households, however, ought not be described as extended or grand families.[6] They were seldom composed of complete multiple families. As both kin and nonkin were included without significant distinction, family is not an accurate descriptive term. Börje Hanssen has suggested "farmfolk" as a more encompassing term.[7]

The composition of the household was adjusted as the labor needs shifted with the life cycle of the core family. The pattern of adjustment for smaller holdings was centrifugal, casting out children as they matured; that of the larger holdings was centripetal, adding the children cast out by the small holdings and concentrating those born to the household. Persons who had the prospect of inheriting a living composed of some land, some fishing rights, some animals, etc., postponed marriage until the living was passed to them. It was customary for sons to inherit real property and fishing rights and for daughters to receive movable property such as household goods and livestock.[8] This usually occurred when the groom was between twenty-seven and thirty years old and the bride between twenty-five and twenty-seven.[9] (Twenty-seven remained the average age of Norwegian brides into the 1960s.)[10] The newlyweds then took possession of the buildings and property and control of the work.

The older couple, the potential grandparents, received a retirement settlement, reserved rights of *kaar*.[11] They were given a place to live, perhaps a part of the main dwelling or a loft above the storehouse. Their needs for food and clothing were provided for by the produce of designated animals or by agreement to a certain amount of each product. Their contributions to the household were also specified. As they aged, their contributions became less; their needs changed; and appropriate adjustments were made.

A younger, unmarried sister of the wife might have come to live in the new household when she was no longer needed in their parents' home and her help was sorely needed in a house with small children. By the time she married, the eldest daughter was old enough to assume some of her responsibilities. If there were no sons, a neighbor boy just past confirmation age (fourteen or fifteen) might join the household and stay for many years. In this way the actual population of the *tun* shifted to maintain a balance of labor resources and labor needs while providing temporary places for young people between confirmation and their own marriages. Many youths passed through this stage of "servanthood"; as there was little social stratification between the family and the servants among the farmfolk, this temporary state was not viewed as degrading. On the contrary, it was sometimes regarded as an education and as an increase in status.[12]

Each household was corporately engaged in a multiplicity of occupations.[13] Individual members were able to do a variety of the tasks involved in the household's economy: fishing, dairying, weaving, farming, etc. This multiplicity of occupations and skills provided the flexibility necessary for survival in an economy of scarcity. In addition to the household, labor was drawn from the neighborhood through customary social arrangements.

Within the flexibility there was a clear pattern of division of labor and responsibility on the basis of age and sex. Women were close to home; men were mobile. Women were occupied by tasks that could not be postponed; men were able to alter their schedule to take advantage of unusual opportunities. Generally, women were responsible for the repetitive, daily work and primary production necessary for the continued existence of the household; men were responsible for the seasonal work.

Ethnologist Brit Berggreen described the yearly cycle of women's work in western Norway at the midpoint of the nineteenth century. In the spring, the adult female members of the household were the first up in the morning so that they could prepare a meal and dress the children. They milked and fed the cattle; they bundled hay for a later feeding. Outside, they cleared and raked fields, built hay-drying racks, spread manure, and fished from the shore with nets or a line. At the end of the day there was another meal to make.

In the summer, women were occupied with baking a six-month supply of flatbread and doing textile work. They cut hay, looked after the dairy production, and took care of the work on the summer farm. "Grown girls" gutted the herring catch. The daily round of meals and child-related tasks continued.

Autumn was particularly busy with outdoor work. Both men and women harvested grain. Women harvested potatoes, made a second cutting of hay, and collected fodder for winter feed by stripping ash leaves. They also dried grain in a kiln. The press of autumn work forced routine tasks to be neglected or done in the evening by artificial light.

Winter brought time for indoor projects: spinning, weaving, and mending. When the men were away, the full load of farm work fell to the women. Always there were "duties connected with nurturance, the taking care of children, sick people, animals, and visitors, work to be done instantly and without delays."[14]

Men were not without work, despite what this list of women's work might suggest. Their labor was extradomestic and organized to exploit whatever opportunities presented themselves. "This could be seasonal work, industry dependent on market fluctuations, crafts, construction work, or other jobs."[15] Men were routinely away from home for extended periods fishing on the sea, working in the lumber industry, or engaging in trade. Extraordinary circumstances, such as a shipwreck or an unexpected abundance of cod, called for immediate attention if they were to be capitalized upon; men were able to respond because women provided a stable work force at home.

A successful household required both male and female labor to run. A one-person household was unimaginable. Everyone was attached to a household. Similarly, every household was linked with its neighbors by social and work ties. The boundaries of these groups were defined in part by proximity and in part by natural barriers. In some areas the ribbonlike pattern of settlement determined that a household would associate with a few others on each side of it. The social-work groups of the next household would overlap with those of the first but were not coterminous. In other areas natural barriers were less rigid and the groups were more fluid. Ecclesiastical and political administrative units did not coincide with these "natural" groups.

The smallest social group was the *grannelag*, composed of the nearest neighbors. These folk provided each other with aid in "any eventuality that went beyond daily need."[16] At the time of birth or death help came from the *grannelag*. The *bedlag* was slightly larger. It included those people invited for important occasions such a weddings or burials. All the member households contributed to the festivities on the basis of their ability to do so. In this way the burden of entertaining 100-300 people at a three- to seven-day wedding was spread out among the guests in a sort of marathon potluck and no one had to forego a celebration because of inadequate means.

Work was shared in two ways. The first, *dugnad*, was organized by household. The nature of the work to be done determined how many and which people were involved. The *dugnad* was activated for projects like major construction and to fulfill common obligations such as poor support and road maintenance.

> It was a form of mutual help which was both a privilege and a duty, and nobody could escape it. A man might join the dugnad many times during his life without ever needing such help himself. But it was *the farm* and not the individual person which received and rendered this help.[17]

Bytesarbeid was work exchanged on a personal basis with some attention to the equability of the exchange. It was used for seasonal chores made more interesting by company: slaughtering, harvesting, flatbread baking. Different sorts of work were bartered; weaving of a blanket might be exchanged for loan of equipment. In both arrangements reciprocity was assumed, as was a basic equity expressive of egalitarian views.

Privacy was limited by available space and social customs. Everyone lived in the same few rooms; one person's business was everyone's business. Family was not distinguished from "servant." Children of the family and the young hired workers, if not the entire household, slept together in a loft in the storehouse or stable. All the farmfolk ate the same food, at the same table, at the same time.

Courtship proceeded in customary patterns. On long summer evenings young men visited young women in their rooms; sometimes they spent the entire night together in the same bed. This practice, night courting, was not unregulated sexual promiscuity. It was a serious relationship governed by clear, local standards. The upper class, nonetheless, found both the standards and the ways of coping with breaches of the standards disdainful.[18]

Elite attitudes toward the peasants were of two sorts. On the one hand there was an idealistic attraction to their rustic life. At the other extreme there was shocked disgust at their lack of sophistication. Distaste for peasant life prompted some Norwegians to undertake reforms designed to bring them into the modern world by raising standards of cleanliness, privacy, sexual morality, and drinking habits. For example, health regulations were enacted forbidding pigs in residences.

Eilert Sundt's remarkable studies of country life were the direct result of these concerns. In his first years of research Sundt was inclined to ally himself with upper-class standards; after prolonged contacts with the people, he saw their life as worthy of respect.[19] In the so-called porridge war, a literary exchange, Sundt defended the traditional method of making porridge against P. Chr. Asbjørnsen's charges that it was wasteful: Asbjørnsen calculated that one-sixth of the flour was wasted. The Society for Promotion of Popular Enlightenment opposed Sundt but he and the traditional porridge makers were later vindicated by scientific experiments.[20] In his *On Marriage in Norway*, the pioneer sociologist asserted that the increased number of births in the early 1800s was not the result of wantonness but the logical outcome of an earlier baby boom, one generation before.[21] Sundt's defense of the peasants did not change the fact that Norway's population was growing rapidly.

Other factors contributed to reorganization of peasant life. Agriculture was shifted to a capitalistic, market orientation. This was accomplished by changed patterns of landholding brought about by partition of old holdings, by breaking of new land, by consolidation, and in the 1880s by enclosure, *utskifting*. Norway was slow to adopt these reforms because the profit motive was so weak for people whose "farms were too small and the soil too poor to produce a saleable surplus."[22] New techniques and improved machinery and tools helped to produce such a surplus. Agricultural schools and organizations encouraged changes in animal husbandry as well.

By midcentury most of these reforms were in place, benefiting the *bonde* families who owned their land. The results were less helpful for the *husmenn*, or cotters. The later's economic position declined.[23] As it became more difficult for a young couple to secure a livelihood, servanthood ceased to be a transitional state. The number of nonlandowning cottagers, farm laborers, and domestic workers grew and solidified into a permanent group. Social differences between the *bonde* and the *husman*, which had been largely unarticulated, were highlighted by attention to profit. Segregation of the family from the servants at meals and in sleeping quarters accentuated the stratification.[24]

These material and economic changes facilitated changes in relationships of men and women and in sexual division of labor. Night courting fell out of use. Affection and romance played a larger part in marriage. The emotional bonds of kinship may have intensified as a result of both this development and the differentiation of family and servant within the household.[25]

Men assumed responsibility for the more productive agriculture, both crops and animals. When the Norwegian Dairymen's Association was founded (1881) it had no female members despite women's age-old responsibility for dairying. Genteel values discouraged peasant women from displaying their hard labor. Likely they continued to work just as hard, but their efforts were deemphasized and "undercommunicated."[26] In addition to traditional tasks, women gained new, nonproductive jobs related to increased attention to domestic space and acquisition of the material "props" of elite standards. Glass windows, for example, required washing, and decorative objects required dusting.

Women ceased to be viewed as partners in the household; rather, they were seen as helpers. Upon marriage they no longer took possession of the farmstead keys, which had been a badge of female responsibility since Viking days. This loss coincided with the trend toward women adopting their husbands' patronymic in place of their own -datter surname. Ironically, legal developments appeared almost contradictory. Equal inheritance rights were extended to women in 1854; the last stipulations that relegated unmarried women to the status of minors were removed in 1863.[27]

Elite women were more thoroughly influenced by nineteenth-century European ideals of appropriate female behavior, which emphasized their domestic and decorative role. Some daughters were educated privately in the last years of the eighteenth century. They acquired skills in languages, music, and the arts, all considered "matrimonial assets."[28] Girls were admitted to the Realskole in Trondhjem in 1804 and a girls' school was opened in Christiania in 1849.[29] Other daughters were sent to boarding schools in Denmark and Germany.

The stirring of Norwegian feminism began with publication of *Amtmandens Døtre* (*The Governor's Daughters*) by Camilla Collett, sister of Henrik Wergeland. Collett protested identification of women with the "Christian virtues of long-suffering and patience" and the increasing polarization of the sexes. Rather, in her view, women should receive their rights as individuals equal to men. Both Henrik Ibsen and novelist Jonas Lie were influenced by Collett's position and portrayed with realism the tragic consequences of unhappy marriages and circumscribed personalities in their work. Ibsen's play on this theme, *A Doll's House*, quickly gained a reputation worldwide.[30]

Founding of *Norsk Kvindesagsforening* (Norwegian Society for Women's Rights) in 1884 marks the beginning of the organized women's rights movement. Its first president was a male journalist who seceded to Gina Krog. Under Krog's leadership the society conducted educational work in support of opening professional positions to women and granting legal rights to married women. All university degrees were made available to women in 1884; women were granted positions as teachers in common schools after 1869. It was some years before women took full advantage of these opportunities. Efforts to secure the vote were successful in 1906.[31]

Hanna Winsnes, the wife of a pastor, was more typical of women in the late nineteenth century than Collett or Krog. The stories she wrote under a male pseudonym were popular, but her most successful work was a widely used cookbook and household guide. While Winsnes recognized that women's work was "less esteemed" than men's, she also judged it to be equally demanding and valuable. Nonetheless, she was not a vocal feminist.[32]

Norwegian women who immigrated to the United States were most likely to be hardworking *bonder* or *husman* women. The majority were unfamiliar with the stirrings of feminism among their countrywomen. Even women from the elite were more like Hanna Winsnes than her more radical contemporaries.

Christianity in Norway

From Christianization to the Nineteenth Century

Among European nations Norway came to Christianity rather late. The ill-fated missionary efforts of Archbishop Ansgar of Bremen in the 800s did not extend into Norway. The Old Norse religion of Thor and his court continued. Certainly the northerners were exposed to Christianity on their extensive forays throughout western and southern Europe. They were, however, not in search of religious truths on those voyages. And the terrified Christians were not in a position to instruct their attackers. Only as the Viking age was drawing to a close in the late tenth century did the warriors bring Christianity home in their longships.

The Christianization of Norway took place simultaneously with the uniting of the scattered jarls (local chieftains) under Olaf Tryggvessön. Dynastic struggles forced the young Olaf to protect himself by residence in the court of Olga, the first Christian queen of Russia. He took part in Viking raids in the British Isles and France. It was in England that he was converted to Christianity through the agency of a hermit.

Due to the inhospitable situation in England he returned to Norway, where he commenced his campaign to gain political control of the country and to bring Christianity to the people. He was largely successful in the latter, using methods varying from persuasion to threats and bribes. Continued political disputes resulted in Olaf's death in battle in 1000. (Leif Ericson's alleged visit to North America took place the same year.) There followed an interim of fifteen years in which the people reverted to their prior religious practices.

The work of Christianization was taken up by Tryggvessön's kinsman, the sainted Olaf Haraldson. Legend has it that the younger Olaf was baptized as a child in the presence of the elder Olaf; other accounts say that the sacrament was performed at Rouen during Haraldson's Viking career. In any case, he completed what had been begun by the first Olaf. An Icelandic monk gave account of the two men's work. "Olaf Trygvesson prepared and laid the foundations of Christianity, but St. Olaf built the walls." His picturesque account of the relationship continues, "Olaf Trygvesson planted the vineyard, but St. Olaf trained up the vine covered with fair flowers and much fruit."[33] St. Olaf was advised by churchmen. In the decade and a half of his reign he established Christian laws and practices. Infanticide was forbidden; *thralls* (slaves) were to be emancipated rather than sacrificed. Churches were built. Church officials were appointed. Christian feasts were held and new interpretations were given to old Norse ones.

Opponents of these changes and of Olaf's none too gentle methods of making them allied themselves with the Danish contender in a successful effort to force Olaf off the throne. At Stiklestad (north of Trondheim) he went to battle to regain his kingdom; in July 1030 his supporters rallied with the cry "Christ's men; cross men; king's men." Olaf was killed and his army was defeated. Under Danish rule, the people soon had cause to regret both losses. Stories of miracles were immediately connected with the slain king. Bishop Grimkell declared him a saint in 1041. The king's body was exhumed and enshrined over the high altar of Nidaros Cathedral in Trondheim. Some would say that he took Thor's place at the head of the gods. Certainly he came to stand as a symbol of Norwegian national identity.

The unity and independence of Norway were thus linked with Christianity in the person of St. Olaf and the potent aura that came to surround him. On a mundane level the effect of Christianization was less dramatic. Age-old attitudes, folk wisdom, and practices did not disappear entirely and certainly not immediately. The Christian gospel was introduced by force; it permeated the culture only gradually.

This pattern of abrupt introduction followed by slow adaptation was duplicated by the sixteenth-century Reformation. Historical interpretation of the Reformation in Norway was classified by K. E. Christopherson as being of three successive sorts.[34] Earliest historians viewed it as an entirely beneficial event. Nineteenth-century historians, influenced by growing national pride accompanied by anti-Danish sentiments, viewed it as an entirely foreign event. The two views coincided in their stress upon the sudden and forceful character of the reform. The church in Norway had escaped many of the antecedents that prepared the way for reform in other parts of Europe. There was less corruption in the hierarchy and among monastics; there was little mystical piety; there was scarcely any contact with humanism; nor were there any notable popular religious awakenings.

The Reformation came to Norway by royal declaration. In October 1536 Christian III, the Danish king, announced that the Danish church was reformed and that Norway would henceforth be a province of Norway, no longer a cokingdom. The following year he published a new Church Ordinance establishing a Lutheran church. As Christianity had been tied to Norwegian unification, the Reformation was tied to loss of autonomy. As Lutherans, the Norwegians have rejoiced in the Reformation; as Norwegians, they have "held it in contempt."

Only recently has the third interpretation transcended such conflicts of loyalty to "be clear about what the Norwegian Reformation was." Andreas Slirstad delineated three phases of reformation: awakening movements, shifts in government and law, and church evangelization work. In Norway, the third phase was most significant.

[The Reformation] was a work of spiritual education which went on for two or three generations from about 1539 into part of the 1600s. The Reformation was not something that happened in 1537 [with the new Church Ordinance] . . . the Reformation did not come with us as an awakening but as a movement of spiritual education with the initiative from above.[35]

Carl Wisløff suggested similar stages dating their completion as follows: legal break, 1537; development of evangelical tools (viz., Bible translation, hymnbook, and liturgy), 1560; education, circa 1640. The process of reformation took at least a century.

The religious situation of Norway in the late eighteen and nineteenth centuries must be seen in light of the both politically sudden and religiously gradual character of conversion and reformation.

> Indeed it has frequently been remarked that, until the late eighteenth century, the mass of the Scandinavian population had never experienced a true religious awakening. Christianity had been introduced by compulsion; Lutheranism had been dictated by the state. Neither had sprung from a deeply felt need for religious expression. Lutheran Christianity was still, in the eighteenth and early nineteenth centuries heavily tinged with animistic hold-overs. . . . This ancient body of folk superstition existed peaceably alongside the body of elementary Christian teaching which people had assimilated over the years.[36]

Lutheran orthodoxy did little to alter this situation. Emphasis on right doctrine and proper forms did not stimulate religious awakening.

The reign of Christian VI, Danish king, coincided with "the first religious revival which the Norwegian people had ever experienced."[37] The king was profoundly influenced by pietism of a sort that called for stern morality and high regard for things spiritual. His way of sharing these concerns with the Norwegian and Danish people was not unlike that of previous rulers: he enacted laws. The Sabbath observance law of 1735 imposed a fine or imprisonment for neglect of Sunday worship. Confirmation, a public renewal of baptismal vows, was made compulsory. A short-lived attempt was made to establish mandatory public schools using religious textbooks. Although Christian's methods were as external to the people as those used by Olaf and Christian III, his actions received a more sympathetic reception, especially among those clergymen who were influenced by pietism.

During these same years Erik Pontoppidan, bishop of Bergen, wrote his explanation to Luther's *Small Catechism*. This small book, *Truth Unto Godliness*, shaped the religious sensibilities of Norwegians for generations. Its readers absorbed a sense of a sharp distinction between the children of the world and the children of God, which undergirded profound moral seriousness.[38] Nonetheless, pietism in Norway remained primarily a movement among the clergy and upper classes; this "first religious revival" did not awaken the *alume*, the common people.

By the early years of the nineteenth century, rationalist influences began to be felt in Norway through clergymen returning from their education in Copenhagen. Its impact was limited by the opening of the Royal Fredericks University in Christiania in 1811 and the requirement, made in 1814, that all pastors in the Norwegian state church take their theological training in Norway.[39] Svend Borchamann Hersleb and Stener Johannes Stenersen, the first professors appointed, were followers of the young Nikolai Frederik Severin Grundtvig during his antirationalist period. They instilled their students with orthodox, conventional Christianity quite in opposition to the churchly views espoused by Grundtvig in his later life.[40]

Nineteenth-Century Religion

At the beginning of the nineteenth century, worshipers in local parishes had only minimal interest in the views of the few rationalist pastors. The people's religion consisted of conformity to familiar forms that were unaltered by the Enlightenment. These forms became "the framework of the religious revival" that spread from one tip of Norway to the other in the early 1800s.[41] Unlike the initial Christianization of Norway or the sixteenth-century Reformation of the Norwegian church, this turn-of-the-century revival sprang from the people and took deep root in their hearts.

The common people, *alumen*, were most receptive to the revival's pietistic impulse. Without attention to this movement, the religious character of those Norwegians who immigrated to the United States in the following decade and of their descendants is incomprehensible.

Hans Nielsen Hauge (1771-1824), the son of a *bonde* from southeastern Norway, was the coxswain of the early nineteenth-century religious revival; his voice called the people to repent. In many ways he typified those common people who answered his call and were animated by the revival. His rudimentary education enabled him to read generally available pietist devotional works, such as Pontoppidan's *Truth Unto Godliness* and Arndt's *True Christianity*. He took his religious life seriously and was not given to immoral behavior. Rather, Hauge was an industrious youth, well known as a clever worker. Nonetheless, an event that took place on his father's farm in 1796 altered his piety and affected the religious life of the nation. While plowing a field and singing a hymn, he experienced a profound conviction of sin and a release that prompted in him a sense of his own salvation and of his call to God's service. Einar Molland compared Hauge's conversion to John Wesley's.

> It was not a conversion from a worldly life to a godly life. Rather it was a pious and serious Christian experiencing a sudden break-through and from that day on, possessing an assurance and a power he had not previously known.[42]

Throughout Hauge's career the themes of his own experience remained constant in his preaching: intense conviction of sin, repentance, and divine forgiveness followed by the fruits of a godly life and witness to the gospel.

Hauge preached to his countryfolk of moral conversion and new life. He reached Norwegians in all parts of the country with this message through his preaching during eight years of extensive travel and through his writings. In addition to preaching, he passed along practical information about farming techniques and tools, which he gathered on his travels. Along with his religious message came the example of his own industrious life. This was in keeping with his emphasis on Luther's notion of each person's daily work as a divine calling. Fierce concern for experienced, heartfelt Christianity and a demand for a commensurate abandonment of worldly life also characterized Hauge's preaching. His hearers demonstrated their adoption of these views in their lives; they rejected drinking, dancing, and other worldly sins. Positively, many took up the task of lay preaching.

This awakener of the common people was not well received by all his countryfolk. The Conventicle Act of 1741 forbade sectarian religious meetings; despite Hauge's intense loyalty to the Lutheran church, it was invoked against him and his followers, as were vagrancy laws. In part to protect himself from the later charge and in part to support his work, Hauge engaged in several business ventures in Bergen in addition to publishing his own writings in Denmark. Both the business community and the clergy were suspicious of Hauge, who remained a layman and was without formal theological training. He was arrested on several occasions; from 1804 to 1814 he was imprisoned. During that decade he was released for a short time to aid the country by assisting in the construction of a salt work. That plant distilled salt from seawater, providing the essential resource made unavailable by an English blockade.

After his final release, Hauge settled on a small farm. Broken health prevented him from resuming his earlier activities. Nonetheless, he continued to influence the movement of religious awakening that became synonymous with his name.

The effects of Haugean revival were not strictly confined to the religious sphere. In a discussion of social class, Peter Munch described the Hauge movement as

a forceful emancipation of the common people . . . from the control and dominance of the elite . . . an important manifestation, and a reinforcement, of the . . . now reawakened quest for freedom and independence.[43]

It was strengthened by and lent support to both Norwegian nationalism and the political maturation of the common people with which it coincided.

Since 1397 Norway had been linked with Denmark in the Kalmar Union. Originally a dynastic union between equal powers, the alliance had become unbalanced. Norway took the role of the "little brother." This relationship ended with the Napoleonic Wars, in which Denmark allied with Napoleon. At the Congress of Vienna, Norway was given over to Sweden in compensation for the Swedish loss of Finland, with little regard for the internal events of Norway. Norwegian men had gathered in Eidsvoll in 1814 and drafted a modern constitution for a democratic, independent nation. Despite this liberal constitution and much international negotiation, the Vienna agreement was enacted. Nearly a century passed before Norway became totally independent. The years from 1814 to 1905 were a period of simmering Norwegian nationalism, during which shifts in social structure took place. These changes were significant in both the political and the religious institutions.

Approximately a third of the representatives at the Eidsvoll Constitutional Assembly were *bønder*. However, political self-consciousness among the common people grew only gradually through the century. Suffrage was limited to those men who owned land or had rented it for five years or more. They elected their conventional leaders to the *Storthing* (parliament) rather than speak for themselves. An increasing number of representatives came from the *bonde* class. The right to vote was extended in stages: to all men in 1898; to women in 1913. At the same time, a labor movement was slowly forming.

A second revival in the 1840s reinforced the Haugean movement and promoted religious awakening in the elite clerical and commercial class. With theology professor Gisle Johnson (1822-1894) as its leader, this revival spread among the pastors and theological students. Like the earlier movement, the Johnsonian Revival did not place awakening in opposition to doctrine. Rather,

27

the piety of the revival enlivened and strengthened the confessional position of the Lutheran church. This characteristic distinguished Norwegian revivalism from the American Second Great Awakening in the same period. With a few rare exceptions, the awakened believers of both Haugean and Johnsonian revivals stayed inside the state church. The goals of the Johnsonian revival were to awaken spiritual life and to preserve the Lutheran faith from the sectarianism of the few who withdrew from the state church and from the churchly views of the older Grundtvig. The initial influence of Grundtvig's churchly position on American Norwegian Lutheranism was quickly contained and rooted out by Pastor Herman A. Preus.

Gisle Johnson was an unlikely candidate for leader of a religious movement. He came from a family of government officials. His personality was neither charismatic nor dynamic. He had experienced no abrupt religious awakening. Nonetheless, it was Johnson's teaching of public Bible classes in Christiania, his preaching throughout the country, and his influence on his theological students that promoted the spread of the revival. "Johnson sought to imbue his students with a spirit of orthodoxy that blended the passion and subjectivity of a revival preacher with the intellect of an orthodox systematician."[44] The later influence was not confined to the classroom; Johnson and his colleague Carl Paul Caspari invited students to their homes on alternate weekends, where they enjoyed entertainments appropriate to pious Christian life. Johnson's influence also extended to the United States through the pastoral work of his students who immigrated.

Church reform was a byproduct of this midcentury revival. Reforms were directed to morality, church government, missions, and education. As the Haugean revival had silenced the fiddles and broken the dram glasses of the common people, the Johnsonian revival rendered the life of the upper class more quiet and sober. At midcentury a theological student described the changes in parsonage life.

> The custom of inviting guests was discontinued, the card tables disappeared, and with a view to the servants also having a day of rest, the assistant pastor and his family have this last year ceased to visit the pastor on Sunday as before. Instead, these things have been supplanted by the reading of God's Word, singing, prayer, and conversations on spiritual topics.[45]

The temperance movement grew in these years. Many of its goals were realized. Alcohol consumption dropped; distilling came under government regulation.

The Constitution of 1814 placed church affairs under the authority of the Storthing, which administered its responsibility through the Department of Church and Education. The national government had control of finances, appointment of pastors, and educational materials. The exercise of the last jurisdiction stirred a major controversy when a revised edition of Pontoppidan's explanation of Luther's *Catechism* was prepared by a Grundtvigian, Pastor W. A. Wexels. In 1843 the new version was introduced for use in public schools and confirmation instruction. Reactions, especially from the laity, were unambiguously negative. The church people objected to Wexels's lack of clear distinction between the children of the world and the children of God; to his seeming acceptance of immoral behavior such as reading novels, dancing, and attending the theater; and to the suggestion that conversion would be possible after death. In 1852 use of the original Pontoppidan *Explanation* was reauthorized. It was carried along to America, where it continued to be a key component in religious instruction and was cited as evidence in significant theological battles.

Objections to governmental controls were also voiced. The clergy and lay church leaders were concerned that the affairs of the church were placed in the hands of people who were indifferent to true religion, if not in the hands of unbelievers. Some young theological students and pastors seriously questioned the validity of the pastoral office "in a church which practiced compulsory confirmation, retained a general absolution with laying-on-of-hands, required church weddings, failed to exercise church discipline, and the like."[46] These advocates of church reform, Johnson among them, called for a measure of ecclesiastical self-government in the form of a national church assembly and congregational councils. No actions were taken beyond a study group until the 1880s. Congregational councils were authorized only in 1920, long after similar measures were commonplace among Norwegian-American Lutherans. The national church assembly was never organized.

Interest in missions, both domestic and foreign, predated the Johnsonian revival. The Norwegian Mission Society, founded in 1842, had prepared the way for the spread of the awakening. The revival returned the favor by lending its strength to the emerging inner mission societies. At first these groups were local. The focus of their activities was the *bedehus*, prayer house, used for evangelistic, devotional, and prayer meetings. Laymen and -women conducted meetings.[47] A separate building was necessary because Norwegian law forbade the use of a church building for such activities and restricted the pulpit to ordained clergy.

29

Efforts to unite local groups in the national *Den norske Lutherstiflse* in 1868 were hindered by disagreements over the propriety of lay preaching, which seemed to be forbidden by Article 14 of the Augsburg Confession. Professor Johnson, a firm supporter of the Confessions, allowed lay preaching on the basis of an emergency principle. The definition of an emergency sufficient to require departure from the confessional position and allow preaching by an unordained person was unclear and open to dispute. Johnson's compromise was attacked from both sides: by those who objected to any lay preaching and by those who found all regulation excessive. Despite this tension within the inner mission movement, it supported numerous societies and institutions for the spiritual and physical well-being of children, the sick, the aged, seamen, and others.

When the Storthing created a Department of Church and Education, it was following a centuries-old precedent. Religion and education had been linked in Norway since the Reformation. In Christian IV's Church Ordinance of 1552 provision was made for the payment of a special tax, *klokkertolden*. This money was to be used for the salary of the deacon, who was to instruct the children of the parish in "the catechism and the Christian religion" on a weekly basis. No evidence is available to evaluate how well the ordinance was followed or the quality of the education given. Nonetheless, "this was the first germ of the Norwegian public school."[48]

In the eighteenth century, Christian VI, the pietist king, instituted the rite of confirmation. After a period of instruction, young people (usually about age fourteen) were publicly examined and then made a formal renewal of their baptismal vows.[49] In the same years (1730s), attendance in public schools was made compulsory for all children aged seven to twelve. They were instructed for six to seven hours per day for three months of the year. Luther's *Catechism*, Pontoppidan's *Explanation*, the Bible, and a hymnbook were the prescribed textbooks.

After these schools were made optional in 1741, they continued to provide the Norwegian people with a rudimentary literacy and a theology of a particular cast. This background allowed people to sustain their faith even when they did not understand the preaching of rationalist clergymen. It also prepared the ground for the Haugean revival, which animated familiar beliefs and provided the boundaries that kept the enthusiasm within the state church.[50] The tenacity of beliefs learned in confirmation instruction and public schools was demonstrated by the vehement attacks on Wexels's revision of Pontoppidan's *Explanation*.

Public schools were made compulsory again in 1860. The parish was the basis of their organization; it was divided into several districts to make attendance convenient. All children from age eight to fourteen were required to attend. If thirty were able to do so every day, a building was to be constructed; if not, the teacher traveled from home to home to hold classes, *omgangskole*. When they established schools, Norwegian-Americans adapted this system to their new situation.

Church reform and the gradual democratization of the society in the nineteenth century made significant but slow changes in the social composition of the Norwegian church leadership. Training in Oslo reduced exposure to general European influences. This constraint was not absolute, however; Gisle Johnson traveled across the European continent dipping into the resources of its great universities. Many children were privately instructed by Swiss, French, and English governesses. Daughters of some families were sent to boarding schools in Denmark and Germany; Diderikke Otteson Brandt and Christiane Elizabeth Otteson Hjort attended Moravian schools. Both accompanied their clergymen husbands to the United States, where they used their education to instruct the daughters of other immigrants.

Throughout the century the clergy and their families were European rather than national in their cultural views. Their language reflected their former identification with Denmark as servants of the crown; they spoke Norwegian-Danish rather than regional dialects. As part of the upper class, clerical families were intertwined with one another and other professional families. Few men entered the ordained ministry from outside this circle until late in the century.[51]

Even as revivals took place and societies were organized to carry out the church's mission, the ground was being prepared for challenges to Christianity. Literary and artistic figures lauded the common Norwegian as the heir of the Viking age. The years 1844-1872 were colored in vivid hues by romantic retrieval and cultivation of this heritage. Poet Henrik Wergeland gave voice to a profound love of the country and its people. Jørgen Moë and Peter Christen Asbjørnsen collected folktales and gave them classic form. Ivar Aasen gave the vernacular language the dignity of a grammar, a dictionary, and a name, *landsmaal*.[52] Adolph Tidemand preserved the countryfolk's appearance in his paintings. Peter A. Munch asserted the uniqueness of the Norwegian past in opposition to earlier assumptions of a common Scandinavian history. At the same time, the common man became politically self-aware, and by the 1830s the male *bønder* were taking an active role in the national government.

Romanticists in their youth, the generation of the last third of the century turned to realism. In the person of Bjørnstjerne Bjørnson, realism combined with a Grundtvigian view of culture; in his contemporary, Henrik Ibsen, it was combined with free thinking. This combination was perceived by religious leaders as a challenge to morality and the church.

In the closing decades of the nineteenth century the profound and serious piety of the common people was supported by the educational system and found allies among the awakened clergy of the Johnsonian revival; the leadership of the church was primarily the realm of the cultured upper-class clergymen who had been associated with the Danish rule and still were viewed by many as agents of the state. The majority of Norwegians who immigrated to the United States in those years carried with them this distinctive brand of Lutheranism that combined a concern for heartfelt piety with right teaching. The class distinction between the laity and the clergy also continued in the Norwegian-American church. The intellectual movement of free thought that seemed contrary to religion was not well represented among the earliest immigrants, but its influence gradually increased in the new land as well as in the old.

TWO

Immigration
and Settlement

Leave-Taking

Economics, politics, international affairs, agricultural adaptation, religious awakening, and intellectual ferment contributed to the emergence of modern Norway in the nineteenth century. The same factors prompted hundreds of thousands of Norwegians to leave the country in the century after 1825. Each individual's decision to emigrate was a personal response to the general situation and thus unique. The combined decisions placed Norway second only to Ireland with regard to the percentage of its population that emigrated.[1] Despite the personal nature and individual variations of each emigrant's story, the similarities were sufficient to allow their actions to be viewed as a mass movement about which general observations can be made.

A decision to emigrate, to move from where one was to any other place, required that one had some motivation to leave, knew of an alternative place, had the desire to go to a specific place, and had the means to get there. The motivations to leave are conventionally called the "push" factors; the "pull" factors are those that produce the desire to go to one specific place rather than another. The decisive push factor in nineteenth-century Norway was most often economic; there was a lack of opportunity for material advancement or even for maintenance of a former level of prosperity as standards and expectations rose. The matching pull factor that made the United States, particularly the upper Midwest, attractive was the opportunity it provided for achieving a higher level of prosperity while continuing a rural life.

Why did these coalesce when they did to produce three waves of mass immigration? Knowledge of the alternatives and procession of the means to get there, of course, contributed; shifts in the Norwegian situation and the American one also were important. Specific factors included a rapid increase in population, a lag in industrial development, increased material and social expectations, price reductions for the trans-Atlantic fare, publications about the opportunities in the Upper Midwest, personal contacts in America, and the balance of immediate conditions in the Norwegian economy and that in the United States. In various combinations these brought on America fever, which reached its height in the 1860s, 1880s, and 1900s.

As in much of Europe, the population of Norway had been relatively stable for several decades, increasing at one half of a percent each year. After 1815 the Norwegian population grew at nearly three times that rate (1.3% increase per year).[2] Many explanations were advanced for the sudden spurt of childbearing. Some observers blamed the increase on peasant wantonness. Sociologist Eilert Sundt suggested that it was directly related to a previous surge approximately one generation earlier. The children of the baby boom had reached childbearing age and produced a second-generation boom.[3] Other factors included reduction of the mortality rate by introduction of smallpox vaccinations, improvement of nutrition by cultivation of the potato and return of herring to Norwegian waters, and improvements in sanitary conditions.

Whatever caused the increase, it represented children who needed to be fed, housed, clothed, educated, and given a start in life. And these children reached maturity as Norway was passing thorough the significant religious, political, and social changes discussed in Chapter One.[4] The cities, Christiania (Oslo) and Bergen, for example, were able to absorb some of the young Norwegians but, as industrialization was just underway, the urban areas were saturated early in the century.

Agricultural reforms in rural areas increased efficiency so that fewer workers were needed rather than more. In many areas the land could not be divided into smaller pieces, nor was there new land to be broken. The number of landless cotters and day workers grew by 100% and 200% respectively in the first half of the century, while the number of landowners increased by only 27%.[5] The social distance between these groups widened; members of the landless *husman* class were made to feel their lower status more intensely than in the past.

Even in a subsistence economy with a multiple occupational structure, a minimum of land and work was necessary for survival. As standards of what constituted an adequate living were also rising, what might have been considered an acceptable living at an earlier time was no longer acceptable. The open hearth was replaced by a stove; *bønder* began to vote and serve in public offices; women were relieved of some of their heavy labor. The old rural patterns were altered by contact with the city and thence with continental European culture. Even if the former minimum standards could have been met, they were no longer satisfactory. People expected more. Young people in particular expected more.

Historian Ingrid Semmingsen compared the opportunities open to a boy early in the nineteenth century with those of his grandson in the closing years of the century. The earlier lad was likely to stay close to his parents' home. He might have hired himself out as a servant for a few years after his confirmation. When he came into a living, either by inheritance or by taking a *husman*'s place or breaking a piece of new land, he married. He also worked at some additional occupation such as peddling or fishing. His wife's opportunities were parallel to his and neither of them was great.

Although their grandson might not have been able to secure land, he had more varied options. He might have gone to school and fashioned himself into a community leader; he might have gone to a city and become an industrial worker; or he might have gone to America. His wife or sister was not likely to have a career as a public leader but she could have gone to the city or to America.

That many Norwegians did go—to school, to the cities, to America— indicated a new attitude of individualism and an unwillingness to struggle along in the same old way. "Youth felt the desire to make use of the opportunities offered them, even though to do this it was necessary to cut off all ties that bound them to relatives and environment."[6] Those who went to Christiania or Bergen, those who migrated to the northern counties, those who went to school, took part in the *bønder* and labor movements, and those who emigrated to the New World were all part of the same trend.

The traditions of the region, available resources, and personal knowledge all influenced one person or family's decision to make use of this opportunity or that one. From the flatter, lowland areas around Oslo fjord, people were likely to migrate into Christiania. In the highlands the pattern of international migration became well established. High fares in the first years of emigration limited the travelers to those who had something substantial to sell or someone who was willing to back them. By the 1880s that backer was frequently a relative or acquaintance who had already gone to the United States. Even if such a person could not send a prepaid ticket, knowledge that a familiar face and a warm welcome would be waiting in Wisconsin or Minnesota could tip the balance toward America rather than toward Christiania or the less exploited areas of northern Norway.

35

Knowledge of the United States spread throughout Norway as the century progressed. In 1817 a Dutch ship with 500 German emigrants aboard was stranded in the Norwegian port of Bergen; news of the incident traveled and must have given some people a notion that it was possible to go to America. Certainly this was not unknown information. There had been the legendary trip by Leif Ericson several centuries before and a few lone Norwegians had taken residence in the United States in the decades since its founding. Still, such an undertaking was unusual and no significant group had done it yet.

In 1825 this changed. The first group of Norwegians sailed for America in the sloop *Restauration*. There were ten married couples (six of whom had children), eleven single men, and one single woman aboard. One infant girl, Margaret Allen (named for a British Quaker), was born during the voyage, bringing the total number of emigrants to fifty-two. They came from the area around Stavanger on the southwestern coast.

Their leader, Lars Larsen (Geilane) was a member of the Society of Friends, which was illegal in Norway as was any religion other than the state Lutheran church. Larsen and his coreligionists had endured the consequences of their dissent for some years before they determined to emigrate. Likely they were encouraged in their action by non-Norwegian Quakers. Although only Larsen can be decisively identified as a Quaker, some of the others in the group were at least sympathetic. In their desire to emigrate for religious freedom these "sloop folk," as they became known, were unusual among their countryfolk who followed. They purchased their own vessel and loaded it with iron in the hope of making some profit on the sale of both upon arrival in New York. This too was unusual. (It was also less than successful.)

With the guidance of Cleeg Peerson, another legendary Norwegian explorer, the sloop folk settled in the United States. They made their first homes in Kendall County, New York. Their little colony served as a stopping-off point for hundreds of their countryfolk who followed in their path to the New World; however, nearly all of those who followed continued on to the Midwest. Peerson was also instrumental in establishing the Fox River settlement in La Salle County, Illinois, in 1834. Others from Kendall sold their property, headed for Illinois, and joined their "native" American neighbors in the westward migration.

In the late 1830s more groups bound for America left from Stavanger and other European ports. Relatively reliable departures for North America from Göteborg, Hamburg, and Havre made them popular. After weeks at sea the immigrants made their way across the Eastern states to the farmland of Illinois,

Missouri, and Wisconsin. Upon their arrival they wrote to friends and relatives back home; the letters were widely read. Recipients passed them from hand to hand and some were published in the newspapers. These "America letters" provided a trusted source of information about the opportunities waiting in the United States and drew more immigrants to areas already populated by their former neighbors.

Guidebooks also offered the would-be immigrant advice about the journey and getting established. Ole Rynning's *True Account of America for the Information and Help of Peasant and Commoner* and Ole Nattestad's *Description of a Journey to North America* found large, interested audiences. "Women are respected and honored far more than is the case among the common people in Norway," wrote Rynning. With more than idle curiosity Norwegian women read that a servant girl would earn $1-2 per week in America when the wage in Norway was $8-12 per *year*.[7] Wages for a man were similarly better. There was plenty of land to be had. Social equity was a prominent theme in letters back to Norway. In America a man did not have to take off his hat to the clergyman; everyone was equal. One man explained the situation to a friend:

> The native-born Americans are called Yankees. . . . No matter how simple a workingman they may have with them, all eat at the same table, without distinction as to persons. These people work daily at their various tasks even though they are merchants or officials.[8]

One could make a good living—if one was willing to work. Norwegians were accustomed to work.

Enough Norwegians were convinced that going to America was the opportunity they were looking for that an antiemigration sentiment grew up among the elite and patriotic who viewed emigration not only as foolish but also as a traitorous evil. Poet Henrik Wergeland held such views and wrote about them with enthusiasm. Bishop Jacob Neumann of Bergen published "A Word of Admonition to the Peasants in the Diocese of Bergen Who Desire to Emigrate" (1837). He argued on religious, patriotic, economic, and emotional grounds to convince his readers to remain in their homeland.

> Here in Norway rest the ashes of your fathers; here you first saw the light of day; here you enjoyed many childhood pleasures, here you received your first impressions of God and of His love; here you are still surrounded by relatives and friends who share your joy and your sorrow, while there when you are far

away from all that has been dear to you, who shall close your eyes in the last hour of life? A stranger's hand! And who shall weep at your grave? Perhaps—no one.[9]

His appeal was strengthened by reports of immigrants who did not flourish and wished that they could return to Norway.

However, the sight of "Americans," like Ole Nattestad's brother, who returned for a visit with glowing stories and the appearance of success, was far more persuasive. Groups in Muskego and Chicago organized themselves specifically to counteract the bad press about America. The "Muskego Manifesto," signed by eighty residents, was printed in *Morgenbladet* newspaper in 1845. The Vossing Correspondence Society of Chicago made a systematic report of conditions in America and sent a representative to Norway to give personal witness to their testimony.[10]

It was not only the peasant who found America appealing. The professional class had large families and its youth were attracted by the opportunities across the Atlantic. Labor leader Marcus Thrane immigrated, as did some reform-minded people like Johan Reinhart Reiersen and Elise Amalie Tvede Waerenskjold.[11]

Those who decided to leave had much to do in preparation. Spring was the usual time of departure so the previous winter was used to make ready: to mend and manufacture clothing, to build up a store of food for the long trip, to make arrangements for an auction and for whoever was to be left behind. Some Norwegians left with the intention of returning later to buy the old homeplace or restore it to its former glory with American dollars, but most seemed to know that their steps would not be retraced. (Of course, there were some who did return to live in Norway.) For the majority there was no turning back.

Even among the notoriously reserved Norwegians the prospect of breaking off lifelong relationships was not easy. Old parents living on reserved rights continued to receive their agreed upon measures of supplies and food from the new owners of the farmstead, but there was no assurance that the new social relationships would be satisfactory and little hope that they could replace those broken by emigration. Not only aged parents were left behind. American letters were filled with longings to be remembered to childhood playmates, with sharp desires to see newborn nieces and nephews, and with deep sorrow over the death of friends.

The distance to America and separation from the bonds of old relationships and obligations were precisely what attracted some emigrants. Recognizing that the effect of emigration on families was potentially disastrous, members of the Storthing included regulations about those left behind in legislation proposed in the 1840s. The legislation was not passed; however, its contents gave clues to the perceived threats of emigration. Debtors could escape their creditors; irresponsible husbands could desert their families; reluctant wives could cause conflict.[12] America was also a place for hearts to heal. It has been suggested that romantic difficulties contributed to both Ole Rynning's and Cleeg Peerson's decisions to emigrate. Surely they were not the only ones who found solace in a new country.

In the 1840s the Atlantic crossing could take up to three months by sailing ship. From a Norwegian port the passage cost thirty to thirty-five specie dollars. (An average wage for a hired man was ten specie dollars per year.) A less expensive fare could be had from Sweden, France, or Germany, but there was the added expense of travel to the foreign city and waiting there for departure. Changes in British shipping regulations opened up Norwegian trade with Canada; between 1854 and 1865 nearly all Norwegians landed in Quebec. In the mid-1860s steamships were introduced and took over the trans-Atlantic route. Price wars among the steamship companies in the 1880s pushed the fare down and encouraged more Norwegians to emigrate.[13]

The captain provided water, firewood, and closely spaced bunks. The steerage passengers provided their own bedding and food. They were advised to bring dried pork and mutton, salted herring, peas, potatoes, flatbread, grain and flour, butter, cheese, sour milk, and beer. All of the provisions went into large painted wooden chests along with whatever household and farming goods were taken.

The passengers on a ship were often from the same area of Norway. If they did not know one another already, the weeks at sea provided plenty of time to forge new friendships. They took turns cooking over a common fire. The women used their time for handwork, perhaps knitting stockings to be worn in their new homes. If the weather was good and the emigrants were not too pious, there was dancing on the deck, particularly to celebrate Constitution Day, May 17. If the weather was bad, there were the sick to attend. In addition to seasickness, ship fever—typhus—and cholera broke out, depleting the company's number. (In 1861 the number of emigrants was higher than ever before: about 200 people died aboard ship.)[14] As on the *Restauration*, there were births at sea. Both births and deaths called for religious services.

When a clergyman was on board, he conducted worship services on Sundays. If no pastor was along, the ship captain or a devout passenger led the hymn singing and read a sermon.

When the sea voyage ended in New York, Boston, or Quebec, the trip was far from over. Steerage passengers had to pass a medical inspection before being allowed to land. They were immediately confronted with a large, congested city filled with people whose language they could not speak or understand. From this vulnerable position overland travel had to be arranged by steamer, canal boat, and railroad; in later decades tickets were purchased all the way through from Europe to Chicago or Milwaukee. This protected the newcomers from "runners," who proposed to act as agents and instead made off with the immigrants' money. Both Wisconsin and Minnesota employed Scandinavian agents in the 1850s and 1860s to advise Norwegians upon their arrival in Quebec or New York.

Settling

A few travelers brought their journey to a halt somewhere before reaching the Midwest; most continued on to the pioneer settlement in Fox River, Illinois (1834) or Muskego (1839) and Koshkonong (1840), Wisconsin. When the land in these areas had all been taken, newcomers still stopped in; there they found relatives, old acquaintances, or at least someone who spoke their language. They were able to rest for a few weeks or hire out to earn enough money to finance the next step in their trek. People from these first areas who were moving on farther west joined the new arrivals on the trail to St. Ansgar, Iowa, Fillmore or Goodhue Counties in Minnesota, or the Dakota Territory.

Rural settlements clustered in three areas. The first was concentrated in the southern counties of Wisconsin. By the late 1840s there was movement into northeastern Iowa and by the 1850s and 1860s into southeastern Minnesota. The third area, encompassing the Park Region of Minnesota and the upper Red River Valley dividing Minnesota and the Dakotas, was well begun in the late 1860s with continued growth into the 1880s. Settlement followed a leap-frog pattern with residents from the first areas moving on to the second and third along with newer arrivals. As Carleton Qualey pointed out, the history Norwegian immigration is also that of American westward migration.[15]

Norwegian colonies grew up in Chicago and Minneapolis; there were significant Norwegian populations in smaller towns such as Stoughton, Wisconsin, Decorah, Iowa, Northfield and Fergus Falls, Minnesota. Despite these urban concentrations, Norwegians were the most rural of immigrant groups. The Dilligham Commission reported that in 1890 only 20.8% of Norwegians were residents of cities of 2,500 or more; in contrast, 73.4% of Russians and 61.2% of Italians were living in cities.[16]

For those Norwegians who chose the move to America over a shorter move into a Norwegian city, the availability of land was a persuasive factor. Farming in the American Midwest was very different from farming steep fields along a fjord, but it was not industrial labor in a factory. Moving to the United States allowed Norwegian *bφnder* to continue a rural life, if not the same one they had left behind. There were new crops and tools. Agriculture in the United States was a more single-minded affair without the combinations of occupations typical in Norway. There were, however, similarities. Some men spent winters working in the lumbering camps of northern Wisconsin or Duluth in addition to farming. Women continued to work at their conventional tasks: preparing food, manufacturing clothing, looking after the livestock, even working in the fields. Many young women hired out as domestic servants either in other Norwegian households or in Yankee homes, both on farms and in towns.

Norwegian immigration coincided with the settlement of the upper Midwest. The Pre-emption Act of 1841 and the Homestead Act of 1862 made land available to the newly arrived Norwegians as well as to Yankees moving west. Yankees were quick to secure the flat plains sections. Norwegians, in contrast, were first attracted to wooded land near water; it resembled the homes they had left behind. The newcomers were not immediately aware of the difficulties of farming such land.

Nor were they aware of the health hazards of the damp, swampy sections they choose in Muskego and Koshkonong. In those settlements early years were marked by epidemics of cholera and malaria. Nearly one quarter of the 500 or 600 residents of Muskego died of malaria in 1841 and 1843. Danger from these diseases disappeared by midcentury and was never as prevalent in the drier regions of Minnesota, Iowa, and the Dakotas.

Other human and natural dangers continued. Treaties and agreements with the Sauk and Fox tribes in the 1840s and 1850s opened up additional lands for white homesteaders. Nonetheless, Indians were still living in the vicinity of Norwegian settlements. Contact between the two groups usually was peaceful,

41

sometimes it was even pleasant or amusing. A certain amount of curiosity was present on both sides. Indians shared their medical skills and returned strayed children to their parents; Norwegians shared their food. There were, however, violent incidents. The Spirit Lake Massacre of 1857 in northern Iowa and the Sioux Outbreak of 1862 in Kandiyohi County, Minnesota, stimulated fears in other settlements.

The American Civil War had relatively little effect on immigration from Norway, which continued to increase during the 1860s.[17] The brave record of the Fifteenth Regiment from Wisconsin, composed largely of Norwegian men, contributed to the groups' good reputation among Americans.

In the years just after the war the Norwegian crops were poor and prices were low. American expansion stimulated a huge need for people to settle the western territories. The coincidence of these two circumstances stimulated immigration, which took off at an astonishing rate. Mass immigration had begun. In 1866 arrivals surpassed 10,000 for the first time; they did not drop below that figure until 1874. For the rest of the decade the pace continued to be slower, though still steady. The financial panic of 1873 and the subsequent depression made the American opportunities less sure and discouraged Norwegians from undertaking immigration.

By the 1870s Norwegian settlements had reached westward to the Park Region of Minnesota, the Red River Valley, and into the Dakotas. Railroad connections, completed to the Red River in 1871, made the trip much easier for those who used them. Settlers continued to move ahead of the railroad using the slower oxcart and covered wagon. Norwegians ventured onto flat, unwooded land of the Dakota Territory. These areas were subject to natural disasters unlike those encountered in Wisconsin. Prairie fires swept across the fields. Plagues of grasshoppers in several counties destroyed crops annually from 1873 to 1876. On the prairie the margin of survival was very narrow.

In each new area the phases of settlement were repeated by newly arrived Norwegians and more experienced Norwegian-Americans. Unlike Yankees, who usually selected their land individually, Norwegians sent a few of their group ahead to scout out the land and choose a place to which the others followed. The provisions of the Homestead Act entitled each adult to 160 acres of government land. Claims were staked out and the process of breaking fields begun. In wooded areas this required clearing away trees before plowing. On the plains, the opposite was done; trees were planted to break the wind and the monotony of the flat horizon.

Some sort of shelter had to be constructed as quickly as possible. Norwegians were familiar with timbered buildings, but frontier log cabins were not exactly like the houses they remembered. There was no time to allow the logs to cure; frequently the proper tools for joining were lacking. The resulting cabin walls were less than weatherproof. Clay caulking fell out in the cold months, leaving gaps that one letter writer described as "big enough for a cat to climb through." An alternative type of shelter made use of the earth by digging three walls into the side of a hill. This sort of dwelling, a dugout, may have been warmer than a log cabin, but it was dark and damp. On the prairies the only building material at hand was the sod, which was cut into bricks and piled up to form a small house.

Concentrated settlements of people from the same small locality in Norway provided a ready-made community in the new country.[18] Familiar patterns of social life continued; the news from across the Atlantic was exchanged in regional dialect; Norwegian foods were shared. Visitors observed the distinctly Norwegian character of some towns in which one hardly noticed that one was in the United States.

Nonetheless, it was a new country that required some new ways. Settlements named Norway Grove, Eidsvold, and Oslo were in the United States and their American setting shaped their residents. Names were adapted to fit the new circumstances. Some families adopted the name of their Norwegian landholding, although in Norway that name was attached to the land itself rather than to people. Other families used the husband's -son name in a static form rather than continuing the Norwegian custom of active patronymics. Use of -datter surnames disappeared. In the first decades there was a great deal of fluidity.[19] Both first and last names were altered to conform to American conventions of spelling and pronunciation. Sometimes the change was initiated by an American neighbor or schoolteacher. Sometimes it was done by a newcomer anxious to fit in. Contacts with Yankee merchants, employers, and neighbors required some ability to understand and speak English. English words crept into conversations among the newcomers when there was no adequate Norwegian expression.[20]

As with all such shifts in behavior and thinking, changes in names, language, food, and dress were adopted with more or less enthusiasm by each individual. There were those who longed for a taste of rye bread like that they had eaten in Norway and rejoiced when they were able to enjoy a good bit of *gammleøst*, a kind of cheese. Others were just as glad to bite into a novel treat like a watermelon. While letter writers complained that the goods for sale were shoddy and ill-made, they gradually replaced their Norwegian wool *skjørt* with a gingham skirt and their all-purpose shawl with a sunbonnet.

Religious Institutions

Personal and familial habits were not all that required adaptation to the new American setting. Old institutions and organizations required a recasting. Although very few Norwegian Lutherans immigrated because of American religious toleration, they made good use of the freedom they found. The most potent institutions they formed were Norwegian Lutheran churches and related institutions such as hospitals and schools. They shared a religious heritage that had been transmitted to them by the combined efforts of the Norwegian state church, the public schools, and the Haugean and Johnsonian revivals.

The Norwegian-American Lutheran church was plagued by debates and divisions from its beginning. In the American environment of religious liberty and voluntary church membership, all the tendencies that the state church had held together found separate expressions and autonomous organizations for longer or shorter periods. The synods and positions seemed to multiply with every decade. Those people and groups who agreed on one issue did not agree on another. The number of issues involved dooms any characterization of the views to inadequacy or oversimplification.

There was, however, one underlying controversy: the relationship of objective doctrinal truth and subjective religious experience.[21] In Norwegian Lutheranism the two were delicately balanced in a pious orthodoxy; religious awakening strengthened the established church and was interpreted through the Confessions. This partnership built on the long tradition of mandatory catechetical instruction and the state church. It evolved gradually through the years of Haugean and Johnsonian revivals.

In the United States this balance was upset, first by the discussions of lay-preaching, then by the slavery debate and its central question of scriptural authority, and most tenaciously by the election controversy that spanned decades. The two extreme positions were held by the Norwegian Synod aligned with the German Missouri Synod on the side of doctrinal purity and the Eielsen Synod on the side of godly life and experience. The place between the two was filled by a shifting set of groups beginning with a short-lived affiliation of some Norwegians with the Synod of Northern Illinois and most vocally by the Norwegian-Danish Conference (the Conference, 1870-1890) and its successor the United Norwegian Lutheran Church of America (the United Church, 1890-1917).

Disputes arose both between these organizations and within them. The "subjective" wing had both the Eielsens and the Hauge Synod; The Norwegian Synod had the Anti-Missourians; the Conference had an Old School and a New School. In addition to doctrinal issues there were disputes about liturgical practice, church discipline, language use, and polity. Personality and social class also played a part, as did control of educational institutions. The single point of agreement seemed to be that the points at issue were worth fighting about.

The controversies were not contained within the ranks of the clerical leadership. Lay representatives attended conferences punctuated by vigorous debates. Congregational members read about the situation in the church press and discussed the issues. Local parishes were split. There was competition for members on the home mission field of western Minnesota and the Dakotas. Congregations ejected pastors whose views they disapproved of.

Beneath the seemingly constant and endless disputes there was the common heritage of pious orthodoxy. "A common language, a common hymnody, the same form of catechetical instruction, uniform devotional books, and the like" were both evidence of and grounds for a this religious heritage.[22] These provided a countervailing force that drew the factions back together in two mergers: in 1890 the Norwegian-Danish Augustana Synod and The Conference were reunited with the addition of the Anti-Missourian Brotherhood to form the United Church. In 1917 the United Church joined with the Hauge Synod and the Norwegian Synod to form the Norwegian Lutheran Church of America. Although four Norwegian Lutheran bodies remained outside the new church, it contained the largest share of members (nearly 90%). The total membership in all the churches was about one third of all the Norwegian-Americans.[23]

As few Norwegians immigrated for religious reasons and government and church officials were opposed to emigration, no one was responsible for providing pastoral care to Norwegians in the United States. There was no formal religious leadership in the first settlements. Families conducted their own devotions, relying on standard devotional works such as those by Johann Arndt for inspiration. Groups met together for worship conducted by lay leaders. This sort of exercise was facilitated by the Haugean views of early settlers. Noted among the leaders were Søren Bache and Even Heg, significant figures in the development of Muskego, Wisconsin, from the 1840s. Worship services were lead by Heg in his large barn, which also served as the first home of many newly arrived immigrants.

Other settlements depended on the visits of traveling evangelists. Elling Eielsen (1804-1883) arrived the United States in 1839. His simple message emphasized a personal experience of salvation and the need for a godly life; Norwegians whose faith had been shaped by Pontoppidan's *Truth Unto Godliness* and Haugean revivalism responded to these familiar themes. Eielsen's ministry was not confined to legalistic prescriptions against "dancing and drinking, riotousness and revelry." His efforts to keep his countryfolk supplied with Luther's *Catechism*, a central document of their religion, were legendary. When he was unable to secure English copies of the *Catechism* he made a trip to New York to buy some and also have Pontoppidan's work printed. Difficulties obtaining the proper type delayed him until winter travel conditions forced him to make the trip home on foot. On 3 October 1843 Eielsen was ordained by Pastor Francis Alex Hoffman of the Ministerium for the Lutheran Church of Northern Illinois. The Haugean lay evangelist thus became the first ordained clergyman to serve the Norwegian-Americans.

A second lay preacher arrived in the summer of 1843. Claus Laurits Clausen (1820-1892), a Dane, had been attracted to mission work in Africa. During a walking tour of Norway, he was persuaded by Søren Bache's father to forego the African missions and instead to accept a call to Wisconsin as a teacher of religion. Clausen and his new wife, Martha Frederikke Rasmusdatter, established themselves in Muskego with the aid of Bache and Heg. Besides his ministry in Muskego, the evangelist made trips out to the surrounding settlements. On October 18, just two weeks after Eielsen, Clausen was ordained by Pastor L. F. E. Krause, a German Lutheran, on the basis of a letter of call issued to him by the Muskego congregation. Fevold and Nelson date the birth of the Norwegian-American Lutheran church from that call, 13 September 1843.

The following summer a third pastor came to the United States "to assess the religious situation and to establish the Church of Norway among its members 'in exile.' "[24] Johannes Wilhelm Christian Dietrichson was unlike his predecessors. His family was a part of the professional elite. He had been trained at the university and ordained by a bishop of the state church. He represented the conventional Norwegian Lutheran clergyman of the nineteenth century. He was an opponent of immigration.

Dietrichson was interested in the quality and validity of the religious leadership being given. He found Eielsen's ordination lacking; Clausen's he judged to be valid in that it was based on a call and involved both an examination and a consecration. As might be expected, Clausen and Dietrichson were able to forge a working relationship while Eielsen and the newcomer were on unfriendly terms. The charges they leveled against one another were indicative of what each man held to be central to their faith. Dietrichson's concern was for good order. He declared that baptisms conducted by Eielsen were invalid since Eielsen's ordination was invalid. Eielsen looked for behavioral evidences of true religion. Charges of drunkenness and Sabbath breaking were made against Dietrichson as signs of his unworthiness. In their personal relations the three men acted out the potential conflicts dormant within the Norwegian state church. They prefigured the positions taken by Norwegian-American Lutheran synods throughout the century and until 1917.

Initially Dietrichson based himself in Muskego, with Clausen, while he made visits to the Norwegian settlements to assess their religious state and plan his work. He then established himself at Koshkonong. In October of 1844 Dietrichson organized two congregations, East and West Koshkonong, according to a platform of Four Points. All confirmed members, female and male, were asked to subscribe to the platform, which was a compromise with the American situation. Dietrichson recognized that the voluntary nature of church membership in the United States required that his potential parishioners take a clear stand, stating their beliefs and acknowledging their responsibilities. While the pastor thought himself to be in accord with accepted church practice in Koshkonong and the other congregations he organized, as repeated references to the Order and Ritual of the Norwegian Lutheran Church indicated, later immigrant pastors would find it necessary to purge the constitution he wrote for the Spring Prairie congregation of latent "churchly" Grundtvigianism.[25]

The forty families of the East congregation and the thirty families of the West applied themselves to the task of constructing a church building. Identical log buildings were completed and dedicated within three months. Responsibility for the congregation's life fell more heavily on some members than others. The combined Koshkonong churches elected Ole Knudsen Trovatten as *forsanger* to lead the singing and liturgical responses. His duties were expanded to include teaching school and, likely, the additional liturgical role of *klokker*, a lay assistant who read the opening and closing prayers and

47

answered for the congregations in the baptismal ritual. Four men from each congregation were elected as a board of deacons to assist Pastor Dietrichson. Clausen and Dietrichson traveled among their countryfolk, providing ministerial services in barns, in log cabins, and in the open air. They organized immigrant settlers into congregations. However, the need for additional pastors was glaring. Without the guidance of Lutheran clergymen some Norwegians neglected their religion altogether. Others were attracted to "American" religions. The situation in Fox River, Illinois, was notoriously unsettled. Proximity to Nauvoo exposed Norwegians to the Church of Jesus Christ of the Latter-day Saints. When the Saints trekked on to their holy land in the West, there were Norwegian converts in their number. Baptists and Methodists also gained members from among former members of the Church of Norway.

Clausen was not the only one who came to America rather than become a "foreign" missionary. The life of a Lutheran pastor on the American frontier was perhaps well compared to the foreign mission field in its contrast to the sedate life of the clergy in Norway. Several of the men and their wives arrived to find that promised parsonages were still only promises. Those which had been built were like any other pioneer cabin and most unlike a relatively elegant *prestegaard* in Larvik or any other Norwegian parish. The salary was not always forthcoming. In Norway the *prestefru* ran a large household with the help of servants; in America the pastor's wife had only a confirmation student to help her so she herself was often busy with daily work and seasonal chores such as butchering. The parish was large, composed of as many as twenty congregations spread over an area "as big as Denmark," requiring many days of travel in all sorts of weather. Distances isolated the clerical families from one another; there was longing for "cultured" contacts and conversation. Even longer distances separated them from their families and friends in Norway. By 1857 there were about a dozen "university men" serving on the frontier, most with wives and children. Some, like the Dietrichsons and the J. S. Munches, returned to Norway; others—the H. A. Stubs, H. A. Preuses, V. Korens, Laur. Larsens among them—made America their permanent home and impressed their views on the shape of the developing Norwegian-American Lutheran church.

These young, often unexperienced pastors served an unformed church in which everything was new and there was sometimes a "deep prejudice" against the clergy among their parishioners.[26] Herman Preus noted some of the obstacles he encountered in 1859. The attendance at regular worship, midweek devotional services, and Bible studies was disappointing and fewer families conducted devotions in their homes than he thought should. Along with this seeming indifference to religion was the problem of drunkenness, which several observers noted. Preus was not opposed to alcohol; he was concerned about the widespread abuse, which he attributed to the "deeply rooted tradition of the Norwegian, acquired at home that whiskey is necessary partly because of its strengthening to the body, partly because it is conducive to animated sociability and is an evidence of friendship and affection."

Records from H. A. Preus's congregations show that he took his responsibility for the spiritual well-being of his parishioners very seriously and inquired carefully into their personal lives. One couple's request for membership in the congregation was deferred by the council "until such a time as there is evidence of improvement in their marital relationship." A woman was required to "present a certificate from minister and also clear up a rumor implying moral laxity in her past" before she was admitted.[27] In some congregations public confrontations occurred over matters of discipline. Pastor Dietrichson found himself brought to trial by a member of the Koshkonong parish.

Along with the troublesome members there were many who were glad to have the services of these pastors. "As a rule, no major difficulties arose in persuading the people of a settlement to organize a congregation, to call a pastor, and to build a church," observed one of Preus's grandsons. "The great majority were in favor of all these moves from the beginning."[28] Elisabeth Koren's diary from the 1850s was filled with comments upon the kindnesses she and Pastor Koren received from their parishioners.

When the clergymen made their overlapping circuits to the western settlements, the people gave their own beds and the best their larders had to offer to the pastor. They lent their freshly scrubbed cabins for a church building and their immigrant chest, with their best cloth to cover it, for an altar. The pastor brought out his gown, fluted collar, and altar book and conducted numerous baptisms along with confirmation and Holy Communion, often all on the same day—for a congregation assembled from farms for miles around.[29]

The necessity of these trips meant that even those who had issued the call and provided the pastor and his family with a home could expect his presence only every few weeks. On those Sundays when he was away the deacon conducted a worship service according to a prescribed order such as the one laid out by Preus and the council at Spring Prairie:

> When a prayer has been offered, or read, and a hymn has been sung, the Gospel shall be read together with a meditation based on it from some approved sermon collection. Another hymn is sung before the closing prayer.[30]

Following the service there was Sunday school to edify and instruct both young and old.

Growth of the churches followed the arrival of newcomers from Norway and the movement of both old and new settlers westward across the midwestern states. Until late in the nineteenth century Norwegian Lutherans were primarily engaged in ministry to their own as defined by national origin and religious confession. There were instances of cooperative efforts with other Lutherans as in the Scandinavian Augustana Synod and its successors, which included Danes and Norwegians. In some areas Finns were included in early congregations. However, once there were sufficient numbers to allow separate organizations, the Norwegians usually separated to form their own group.

Loss of Norwegians to the Church of Jesus Christ of the Latter-day Saints, to Baptists and Methodists, to Kristofer Janson's Norwegian Unitarian church or to religious indifference stirred Lutherans to their responsibilities. America letters included comments on the variety of religions. One writer, who found little he liked in the United States, described the Mormon religion as "the most miserable sect you can imagine," and related his own views of its teachings to his parents.

> I do not understand this religion, and I do not want to understand it. They believe that their baptism is the gate to heaven, and that it is easy to go there once you have been baptized. They believe they can cure the sick, even that they can help those of the dead who in their opinion have not been saved to enter heaven by means of their baptism. There are many Anabaptists, but none are so ridiculous and detestable as the Mormons.[31]

An effort was made to reclaim Norwegian Mormons for the church of their childhood through a mission established in Utah in the 1890s. It was closed after a short life and little success.[32]

Contacts and confrontations with American "sectarians" were often at a personal or local level. Elisabeth Koren, for example, found "two rather unpleasant-looking women" outside her door. She judged at least one of them to be a Methodist; if the Lutheran pastor's wife was right, the woman probably belonged to the congregation of Methodists that was organized in the area in 1850s. The other woman, Elisabeth thought, belonged to the

Lutheran Franckean Synod. Not long before Pastor Koren had a conversation with one of their lay preachers during which Elisabeth "expected several times that they would come to blows."[33]

Fifteen Norwegian Lutheran families in Grand Meadow, Minnesota, were so offended by the elitism of their clergyman that they joined the Swedish Methodists. The Rev. Steen's behavior in the 1860s was still remembered when the congregation celebrated its hundredth anniversary.

> He showed his disposition as well when he ordered a woman to bring him a cup of coffee or brush his clothes, as when he presided at a church business meeting, and for the least little act by his parishioners that didn't suit his notions, he lost his patience and calm temper and broke out in intemperate language.[34]

When Steen was replaced by J. A. Thorsen, a more congenial man, the diaspora ended and the families returned to their accustomed ethnic and religious fold.

In the 1880s Kristofer Janson was a missionary on behalf of Unitarianism among his countryfolk of Minneapolis and rural Minnesota. In his view the immigrants who joined Lutheran churches merely placed themselves under a clerical tyranny and might as well have remained in Norway. Leaders of the Lutheran churches did not take such criticism without response; they and Janson carried on public debates in their respective publications. His lectures were well attended and for a time his congregations grew. Unitarianism, however, posed little real threat to the Lutherans. Janson himself suggested that he lost male members when they married "orthodox" women and returned to Lutheran congregations.[35]

To protect their country-folk from falling into the hands of these rival groups and to aid them in their initial encounter with America, immigrant missions were set up in major ports of entry beginning in the 1870s. These were linked with seamens' missions. Before the First World War slowed the rate of arrivals, special ministries to immigrants were operating in New York, Boston, San Francisco, and Galveston.[36]

Despite cooperative efforts with other Lutherans, attempts to forestall the recruitment efforts of other religious groups, and work among their own at the point of arrival, Norwegian Lutherans devoted most of their energies to building up their churches in the Middle West. Expansion into the western counties of Minnesota and the Dakotas required continued attention to home mission. Each synod had its own method of providing ministry to the growing

Norwegian-American population and securing its share of the potential membership. Pastors and lay evangelists traveled extensively to hold services and organize congregations in new settlements.

At the local level the church was involved in every aspect of its members' lives. In addition to Sunday worship there were special services for holy days such as Christmas and Easter. Important personal events received religious notice. Baptisms, weddings, and funerals were also social occasions. After the service the whole congregation might have been invited to share a festive meal. Two hundred people attended the wedding of Dina Samfor and Lawrence Peterson in Hawley Lutheran Church without any invitations being sent out. When the ceremony was over, the father of the bride announced: "Today I have given away my only daughter, and now I invite the whole company home to lunch." A similar invitation was issued by Mr. Holm after his children were baptized.[37]

Education of children was a major concern. As early as 1849 Pastor Hans Stub described the need for parochial schools and made suggestions for dividing the parish into districts.[38] At first one of the more educated members of the congregation would be called upon to teach. Parents gave the use of their homes for classrooms. The teacher traveled from one to the next, teaching a few children at each place. Frequently the position was combined with that of *klokker*, lay worship assistant. An advertisement placed in the Norwegian Synod newspaper in 1864 gave the particulars of such a job.

There is a vacancy at West Koshkonong Church for a precentor and schoolteacher which we wish to have filled as soon as possible. The song leadership usually commands an annual income of from $60 to $70, while the teacher, who will conduct at least a ten months' school, is paid at the rate of $15 per month and free room and board while the school is in session. The school is conducted on the peripatetic (*omgangsskole*) basis and over four different routes about six to seven miles apart.

Although we prefer that the schoolteacher also assume song leadership in the church, there is no objection to applications from capable teachers who are unable to qualify for the latter.

In any event the applicant is requested to state to what extent he is able to direct singing, to instruct a choir, or to play some instrument. Applications, accompanied by recommendations, should be sent as soon as possible to the undersigned.

> Koshkonong Parsonage, April 11, 1864
> Jacob Aal Ottesen
> Parish minister for Koshkonong[39]

Instruction was modeled on that given in similar Norwegian schools. The Bible, Luther's *Catechism*, Pontoppidan's *Explanation*, and a hymnbook were the principal texts. Attention was given to religious knowledge and Norwegian language. Sometimes a special schoolhouse was constructed, as the one built in Holden Parish, Goodhue County, Minnesota; in its sixteen-by-twenty-foot space Ole Solberg taught seventy students.[40] An alternative arrangement used the public schoolhouse for "Norwegian school" during the months that the American school was out of session.

Adolescents were given additional instruction by the pastor in preparation for their confirmation at age fourteen or fifteen. Pastor B. J. Muus's daughter, Birgitte Muus Klüver, recalled how she and other children in Holden congregation were prepared.

> The whole life of the confirmand was to be directed by the instruction. . . . Some young people used two or three years for receiving instruction preparatory to taking the confirmation vow. And usually they regarded such a practice as perfectly proper. I attended the confirmation class for three years. I committed to memory, word for word, Pontoppidan's *"Double" Explanation.*[41]

Public examinations were held with the assembled congregation as onlookers. Students who lived a long distance from the church stayed in the parsonage for weeks at a time while they were being taught. In return for their lodging and food they helped the pastor and his wife with all the work that needed to be done.

The heavily religious content of the instruction children received in parochial schools was in keeping with the experience of Norwegian immigrants who had attended public schools in Norway. It was, however, very unlike the instruction available in American public schools. Congregational schools used Norwegian; "Yankee" schools, of course, used English. The language used in each type of school emphasized the differences in subject matter and goals. In addition to teaching students the three R's, the Norwegian schools were to "safeguard the influence of the church, the Lutheran faith, and a Norwegian-American group identity."[42]

Reactions to the public schools were indicative of attitudes toward Americanization in general. Some parents urged their children to attend and take full advantage of the opportunities offered. Others were distressed by the young, female Yankee teachers who gave their students American names. In the mid-nineteenth century, pastors of the Norwegian Synod objected to the common schools, charging that they were "heathen" and their instruction was inferior. These men hoped to establish a system of parochial schools alongside the public schools in the manner of the Missouri Synod. The plan for elementary level schools was doomed by lack of resources and lay disinterest or outright opposition. At the secondary level, nearly seventy-five academies were operated by the various synods for longer or shorter periods. Expansion of public high schools at the turn of the century contributed to the demise of almost all the academies.[43]

In the 1870s and 1880s *Kvindeforening* (women's societies) were formed in many congregations. The women met regularly to do some sort of handwork, which was sold. They also had a devotional exercise involving singing hymns, a reading from a missionary publication or the Bible, and prayer. The hostess provided a meal or two. The items produced at the meetings were sold at a combined dinner and auction; the profits were added to the dues paid by members and used to support various aspects of the church's work.

The women's societies' contributions recorded the development and maturation of the church. In the earliest years the money was used to support the parochial schoolteacher or to pay for the first building. When the congregation stabilized, the women's purchases often included pews, an organ, or an altar painting. They also gave a substantial portion of their treasury to foreign missions and the charities of their own synods.

Concern for foreign missions increased in the last quarter of the nineteenth century. Norwegian-American interest in world missions was initially directed to the work of the Norwegian Mission Society. J. P. Hougstad and E. H. Tou, the first Norwegian-Americans to be sent out, went to Madagascar under the auspices of the NMS in the late 1880s. Support was also given to the Schreuder Mission in South Africa, particularly after Hans and Nils Astrup, who had relatives among the leadership of the Norwegian Synod, were called to that field in the 1880s. Attention was drawn to China by the formation of the Norwegian Evangelical Lutheran China Mission Society in 1890. Thea and Pastor H. N. Rønning, a sister and brother team from the Hauge Synod, were the first missionaries sent by the intersynodical society. Enthusiasm for mission work was built by visits from missionaries as well as by publicity about their activities in the church press.

Parallel to growing interest in foreign fields was increased attention to works of charity among the Norwegian-American community. Pastor Even J. and Ingeborg Swenbolt Homme were the pioneers in this work. Using Mrs. Homme's inheritance as capital, their first undertaking was a small orphanage in Wittenberg, Wisconsin. From that beginning in 1883, they built a complex of institutions that included a home for old people, a normal school, and a mission school for Indian children.[44] Similar work was taken up both by church bodies and independent groups of church people. During Sister Elizabeth Fedde's years in the United States (1883-1896) she founded three deaconess centers. The deaconesses operated hospitals in Brooklyn, Chicago, and Minneapolis. In addition to treating patients they administered nurses' training programs.[45]

By the turn of the century, church leaders were aware of the need to turn their efforts to the city as well as the rural areas. The Norwegian-American population of large towns and cities was increasing as the children of immigrants moved into urban areas. Immigrants arriving in the first years of the new century were more likely to settle in a city than those who had come in the previous decades.

In the cities the inevitability of a shift from Norwegian to English was clear. Despite loud voices in favor of retaining Norwegian in worship, it was impossible to do so. Although some second- and third-generation Norwegian-Americans could speak Norwegian, it was not the language "of their heart." Many had learned their catechism lessons in a language they did not understand. The change came gradually, sooner in the oldest areas of settlement and in the cities. First the Young People's Society spoke English at their devotion; then Sunday school lessons were given in English; then the Ladies' Aid followed. Once a month there was an English sermon; the next year, twice a month. By the merger of 1917, about one in four or five services was conducted in English. In educational settings English was used nearly half the time.[46]

As they had learned to eat new foods and wear new clothes in the process of becoming Norwegian-Americans, the immigrants and their children learned to speak the religion of their hearts in English. They adapted their shared religious heritage to the American setting of religious variety and voluntarism. Through years of debate and years of living together they shaped a Norwegian-American Lutheranism characterized by pious orthodoxy and mutual concern.

THREE

Home and Family

Remember that you are born and brought up in this country and have absorbed the ideas habits and tastes peculiar to this country from your babyhood. . . . Your associations habits and modes of thinking talking and reasoning are all american. Your notions throughout even to housekeeping and entertainment are all american. You so to speak move in an atmosphere that partakes of the liberal nature of american institutions. There things have become part of your nature as they will to anyone who is exposed to them for any length of time while young. . . . He is diametrically the opposite. . . . In the society which you as an american woman (I mean american in ideas) will feel most at home he will be a stranger.[1]

Bella, a young Norwegian-American engaged to a "newcomer," received this bit of advice from her brother-in-law. In his view she and her husband-to-be were "as near antipodes . . . as any two persons well can be." His explanation of why this was so revealed some of the adaptations made in the new land and some of the consequences of an overlap in waves of immigration.

The process of becoming first Norwegian-American and then American was both individual and corporate. In each case it was gradual. While newcomers slowed the process as cold water added to a boiling kettle slows the boil, they were heated by those who preceded them. Those who arrived first had to make adjustments. Children born after the crossing were immediately American citizens whose memories of Norway and old ways were all secondhand. The youth of this "second generation" coincided with the arrival of another "first generation" of immigrants who came from an altered Norway and whose adaptation to America was just beginning. Thus the process was repeated again and again with variations on the theme.

The Norwegians who immigrated to the United States could be divided into groups by any number of criteria: they came early or they came later; they identified themselves as from one Norwegian *bygd* (region) or another; they associated with one Lutheran synod or another, or with the "sectarians," or with no religious group; they were anxious to learn English, Americanize, and fit in among the Yankees or they preferred to speak their own dialect and hold on to as much of the old way as possible; they were of peasant stock or they were from the people of quality. They were men or they were women.

All of these factors affected an individual's reaction to America. Coming earlier meant arriving in an unknown place with no experienced countryfolk to lend advice and assistance. Being from one region influenced the choice of destination and provided ready-made links with earlier arrivals. Association with any religious group served social as well as spiritual needs; it sometimes hastened and sometimes retarded contacts with non-Norwegians. Curiosity and openness to new ideas and ways of doing things propelled a person beyond local circles and into business, or politics, or education. A refined background could be either a burden or an asset. Longing for culture could bring on depression; acquaintance with literature and music could provide needed distractions on long winter nights. Familiarity with scarcity and hard work gave peasant immigrants a head start on the rigors of frontier life; it certainly did not make the life easy.

The difference being a man or being a woman made in an immigrant's experience was noted in early letters that recorded the wages each received: "a halfdollar and board a day for a day laborer in the winter, and $1. to $1.50 a week for a servant girl. She receives as much as $2.00 if she understands the language." Søren Bache and Johannes Johansen suggested that the male advantage in wages was offset by the fact that it was "easy for girls to find work at any time, whereas it is sometimes hard for men to find work in the wintertime, since the farmers themselves have little to do then."[2] The opportunities for women in America were not limited to good wages; in the view of Norwegian immigrants, women were also respected and thus protected from hardship.

> January 11, 1841. Iowa County, Wisconsin. What I have said thus far about working conditions applies to men. Women, especially young girls, will be able to do relatively better. Even in Chicago, through which so many emigrants pour, Norwegian girls are in great demand. Until they have learned a little English, they get only a dollar a week, but later from $1.50 to $2.00, and because of the high regard in which women are held in this country, they are exempt from all kinds of outdoor work and so are far less exposed to disease.[3]

Immigrants observed the lives of American women and noted particularly the ways they contrasted with the lives of Norwegian women. Certainly not all nineteenth-century American women were accurately described as "painted angels"; nonetheless, it was the women of the leisure class who were commented upon. Gro Svendsen, a settler in northern Iowa, remarked upon the discrepancy between what she had heard and what she saw. "We are told that the women of America have much leisure time, but I haven't met any woman who thought so!"[4] Perhaps there were Norwegian women who immigrated in the hope of leaving their days of labor behind and becoming women of leisure. Many—like Guri Sanders-datter near St. Peter, Minnesota—found that although they had not left hard work behind them in Norway, life in America was good.

> Now, to give you our honest opinion about emigration, which I know many of you want to hear about, I can say truthfully that I do not regret our coming here, especially when I think of the heavy burdens we escaped from. I feel very glad about it all, for example, when I remember the moving to the saeters [summer farms], the plight of the cattle in winter, the difficulty of getting hay, and the problem of subsistence. From all this, with God's help, I regard myself as freed, not that I want anybody to think that we have escaped worry by coming here. Still, there is a big difference, especially for women.[5]

Much of the work done by Norwegian immigrant women was related to the survival of their household as it had been in Norway. However, neither the cabin walls nor the corner stakes of the claim proscribed the limits of their lives; the lives of Norwegian immigrant women and their daughters and granddaughters took place in concentric arenas with themselves at the center. The closest circle was their family, the domestic realm. The next was the local religious arena: their congregation, their personal religious experience, and their women's society. A larger circle included extralocal church activities. The largest, not treated here, took in their local town and extended into the world through schools, secular societies, contacts with friends and relatives, and professions outside the churches. Some women lived entirely in the limits of the first or the first and second arenas; the activities of others spanned all four. Age, martial status, education, economics, location, health, and social background all influenced the ways one woman lived in each of the arenas. The women were themselves links between their several worlds.

Given the fact that over three-quarters of Norwegian immigrants lived in rural settings, it was not surprising that most women lived on farms. Along with their husbands and brothers, they filed claims under the provisions of the Homestead Act. *Bønder* and *husmann* women lent their strength to clear timbered land and to break grassland on the prairies. Many of the skills they learned as children in Norway were useful on midwestern farms. Merely crossing the Atlantic did not abolish the need for self-sufficiency. Elite women also participated in the settling of the upper Midwest. Some came to homestead; others came as wives of clergy.

The occupation of the male head of a household was perhaps the significant factor by which women's lives were determined. Frequently the *prestefru* (pastor's wife) was from a family of the Norwegian elite, she was ascribed additional status on the basis of her marital relation with the pastor. Initially her material circumstances were no better than those of her neighbor women; this changed. Although parsonages were the home of far fewer women than were farms, the background and opportunities of their inhabitants encouraged them to record their lives in letters and diaries that were preserved.[6] Thus the source materials available are disproportionately concerned with the lives of clerical families; however, it must be acknowledged that although these women's life is documented, their experiences were not universal.

Caja Munch, Linka Preus, and Elisabeth Koren were young, newly married women when they journeyed with their pastor husbands to serve the growing communities of Norwegian immigrants in Wisconsin and Iowa. The Munches remained in Wiota, Wisconsin, for only a few years (1855-1859); the Preuses and the Korens stayed to build the Norwegian Synod. All three women left personal records that presented richly detailed pictures of life in parsonages of the mid-1800s.

Reminiscence by children and friends of other clerical families, among whom the Norwegian Synod was particularly well represented, and the recollections of the second generation of pastors' wives provided glimpses of parsonage life in later years. In the 1930s and 1940s the Women's Missionary Federation of the Norwegian Lutheran Church of America gathered this sort of material into two valuable scrapbooks with photographs of many "Pioneer Pastors' Wives." They also published short biographies of prominent women in *Some Marthas and Marys of the N.L.C.A.* and in a pamphlet series, "Little Lutheran Biographies." With eulogies, these last sources shared a tendency to be hagiographic, revealing as much about the ideals and memories of the authors as about the life of the person being discussed. Careful reading allows the individuality of the subjects themselves to emerge.

Preserved sources were not confined to parsonage life; even the diaries of *prestefruen* revealed something of the lives of their parishioners. There were also farmwomen who recorded their lives in letters home, diaries, and recollections recorded in their own hand or in that of their children and grandchildren. They told their own stories at close range, giving glimpses of the unique, personal details of their lives.

Gro Nilsdatter Svendsen, the daughter of an influential Hallingdal family, was notable among such immigrants. Having overcome her parents' objections, Gro married Ole Svendsen and immigrated with him and his family to north central Iowa in 1862. She wrote about her American life, "so vastly different from life in our dear homeland and also quite different from what we imagined when we were at home."[7] Her letters were preserved in Norway and published as *Frontier Mother*.

Because much of women's lives were taken up with the ordinary, repeated activities of daily existence, even the most remarkable story told something about the usual patterns by its contrast with the common and unremarkable. One account of making soap or baking bread or watching a prairie fire could be taken as much like the experience of other women's experience of the same. This allows some generalization but ought not suggest that women's lives were undifferentiated from one another. Discussing the value to be given to private writings by women, Elizabeth Hampsten observed:

> Private chronicles can corroborate public ones; historians record and interpret, novelists imaginatively re-create, and diary writers show us what they meant. We read private chronicles in the expectation that they will be true to life, though we do not expect them to be consistently true to fact or even to be always interesting. Inaccuracy and boredom are true to much of life.[8]

"That they will be true to life"—this is what is asked of the available sources. That they will tell us something of how their writers with all their individual characteristics came to be Norwegian-Americans; of what it meant to them to be women; of how their faith and their church influenced their lives—this is what is asked so that we may paint a picture of their authors that is true to who they knew themselves to be.

Getting to America

Recollections recorded after years in the United States said less about leaving homes, friends, and families in Norway and the trip across the Atlantic and half of North America than about what was found there and of their new homes. Letters and diaries, composed as events happened, told more about preparations and travel. Children and grandchildren of the immigrants also

61

recorded what they overheard or were told about the old country and the trip to the new.

Martha Reishus related in *The Rag Rug* how her grandmother, Ingeborg, encouraged her grandfather, Sondre, to immigrate.[9] The two of them used all their skills to raise money to finance the trip. Thurine Oleson's story, "as told to her daughter" and recorded in *Wisconsin, My Home*, included a detailed description of life in Norway and of the family's immigration in 1866. Thorild was thirty-eight, her husband Mathis was fifty-one, and their seven children ranged from three to sixteen years of age when they left Telemark to join relatives in Wisconsin. Everything for the trip was packed into large chests.

> One large oak clothes chest that we still have in the family measures 50 by 26 by 26 inches. It is so heavy that two men can hardly lift it empty. It has a rounded top, and is bound all over with fancy iron bands. The enormous lock of iron has a key as long as your hand. On the outside it is covered with *rosemaleing* (flower paintings) in faded red, white, and black designs. The background is a soft dark green. . . . The inside of this chest is most interesting. On one end is a long box with a lid, a compartment for trinkets and papers.[10]

Food to feed the nine people for the nine weeks at sea was stored in "the biggest chest of all."

> This chest was huge but plain, made of maple or birch, painted red. It was about six feet long, as high as one's head, and about three feet wide. . . . It hinged about halfway down the front and was fastened with a hasp at the top. In the bottom were deep bins which reached up to the hinges. In these [Thurine] put flour, cornmeal, graham flour, and other staples. They must have had dried beef and pickled herring and salted meats and fish. . . . Above the bins in the bottom of the chest, half-way in depth, was first a shelf lying on the bins, then above that another where she stored butter, cheese, *flatbröd*, and other things.[11]

The weeks at sea could be stormy. Seasickness was common. Viking heritage was of little use to farm women who were more acquainted with fields and fjords than with the Atlantic. In the midst of an April storm Gro Svendsen confided her fear and her comfort to her journal.

> May the Almighty God keep us. We are all praying to Him, our true Guide and Skipper, our comfort in our hour of need. Without His help all captains, mates, sailors, and passengers are as nothing. Yet I think they are all of them good folk.

. . . Every evening the captain reads a passage from Skriver's *The Soul's Treasure*. It is a great comfort.[12]

Steerage passengers shared fires and waited their turn to cook their porridge. Fresh water sometimes ran out. Space was limited. There was little to do, especially for those accustomed to a busy schedule of work. Women occupied themselves with sewing, knitting, cooking, and tending to the sick, the dying, and the newborn. June 3, over a month after the storm Gro Svendsen recorded, her mother-in-law gave birth; recently married and without children of her own, Gro felt her lack of skills.

> I trembled like an aspen. My help was less than nothing. I was completely helpless. But God—and one of our good friends—did not forsake us. The little one is quiet, and the mother is as well as can be expected.[13]

First-class passengers had an easier voyage than many of their countryfolk. They had staterooms and ate meals prepared by the ship's chef at a table with the captain. *Fruen* Preus, Koren, and Munch, the three young pastors' wives, traveled in the early days of immigration; they used their days at sea to record their impressions of the trip and their companions. Linka Preus noted that she felt "odd about our eating with silver while the others use tin."[14] Although there was an outbreak of cholera among the non-first-class passengers on the Munch's trip, neither the wives nor their husbands were seriously ill.

Nonetheless, the young women's trips were not uneventful or without diversions. Elisabeth Koren occupied herself with reading Dickens and Schiller. She recorded her impressions of the character and behavior of her fellow passengers. Special attention was given to their meals. If these were not elegant, they were still several steps up from the meals the steerage passengers prepared for themselves.

> In honor of the doctor['s birthday] there was a really festive touch to the dinner. We had chicken broth, roast chicken with peas and potatoes, and a compote of pears, or whatever it was. The captain served Rhine wine and champagne. As nearly all the steward's wineglasses had been broken, the doctor's health was drunk in a beautiful medley of coffee cups, big German beer glasses, and wineglasses. Well, it all tasted good. . . . For dessert our steward had baked macaroons and other cakes, all very excellent, and a welcome change from pudding.[15]

Linka found time and subjects for sketching, an activity she continued in the United States.[16] An Ascension Day worship service provided her with an opportunity to observe the other shipboard Norwegians, potential neighbors in Wisconsin.

> For a long time, even during the singing of the hymns, the sight of this fine appearing congregation delighted my eye. They sat on the deck in two series of rows, the men on one side, the women on the other. From above, the sun in all its glory poured its cheering light upon the entire group. The glittering buttons of the men, the spangles and filigree brooches worn by the women, vied with the beautiful beaded embroidery and the gleaming white linen sleeves among the dark dresses, as to which might radiate the purest light, the most sparkling rays.[17]

A few days before reaching New York she was asked to be godmother to Anne Olafsdatter, who had been born on the ship; Mrs. Preus reflected, "the minister's wife is beginning to assume her functions."[18]

Caja Munch was less enchanted by the trip and her "traveling company" on her voyage in 1855. She wrote to her parents that they were "less than fortunate, all of them Low Germans except a Doctor and an American." (She refers here only to the first-class passengers.) Although seasickness limited her meals to one per day, she pronounced the food excellent. That meal seemed to be the high point of Caja's shipboard days, which passed slowly, with few other distractions.

> In the morning, Munch and Emil [her younger brother] got up first and brought me a cracker and whatever else they thought would please me as I was very particular. Then they went up on the deck while I dressed, reeling from pillar to post, and usually did not manage to get ready before the steward rang the bell for breakfast, after which we again went up on the deck and were awfully bored. I would knit a little on a poncho, receiving some assistance from my friend the American. . . . Time went slowly until the steward finally, at 3:30, rang the bell for dinner, which went on in a very amusing way. We could never put down our plates, one had to balance it with one hand and eat with the other, sometimes we had to use cups. However, we could never be quite certain that we did not get dishes and food all over us. When we finished eating, we usually took a nap, which could last until evening, but note that we seldom finished our dinner until after 5. Afterwards they played cards, but I was busy just hanging on.[19]

Immigrants formed their first impressions of America in large, congested cities long miles from where they would make their homes. They were confronted by a mass of people and a foreign language. Trust was likely to be returned with fraud. "I do not believe a single person in New York," wrote Linka Preus. Her response was based on a short stay in that city, which she described further in her journal.

I gathered up a sizable bundle of personal effects and made my way through a crowd of dock hands, laborers, horses, and vehicles, leaving Herman to guard one of our large chests which had broken in two, while Ziølner argued with a sharper who was charging a half dollar for lifting a small trunk onto a cart. I trudged along through several streets, staring at the walls in search of the hotel name—finally, Scandinavia Hotel. Now came Ziølner with the cart, once more an argument, the men refused to get off the cart before being paid twice the amount agreed upon. The captain backed up Ziølner in the dispute and the efforts of the sharper were foiled.[20]

A family traveling on the same ship with the Svendsens were not so lucky as to have the captains help when trouble befell them. One of their chests was dropped into the water while being unloaded in Montreal.

[T]he cover flew open, and the contents floated around. It held all the possessions of a very poor family. They lost everything. They had four children—no money, no clothes but the ones they were wearing, and almost no food.[21]

Most of the distance from the port of entry to the Midwest was traveled by rail and steamship. One traveler advised his correspondents of the potential difficulties.

For one who cannot speak the American language, the trip from New York to Milwaukee is more difficult than that across the ocean, because of the problems involved with transportation changes, illness, provisions, contracts, tickets, and interpreters. However, it happened with us that there was no difficulty, only pleasure. We kept well and had friends in our company who knew the language, traveled the whole distance with us, guided and instructed us.[22]

Martha Juel, mother of the Lutheran historian Olaf Norlie, traveled from Trondheim to Quebec in the 1860s as a first-class passenger. The crossing took fifteen weeks. Her trip to the United States was completed with an unpleasant train ride.

> She . . . told that they were herded into freight box cars, driven into the cars pell-mell by men using blacksnakes and frightful cursing, and then the doors of the cars were locked from the outside. There was hardly standing room in the cars, and no toilets, and no beds but there they were confined until they reached Chicago a week later.[23]

The Munches used both rail and steamship on the American portion of their trip. Along the way they were able to take in Niagara Falls, which Caja enjoyed. She was less satisfied with the rest of the journey: the benches were hard, the trains were crowded, the other passengers smelled, and the stoves worked so well that "we most certainly would have fainted if we had not been able to open our window."[24]

Interactions with Yankees began upon landing and continued during the inland trip. In the 1840s Gunhild Larsen traveled by a canal boat on which a little Norwegian girl attracted the admiring attention of an American boy; he persuaded the Norwegian boys to teach him a few winning phrases in Norwegian:

> Kari, Kari, *jeg liger dig, kan du like mig, jeg er ikke rig, ikke pen heller styg som synden men jeg elsker dig.* (Kari, Kari, I like you; can you like me; I am not rich, or handsome, rather ugly as sin but I love you.)[25]

The Svendsen party took a steamer from Montreal to Chicago. Although Gro found the locks and dams along the way interesting, the boat itself was crowded and uncomfortable. She met the cook, the first black man she had ever encountered, and managed to convey her regard for his culinary skill. The women (Americans or Canadians) on the steamer did not earn any respect from Gro.

> On our steamer [were] the vainest women I've ever seen. They were loaded down with golden trinkets. No moderation, no taste. They seemed to be interested only in themselves and their finery. Such vulgar looking women![26]

The sailors she judged "most annoying and disgusting."

Thurine Oleson and her family also traveled by boat from Canada to Winneconne, Wisconsin. At the dock they were met by relatives whom they had not seen for several years. Excited greetings were exchanged before everyone climbed into wagons for the last few miles of their trip to the relatives' waiting homes.

For others the journey was longer. The Korens left their belongings behind in Wisconsin to be sent along in the spring because they had to cross the Mississippi in a canoe. An obliging Norwegian took the pastor and his wife the rest of the way across Iowa in his wagon, despite the harsh winter weather. Once the couple arrived in their parish they were taken in and given a place to live.

Not everyone received such hospitable welcomes as the Olesons and the Korens. In September of 1847, four and a half months after they left Vang, Kari Bunde and John Veblen (parents of the yet unborn Thorstein Veblen) arrived in Milwaukee with less than three dollars and no one to greet them. Typhoid fever had so weakened John that he could not walk alone when they landed in Quebec; nonetheless, the day after arriving in Milwaukee he walked twenty-five miles to secure a job with an old friend. Kari found work as a domestic and saved her wages toward purchase of land.[27]

In later years many immigrants traveled on prepaid tickets that included both transatlantic passage and inland travel to Chicago or another midwestern destination. This arrangement guarded immigrants from being stranded short of their final goal by dwindling funds as happened to some of Gro Svendsen's fellow travelers. Even if most Norwegians arrived safely at their destinations, all the dangers along the way were not removed. Trains were missed; misinformation was given; sickness struck.

Women traveling alone were particularly vulnerable. The Immigrant Protection League of Chicago received lists of single women who left New York for Chicago; in the early 1900s its staff made heroic efforts to ensure that the women arrived at their intended destinations.[28] Linguistic ability eased the staff's work and reassured the women they served. Among themselves the league staff and volunteers spoke fourteen languages; Norwegian was one. Helping newcomers to find their relatives or other contacts was one of the league's activities. The task was made difficult by unreliable transportation schedules and confused addresses.

This sort of problem was not confined to cities. A young woman was sent a ticket to travel from Norway to western Minnesota, where she was to be employed by the Charles Nord family of Wolverton. Everything went well until she misheard the conductor and got off at the wrong train stop; no one was waiting to meet her. Without confiding her predicament to anyone, the woman found a job in the local hotel. It was there that Mr. Nord found her some weeks later and took her back to his farm.[29]

Once immigrants reached the places in which they would settle, seasickness gave way to homesickness. As the degree of illness on shipboard varied, so did the intensity of loneliness and longing for Norway. Postal service was slow and expensive. The Korens waited five months before they received their first letters from Norway. Each communication was anticipated and savored. Those who could not write for themselves depended upon their neighbors to send messages and to write letters home for them. Gro Svendsen apologized to her family for neglecting to write to them; she had been occupied writing for others.

Women in the United States imagined the reception their letters received "back home." They longed to see loved ones and to know all the details of their lives. Letter writers shared with their readers the comfort they derived from the knowledge that all would be reunited in heaven; there would be "no more partings, no sorrows, no more trials, but everlasting joy and gladness."

> My dear sisters, it was a bitter cup for me to drink, to leave a dear mother and sisters and to part forever this life, though living. Only the thought of the coming world was my consolation; there I shall see you all.[30]

The "dull pain of loneliness" mixed with a sense of abandoned responsibility in Gro Svendsen's letters to her family. The sorrow of separation was made more keen when she realized that she would not be able to care for her parents in their old age.

> New Year's Day, 1868. I think that my sister and brother at home are especially favored because they can be near you, can see you, can talk to you. And in the years to come they will be able to nurse you in illness and the frailty of old age. I should feel blessed if I could ever help you, and I am confident that there the others will feel as I do. However, I do think that it is impossible for them to feel quite the same as I do, because I am so far away. Oh, my dear mother, can I expect forgiveness from you, and will God in His mercy forgive me for my willfulness that brought you this bleak sorrow and bitter tears.
> Had I remained at home, my conscience would not have tortured me as it does now, and who knows, it might have been wiser to have remained with you.[31]

Whether or not it might have been wiser to have stayed in Norway, homesickness and loneliness had to be put aside if new homes and new lives were to be made in America.

Life on Farms

Immigrants were advised to arrive on their new land early enough in the year to build a shelter and to get some crops in. The first months were filled with such essential jobs. The wagon that had housed a family on the westward trek sometimes served further as their first temporary home. If they were joining relatives or friends, newcomers often moved into the established settlers' cabin or dugout. The nine members of Thurine Oleson's family spent their first winter with her widowed sister: there were fourteen in the cabin.[32]

While waiting for her own house to be built, Elisabeth Koren visited people around Washington Prairie. She found that many families had arrangements like the Knud Aarthuns'.

> It is a poor house that Knud has, and too small for his large family; he has eight children and this winter his paternal uncle and family are living with him. He is a handsome old man, the uncle, though he did not seem very happy at having emigrated; he felt that they were in straitened circumstances—the house and other things—in which opinion, indeed, he may be right.[33]

Cabins were as small as ten by twelve feet. One of the first Norwegian settlers in St. Ansgar, Iowa, married Assur H. Groth shortly after her arrival.

> Our first house was a small log cabin thatched with sod. After a while a new family came to the settlement, and we let them stay with us in our cabin. We were then seven persons in all in our little home. The cabin had no upstairs, but some boards were laid across the beams under the rafters, and there some of us slept on a tick filled with straw.[34]

Thalette Brandt, who did not live in one, judged sod houses on the Dakota prairie to be an adequate, perhaps even pleasant, type of shelter.

> It was wonderful how neat and cozy sod houses could be made. When floors were scrubbed, walls freshly whitewashed, and the broad window sills filled with blooming geraniums, such homes were by no means unattractive in the pioneer country.

She also recognized the potential disadvantages.

> Of course the coziness and attractiveness depended pretty much on the people living in the home. I must admit, however, that such houses had their

drawbacks. They were apt to become damp and in time would settle so that the roof and walls would become lopsided. They were not very roomy for growing families.[35]

These sorts of arrangements were intended to be temporary. As soon as possible improvements were made by adding on or by replacement. Gro Svendsen told her family:

> Our house is very small and humble, but it's a shelter from the cold winter. I shall say no more about it. However, next spring, if we are all here and all is well, we hope to build a large and comfortable house. We shall build even though it costs a great deal of money to build houses in this country.[36]

Mary Syverson Torbenson's family accomplished a great deal during 1880, their first year in Moore Township, North Dakota. They broke sod, plowed five acres for wheat, built a sod house and stable, dug a well, and constructed a firebreak. After two years they built a log house and planted trees: box elder and cottonwood.[37]

Ole S. Johnson, a historian of Spring Grove, Minnesota, described the steps by which a farm was established. Over the years it was developed into a going concern.

> On such a place there gradually grew up a number of small houses, including a horse stable, cow barn, hog house, sheepfold, doghouse, chicken house, wagon shed, corncrib, granary, hay shed (usually merely a roof supported by four posts), smokehouse for meats, privy, and the livinghouse house, which was first erected. . . . After the living house had been sufficiently completed to permit the family to move in, the next thing was to procure a cow and erect a cow barn. Then a hog or two were obtained, and soon a sheep and a few more chickens.[38]

In the first years on a farm immediate needs were the impetus for ingenuity and improvisation. The furnishings of tiny cabins were made from materials at hand. A table was made of the sturdy immigrant chest or from a plank laid on fresh saplings. One woman reported to her correspondents that the legs of her table grew leaves. Saplings were also used to construct rope-spring beds. In some cabins fabric curtains separated beds from the rest of the living space; children's trundle beds were pushed out of the way during the day. Mattresses were stuffed with corn husks or hay; when there was a shortage of bed frames, the mattresses were placed directly on the floor of the loft, which also provided storage for out-of-season clothing and foodstuffs. Back issues of newspapers, such as the *Decorah Posten*, covered the cabin walls; cut in scallop patterns they also lined the shelves.

As the times improved, so did household equipment. Ingeborg Reishus began housekeeping with only a teakettle, an iron kettle, and an open fireplace; later she acquired a cookstove, which came with pots and pans. Chairs, tables, benches, chests, and cupboards were constructed by local craftspeople. While they followed the styles known to them in Norway, they also introduced modifications. A cupboard was a particularly valued pieced of furniture, as it provided essential storage space.[39]

A dirt cellar under the house was used for food storage. The subterranean room was cooler than a kitchen shelf; women noted, nonetheless, that it was more difficult to keep dairy products in the heat of the midwestern summer than it had been in cool Norwegian mountains. Novel methods of food preservation evoked comment.

> It's difficult, too, to preserve butter. One must pour brine over it or salt it; otherwise it gets full of maggots. Therefore it is best, if one is not too far from town, to sell the butter at once. This summer [1863] we have been getting from eight to ten cents a pound. Not a great profit. For this reason people around here do not have many cows—just enough to supply the milk needed for the household. It's not wise to have more than enough milk, because the flies are everywhere. Even the bacon must be preserved in brine, and so there are different ways of doing everything.[40]

Mathilde Berg Grevstad recalled that fish were cleaned, split, and hung on the clothesline to dry.[41] Vegetables and fruits were preserved in syrup by sand-packing in stone crocks. The crock was filled then covered with a sheet of wrapping paper that had been dipped in lard. Layers of newspapers were wrapped around the neck of the container and secured with bands of wet muslin. Finally, quicksand was heaped on top to complete the seal.[42] Other staples were dried for winter use.

In the earliest years, diet was determined by what was available. Within these limits, food preferences based on Norwegian customs endured. Dairy products—several sorts of cheeses, milk, cream mush—continued to be favored elements in immigrants' meals when they had a cow, or access to one. Ingeborg Reishus purchased a half share in a cow; every other day she walked miles to milk it. Coffee and home-brewed beer were common drinks. Germans were not the only brewers in Wisconsin.

71

The malt beer that Mother served so freely was made of hops, malt, syrup or molasses, and water according to the other ingredients. They made the malt themselves, out of barley. It was first wet, then laid in a dry place until it started to sprout. After the malt was made, it was boiled with other ingredients, then strained and yeast added to make the brew "work" for a few days. She then skimmed off the yeast and put the brew in kegs. This crude beer was just a mild drink. You could take any amount of it and never get lightheaded.[43]

Of course, the stricter moralists abstained even from this home brew. Pork was a frequent item at meals, much more so than in Norway. The seeming ubiquity of fried pork was often commented upon by newcomers. While *lefse* and *flatbröd* were still made and eaten, iron stoves with ovens gave cooks means to bake yeasted wheat breads. Along with the stove came useful tools: two kettles, a five-pail boiler, a teakettle, a coffeepot, a frying pan, and five bread pans.[44]

New equipment and new foodstuffs—such as pumpkins and watermelon—prompted women to learn new culinary skills. Daughters returned from working in Yankee kitchens with expanded repertoires. Menus for church women's group meetings revealed gradual adoption of American foods, including pies and fancy cakes. St. Olaf students produced a cookbook in 1906. A separate section in the back of the book gave directions for preparing Norwegian foods, *lutefisk, flφtegrφte, fattigmads bakkels*; the front section included recipes for American favorites, baking powder biscuits, macaroni and cheese, and banana cake.

Clothing continued to be homemade for several decades. In the earliest years women executed every step of the manufacturing process: carding wool, spinning yarn, weaving cloth, and sewing garments. Increased prosperity made purchase of inexpensive, commercially produced cloth possible and eliminated the initial stages of home production. Sewing machines eased the task. A seamstress could be hired to come and sew for the family for a few weeks. As old Norwegian clothes wore out, they were replaced with American styles.

Knitting remained popular. Kari Veblen was well known for the mittens she knitted in the mid-nineteenth century and gave as gifts to her guests. They were easily identified as her handiwork by their ornamental cuffs. Barbara Levorsen told that in the early twentieth century her mother used an ingenious pin to attach a ball of yarn to her skirt allowing her to knit stockings while she walked.

Cleaning supplies were also made at home. Soap was manufactured by boiling fat, saved from cooking, together with lye, leached from hardwood ashes.[45] Elisabeth Koren was forced to escape from the house by her hostess's determination to get as much cleaning power out of soap as possible. First she washed clothes; then she used the strong soapy water to wash the floor. Sand or particles shaved off a brick were used for scouring powder to keep wooden floors gleaming white.

Women's work was not confined to the interior of their houses. Gro Svendsen was able to report on crops and livestock. In her letters to her parents she told each year's yields and the number and types of animals on the farm. She explained the advantages of oxen over horses with authority. Looking back to the early years of the twentieth century, Eva Thortvedt recalled that in the Red River Valley area

> The only field work we girls ever did was cultivating potatoes, mowing, raking but never any pitching of hay or shocking of grain. But milking and cleaning the cow barn was our job.[46]

During World War I the girls also did the plowing.

Barbara Levorsen noted that her mother did things the way they were done in Norway. While other women stayed away from the stable except to milk the cows and gather eggs, Mrs. Levorsen

> . . . carried pails of milk into the house and carried the skimmed milk back to the hog pen, to the chicken feeder, and to the calves. She hoisted water from the well in old wooden buckets and brought it in by the pailful. She carried coal for the stove. These were the everyday chores. The water trebled on washdays, at butchering season, and at other times. She made all the butter, baked all the bread, prepared five meals a day, knitted our stockings, sewed her own and my everyday clothes and often helped Papa in the fields.[47]

Both young Barbara and her mother helped to plant potatoes. When the young girl complained of her sore back, her mother reminded her how much she enjoyed eating *lefse* made from the potatoes. Anne, a friend of Barbara's, began plowing with a gang plow and five horses before she was eleven years old.[48]

The women who joined men in the fields during harvest, following the reapers and binding the sheaves, were not always family members. "Hired girls" were known to desert their domestic posts for the outdoors in the late summer. Linka Preus was understanding when her newcomer girls left her to earn the higher wages offered by farmers.

Anne, a newcomer girl, and Turi, were living here, but as the wheat harvest and the haying were on, just at that time [August 1855], they preferred to work elsewhere and earn a half dollar a day, a wage I could not pay for washing kettles and the like. They did the morning milking and evening for the privilege of sleeping here.[49]

The report in a Minnesota newspaper of 1868 suggested that the Yankee families of that community were perhaps less sympathetic.

From the Northfield Recorder, 31st. Harvest work commenced in good earnest last week, as a number of persons who had Norwegian girls working for them found out, they have left to work in the harvest field where they can earn nearly the same wages as men.[50]

Anna Hedalen left a job as a servant in the Wisconsin governor's residence in the late 1850s to work on a farm, where she "toiled in the fields along with the men from the melting of the snow in April until the last bundle had been threshed in November."[51]

Hannah Harris moved from pitching hay to cooking for the threshing crew. As the sole cook she provided the workers with five full meals: breakfast at 5 A.M., lunch at 9 A.M., dinner at noon, lunch at 4 P.M., and supper at 7:30 P.M. After five days of this labor in the late 1880s Hannah was paid $5.00.[52]

Dangers to settlers were both natural and human in origin. As they moved west from Wisconsin there were encounters with Indians. In the violence of 1862 Guri Olsdatter Endreson's family paid a heavy price for their new home in Kandiyohi County, Minnesota. Her husband and one son were shot to death; two daughters were captured by Indians but later escaped. Guri herself was remembered for her bravery during the attack; her statue was erected. She and her youngest daughter hid in the cellar until the following day, when they found that one son had survived. The three made their way to safety farther east. It was not until four years later that Guri wrote about the tragedy to her daughter and parents in Norway.[53]

Other women recalled less tragic, even amusing contacts with Indians during approximately the same time period. In the Red River Valley Mathilde Berg Grevstad remembered that an Indian woman once begged for a dress and that a blanket once disappeared from the clothesline.[54] Martha Hove Hougstad heard her mother tell about giving the Indians near their Worth County, Iowa, home some bread and butter; to her surprise they would scrape the butter off once they were out of the house. The Hove family bought deer meat from the same people.[55]

In the pre-Civil War years, immigrants in Wisconsin were subject to epidemics of malaria, cholera, and other diseases. Henrietta Jessen's graphic account of her husband's illness begins with stereotypical Norwegian understatement.

> February 20, 1850. I have not had so pleasant a winter as I might have had. My husband fell ill in the middle of September and had to keep to his bed until eight days before Christmas. Then he began to sit up a little and now he is up most of the day, but he is so weak that he cannot think of beginning to work for two months and perhaps not then. The doctor calls the sickness dysentery. Yes, my poor Peder has suffered much in this sickness. The doctor gave up all hope of his life and we only waited for God's hour, but at twelve o'clock one night his pulse changed and the doctor said that now it was possible that he would overcome the sickness, but he said that it would be very stubborn and [the recovery] slow.
>
> That Sickness I can never forget. Think, in one terrible day and night my husband lost eight pots of blood. That was the night before he was near death, and I was alone with him and my children. But afterward there were a few of the Norwegians who were so kind as to help me for a time watching over him, the one relieving the other. For seven weeks I was not out of my clothes.[56]

Because there were few doctors on the frontier, the immigrants had to depend upon themselves and one another in times of medical need. When her neighbor contracted the feared smallpox, Ingeborg Reishus nursed her through her last hours and promised to look after the woman's young son. After the woman died, Ingeborg began to worry about infecting her own family; her husband put the matter in a different perspective. He assured her that even if they caught smallpox she had done the only right thing: ". . . remember a soldier of Christ never shirks his duty at any time. We must rely on God for the rest."[57] In an emergency or an accident Ingeborg could be depended upon to take the situation in hand. One of her sons choked on a fruit pit; she took her knife and performed a tracheotomy. Another son cut off the tip of his finger; she stitched it back on and splinted the digit with a bottleneck. Gro Svendsen took the initiative before disaster struck. She wrote to her father in Norway asking him to send her smallpox vaccine. Although not all the bottles survived the trip, she was able to inoculate her children.

Some settlements had a person well known for medical skill acquired either by formal or informal methods. The Norwegians of St. Ansgar, Iowa, relied upon two women when they were sick.

> At first there were no doctors and no medicines. Rev. Clausen helped those who were sick, as far as he was able. Mrs. Mikkel Tollefson Rust served as midwife, and Sønnøva Knutson, a trained midwife from Norway, served as midwife and also as doctor, practicing both cupping and bloodletting.[58]

The "pioneer nurse and doctor" in another settlement was Mrs. Vie. She had learned her trade, in part, by tending to her own large family. Despite their demands, "she was never too busy to help a friend in time of need."[59] In the area of western Minnesota where the Berghs lived, Mrs. Ingeborg Stensrud (a widow known as *gamlemor*, grandmother) was always ready to give assistance to anyone who was sick.[60]

Clergymen and their wives were called upon to minister to physical as well as spiritual needs. Elisabeth Koren was asked for medical advice from the first weeks of her life in Iowa. In the midst of the blizzard of 1880-81, Pastor Bergh, armed with grape juice and rusks supplied by Bolette Stub Bergh, went to attend to a neighbor suffering from typhoid. A few parishioners were skeptical about Pastor R. O. Brandt's ability to administer a smallpox vaccination. They were, however, persuaded to give him a chance and were thus protected from the disease.

The months of pregnancy and the event of birthing were particularly dangerous times for women. The depended upon each other for assistance at the time of birth and in the days after. Aagot Raaen's mother often made a rich cream porridge and took it to new mothers. Reminiscence suggested that death in childbirth was not uncommon. Gro Svendsen's mother-in-law stayed with her as a "nurse maid" after one of her children was born. She was "quite well although . . . still weak" following the birth of her fifth son in seven years. Gro confessed to her parents that she had wished for a daughter, "but it was not to be."

> I had intended to write to you just as soon as I was strong enough, but during the first two weeks after my son's birth I was not able to read or write because my eyes were so tired. . . . My eyes gradually grew stronger, but then my breasts became inflamed. We succeeded in getting the infection stopped, so that I escaped with not too much suffering and pain.[61]

Not long after the death of little Siri, another daughter, the ninth child, was born. The pregnancy was difficult for Gro, who was always weak. When the baby was born, the mother had no milk and was forced to feed tiny Sigri Christine from a bottle.[62]

In her study of Norwegian women on the Wisconsin frontier, Monys Hagen found that the dangers of childbirth prompted one of the few instances of contact between Norwegian immigrant women and their Yankee neighbor women. During a snowstorm in the winter of 1841, American neighbor women were fetched to assist a young, first-time mother when no Norwegian woman was available to help her through labor.[63]

Death of an infant or small child was a common experience in pioneer families. On April 30, 1871, two cousins were the first children baptized in Richwood Lutheran Church in Detroit Lakes, Minnesota; in less than two years, both children were dead, victims of diphtheria. Of the 133 deaths recorded in Upper Coon Valley Lutheran between 1861 and 1870, 114 were of children under five years of age. Nonetheless, the death of small children was not taken lightly. A photograph of the tiny corpse was sometimes taken to preserve the family's memory of the child's brief life.[64] The Svendsens were not unique in naming the next child with a similar name: Siri and Sigri Christine.

Although the need for self-sufficiency and hard work continued, the initial period of getting settled did not last forever. In her study of the trans-Mississippi West, Julie Roy Jeffrey cautioned,

> All too often, accounts of frontier life suggest that this relatively brief period was the norm for an extended period of time. In fact, settlers came to the frontier quite rapidly, and during the second stage, social and economic conditions markedly improved. This period of community building eventually ended without fanfare as the community came more and more to resemble those to the east. The pioneer generation lived through both periods.[65]

Some lived through the initial period more than once as they followed the frontier west from Wisconsin to southern Minnesota to the Dakotas. Ingeborg Reishus made all of these moves, in addition to her initial migration from Norway to Wisconsin. The saga of settlement included a rehearsal of the pattern: first establishing a farm and then building a community. Each time friends and family were left behind and conditions shifted from primitive to increasingly affluent.

Years of good crops produced extra income that could be spent on luxuries. Frame houses replaced log or sod. Near the new house, a well was dug. Fancy furniture, perhaps a piano or an organ, filled the parlor. Curtains and potted houseplants decorated the glass windows. Barbara Levorsen noted these differences between her aunt's home back east in Minnesota and her more spartan childhood home on the edge of the Dakota frontier. A horse and buggy carried the family to church and visiting. Children went away to college. American food appeared on the table and American styles of dresses appeared on the women. Martha Hove Hougstad, born in 1867, testified to increasing prosperity and settledness. "By the time I appeared on the scene we had a good house and everything was convenient."[66] She had no personal recollection of Norway nor was her conscience troubled by longings for Norwegian friends or relatives.

Life in Parsonages

The lives of early pastors' wives and daughters were somewhat different from those of other women. They came from a more refined background; while they were not unacquainted with hard work, they were accustomed to having domestic help rather than providing it. Their clergyman husbands and fathers were likely to be away from home for extended periods of time. Their livelihood was dependent upon the generosity, dependability, and good fortune of the parishioners, not the government as it had been in Norway. They were responsible for extra tasks such as baking communion wafers and ironing the pastor's fluted clerical ruff. In addition they were called upon for medical advice and to provide food and lodging for their husbands' colleagues and other newcomers.

While the *prestefruen* of the Norwegian Synod left the best documentation of their lives, the first pastors' wives were not part of that group; there was no such group in 1843 when Sigrid Tufte Nelson married Elling Eielsen or when Martha Clausen and her husband Claus immigrated. Sigrid's Haugean family settled in North Cape; evangelist Eielsen became a frequent visitor in their home. After their marriage the young bride (age eighteen) and her husband (age thirty-nine) lived with her parents for some time. Even after the couple moved to Jefferson Prairie they shared living quarters with another family for several years. Their firstborn, Anne Karina, lived only fifteen months; twins were stillborn. Until other children were born, Sigrid was able to take an active part in the ministry. She was remembered as "a good woman; she could read devotions and conduct a meeting as well as any man; she was a woman of great talents; she had an enlightened understanding."[67]

Linka Preus gave a detailed accounting of the sort of life that young *prestefruen* left in Norway and of the decision she and Herman made to come to Wisconsin. Caroline (Linka) Dorothea Margrethe Keyser, the daughter of Rev. Christian Nicolai Keyser and Agnes Lousie Carlsen, was born in Norway in 1829. Before she was ten years old her mother died; she and her sisters then lived with her grandmother. The early pages of her diary, written during an extended visit to her Christie relatives in Askevold, were filled with sledding parties, family theatricals, music, and other amusements. Her activities also included reading and religious instruction from her uncle, culminating in her confirmation in 1845. From her aunt she learned the art of running a large household. In addition to pitching in to stuff sausages, knead minced meat, and help with Christmas baking, her apprenticeship involved learning to make decisions and assume responsibility.

> Meanwhile, all a house-mother's duties have rested on my young shoulders. At first I found it very difficult, but now affairs run smoothly as though I had been a housewife for years—the food question was especially worrisome, and Mondays were always filled with thoughts of food for the ensuing week. A couple of days ago I was in a great pinch and we had to butcher a calf, but the old saying, "Out of season the trolls shall be killed," indeed came true, for no sooner was the animal slaughtered than Uncle was presented with a hind quarter of beef, and the self same day other gifts arrived, a great number of large flounders and some lobsters. Could anything have been more awkward? If only the meat and fish had arrived half an hour earlier, then all would have been well. Now I had to salt some of the veal and the beef—but of salted meat we had enough. To provide Uncle with fresh meat had been my plan, as he likes that best; and now perhaps I shall merit a scolding from Aunty because her pretty calf no longer frolics about.[68]

In the midst of this busy year, Linka fell in love with a young man studying at the University in Oslo. Despite her grandmother's objections they made plans to be married as soon as Herman Preus secured a call. Linka's diary entries revealed her emotions during the wait.

> Today I have written two certificates, according to Uncle J. Christie's dictation, for people who plan to go to America. They are Arne Saetre, his wife, children, and maid. Perchance sometime I shall see them in America.—That, however, is in Thy hand, O my God.—Wherever I go the thought of America and the

journey to that country is with me. Occasionally it disappears, shortly to find its way back into both my head and my heart. At times it appears in bright colors, then again in more somber hues.[69]

In the interval, Charlotte Mueller Dietrichson, second wife of Johannes W. C. Dietrichson, the first clergyman ordained in Norway to serve in the United States, gave the bride-to-be some hints about life in America, remarking on the problem of household help.

. . . it is most distressing—the girls use fans and are "all dressed up"—imitators. Not infrequently does it happen, when the house-mother asks her maid to do something, that she will answer: "Do it yourself"—picks up her fan and settles herself in a chair.[70]

During their conversations with the Dietrichsons Linka became aware that Herman's anti-Grundtvigian views did not conform to those held by Pastor Dietrichson and others. Further, the conflict might prevent them from going to America. This realization prompted a dream: "Every night I dream of ministers and discussions—America always in the background, day and night!"[71] As she slept, she anticipated a situation that did develop in the United States in later years: debates about slavery, discussions about common schools, disagreements during the election controversy, and negotiations toward church union. Finally, in spring of 1851, all the obstacles were overcome: Herman was ordained, the couple was married, and they set sail.

The Preuses arrived in Spring Prairie, Wisconsin, to find their parsonage was nothing but a cellar full of water. They occupied a room in Lars Møen's home. Linka made the best of the situation.

Our room is about twelve by twelve feet. We have a bed against one wall and half of another; on one side a red table and sofa (this consists of two chests, filled with clothes, and pillows from my old sofa laid on top). At the end of the sofa is my chest of drawers with a cupboard as a hat, reaching to the ceiling. This occupies one wall. The cupboard serves as pantry, milk shelf, etc. There are two easy chairs, (my treasures), another chest of drawers, and under the bed a low storage-chest on feet. This is the sum total of our furniture. On the walls are bookshelves and a smaller knob shelf, also fire arms, tinware, flat irons, dust broom, paintings, etchings, and—not to be forgotten—our tools; otherwise the room would not be well filled, which it truly is; two persons can barely pass.[72]

Hanna Bugge Jensen, at the sixtieth anniversary of the Highland Prairie congregation, recalled her arrival there in 1859.

> Many came to meet and greet their new pastor. It touched my heart to see the tears of joy as they grasped our hands, wishing us welcome and God's blessing. Many of those who came brought us provisions: pork, flour, potatoes, eggs, etc. It is needless to tell you that all these things were most welcome.

Hanna, Pastor N. E. S. Jensen, and her sister-in-law Sena Jensen shared the Nordbys' cabin while the parsonage was built.

> Being only eighteen years old, I knew very little about housekeeping, but Mrs. Nordby was given to me as a good teacher. She taught me the art of making bread and also helped me to prepare other things.[73]

In 1848 Ingeborg Arentz Stub, the daughter of a clergyman and granddaughter of a bishop, spent her first night in Muskego, Wisconsin, without sleep in a wooden bed that was home to hungry bedbugs. In the morning she and her husband, Rev. Hans Andreas Stub, were shown a little log house. The proposed parsonage was two miles from the church, close to a swamp, and had no near neighbors, except "Indians, rattlesnakes, and mosquitoes." Aware that Rev. Stub would often be away, leaving her quite alone, she refused to live there: "No dear friends! I dare not live here. Let me have a room where someone else lives or share a room with someone in the congregation."[74] So it was arranged that the Stubs share the home of Even Heg, a prominent member of the congregation. Ingeborg, with the help of Heg's daughter, set up a small study for her husband. The two women scrubbed the room, covered the walls with old newspapers, moved in a table and chair, and improvised bookshelves; unfortunately, it was soon ruined by a rainstorm.[75]

Once the couples were installed in their own dwellings the women began to transform them into homes. The Korens spent nearly a year living with various families from their congregation in small log cabins before Elisabeth was able to begin keeping house in the parsonage and plant the flowers for which she would become well known. Vilhelm helped in putting their books in order before the two of them went for a walk and discussed plans for an arbor. Rev. Duus related how their house was gradually decorated in a style drawing on Yankee preferences.

Our parlor on Christmas Eve was so very elegant that I have not for a long time seen anything to equal it. In addition to this when I went to Neenah on business on January 2, I purchased for $8.00 a beautiful mirror two feet nine inches long and proportionately wide, with a real gilt frame, and two small mirrors with mahogany frames edged in gold for $1.50 apiece. Now the old mirror, which cost $.31 and was used by everyone, has been demoted to the kitchen. The table stands between the windows, and above it the new, big mirror is hung in Yankee fashion by a red cord with beautiful red tassels.[76]

Not all *prestefruen* were recent brides accompanying their young, newly ordained husbands to the American mission field. Some women immigrated alone or with family members before they married. Not all were young. Johanna Cornelia Amundson Krogness had married at age twenty-three, been widowed after eleven years, and served as matron at Loftes Gave, a training school for neglected children in Christiania before she married Rev. S. M. Krogness in 1861. Whether they met in Chicago, where Rev. Krogness ministered to Trinity Congregation or in Norway is not known. Caia Holmboe Waldeland came to the United States in 1869; she lived with her sister in La Crosse, Wisconsin, and in Chicago. Six years later, at age forty-one, she became Rev. O. Waldeland's second wife and stepmother to his five children. They had one more. Maren Eline Kristine Johnson grew up in Norway; her father was Kasserer Sahlgaard at the Kongsberg silver work. She immigrated in 1862 to be *guvernante* in the home of Pastor Hjort. The following year she married Rev. Thomas J. Johnson.[77]

Others came with a growing family. Peter and Johanne Brodahl arrived in Blue Mound in July 1856 with four children and a fifth waiting to be born the next month. Fortunately, the reception they received was unlike the experience of the Korens, the Preuses, and the Stubs. The several congregations issuing the call to Rev. Brodahl were prepared for the family. They had dug a well, built a stable to house two horses and two cows, broken a field of five acres and enclosed it with a seven-rail fence. And they had constructed and furnished a parsonage: a two-story frame house lathed and sided on the exterior and plastered inside. It was equipped with a parlor, a kitchen, a pantry, a cellar and a railed stairway.[78] While looking after this estate and five children, it is unlikely that Johanne had time to sit and record her thoughts and activities, even while Peter was off visiting his numerous congregations (at one time he served twenty-one).

Securing domestic help was an immediate problem that became more pressing as children were added to the families. A young girl from the parish sometimes lived in the parsonage to help with the housework and the children; a male confirmand served as an outdoor helper. The turnover among these servants was high and their work was not always up to the *prestefru*'s standards. Caja Munch sent reports of her domestic situation to Norway.

> Now, then, we have three servants, a boy of the confirmation class (whom we furnish only with clothing) to tend the horses, and then I have been so exceedingly lucky as to get a childless widow, the likes of whom hardly is to be found even in Norway with respect to being orderly, thrifty, clever, and decent in every way. I only wish I could keep her, but she is not healthy. For a nursemaid I have so far only borrowed the neighbors' daughters, but I don't think I shall have any difficulty in getting a young girl of twelve to thirteen years for food and some clothes; for there are several poor families in the settlement.[79]

A few months later she was less satisfied.

> . . . America is so poorly supplied with help. Imagine, now I have a young girl, who was confirmed by Munch last year, and who knows nothing, and yet she is supposed to get more than 1 *Spd.* per week. Moreover, one has to beg and plead with her to stay; indeed, she regards it as a favor on her part that she serves us and not with a Yankee.[80]

Nor were the newcomer girls always entirely reliable, as Caja learned one August when her maid was "seduced by a Yankee," ran away, and "left everything as it was, some things clean, others dirty, some things outside, others indoors."[81] As *Fru* Munch was fond of complaining and not easily satisfied, her views on this matter were perhaps more negative than the situation warranted. Regardless of their skills the women's presence provided some company for the *prestefru* during the many days and nights when the pastor was attending to his widely scattered congregations or meeting with other pastors.

The few single women from the Norwegian elite who immigrated and lived with clerical families were perhaps better companions for a refined pastor's wife than was the daughter of the neighboring farm. Hanna Jensen spoke fondly of her sister-in-law, Sena, with whom she shared the sufferings of seasickness and the pleasures of gardening. Henriette Neuberg, Pastor Laur. Larsen's sister-in-law, was for some years resident in the Preus's home. That she was called *Tante* (aunt) indicated both the closeness of the Norwegian Synod families and the place she held in the Preus household. Christine Goli had a similar place in the Jacobsons' Dane County parsonage. Clara Jacobson noticed Christine's special significance to her mother as well as her relationship to the family.

> Mother and she became fast friends and comrades who shared joys and sorrows with each other. Even if Mother was very tired and worn she fathered new life and courage when Christine arrived. Then work seemed like play to them and the whole house resounded with their merry laughter. Christine had a keen eye and a sure ear for the comic and could reproduce incidents in an amusing way. She did not lack seriousness, however, and took and active part in all work pertaining to the church. She was our faithful friend through her whole life . . .[82]

In the early decades the pastor's absences from home could last days or weeks. After Laur. Larsen had been away from the Rush River parsonage for a month in the mid-1850s, his wife Karen met his boat in Hudson in order to give him a fresh supply of linen and to "get a glimpse of him before he set out to finish his circuit in Minnesota."[83] The days without Vilhelm's company made Elisabeth Koren long for his return. Perhaps this desire was intensified by the narrowness of her world, which she described to her father.

> I have now neither politics, literature, social life, nor any such thing to write about—just my own little world; and that comprises only Vilhelm, the baby, my home, and its immediate surroundings, including such appurtenances as the horse, dog, hens, and other animals that we have—and of this little world you shall receive detailed information.[84]

She was most faithful to her diary and to her correspondents in Norway while he was away, as if to compensate for his absence. Writing filled Elisabeth's days and provided Vilhelm with reading material upon his return.

> I am so glad when he comes. He has so much to tell me, and reads my diary to learn how I have fared while he was away.[85]

> I do not know why I am so much more reluctant to see Vilhelm go this time than before. I ought to be more accustomed to his leaving and should be satisfied with his having been home fourteen days. But the feeling is there; I can do nothing about it; and it is not something I can become accustomed to. But I shall manage to be in good spirits before he returns.[86]

In addition to loneliness and longing for her husband's company there was the worry about the disasters that might befall him in foul weather or times of epidemic sickness. When H. A. Stub was late returning during the 1850 cholera epidemic, Ingeborg sent someone to check up on his health.

Of course life did not stop while the pastor was away. The time was well used for heavy cleaning, exploring, visiting, and letter writing. During one of Rev. A. C. Preus's absences his young wife, Engel Brun, received an unexpected visit from Fredrika Bremer. The Swedish traveler was taken by the young Norwegian woman, who received her with "true Northern hospitality and good will."

> She was pretty, refined, and graceful; her whole appearance, her dress, her guitar which hung on the wall, every thing showed that she had lived in a sphere very different to that of a loghouse in a wilderness, and among rude peasants. The house was not in good condition; it rained in through the roof. Her husband, to whom she had not long been married, and whom for love she had accompanied from Norway to the New World, had been now from home for several days; she had neither friend nor acquaintance near nor far in the new hemisphere.[87]

The pastor's wife had other tasks beyond keeping house for her own family. Elisabeth Koren noted that she was called upon to give medical advice and to nurse the sick in the community despite her lack of training.

> Guri sat there awhile with her knitting and asked my advise as to Eli's indisposition. I have gone through my medical books without finding anything. People come and ask for help, but those they come to are only indifferent counselors. Yesterday Iver Kvale was here for advice and medicine for his child. That medicine came in handy, indeed; I wish we had more of it.[88]

On the occasion of a marriage she might be expected to provide the wedding meal and to stand as witness to the ceremony. Frequently she found herself as godmother at baptisms. In the early years Ingeborg Stub traveled with her husband to his charges and led the singing in worship.[89] The *prestefru* could spend hours laundering, starching, and pleating white clerical ruffs. No less time-consuming, she also made communion wafers. One of Diderikke Otteson Brandt's daughters recalled that her mother had turned these tasks into a source of income for worthy purposes and an opportunity to instruct her children.

Besides making and laundering the pastors' collars used in the synod, she also made all of the communion wafers. For one thousand communion wafers mother received a dollar, each one thousand taking, of course, many hours and for ironing the collars, which took at least two hours, she received fifty cents a piece. All the money she received from these things was set aside for needy students and at the time of her death she had given away six hundred dollars from this fund alone. . . . She was very fond of poetry and could give many psalms and hymns and great portions of the Bible. She used to teach me many hymns and poems when she was cutting out communion wafers.[90]

The parsonage sometimes served as a sort of boarding school and hotel. Confirmation students might stay in the pastor's home for several weeks at a time when preparing for their entrance into the church. When the pastor was away, the task of instruction fell to his wife along with her usual duties.

In her "Memories of Koshkonong Parsonage," Marie Lee described the tradition of hospitality and hinted at the discontent some *prestefruen* felt.

It was very often abused;—guests continually, friends and strangers seemed to feel free to come and make themselves at home. The minister struggling along on a small salary, the wife overworked, and both trying to make ends meet. One said, "We are supposed, sometimes, to entertain angels unawares, but most often I listen in vain for the flapping of their wings."[91]

Mrs. Lee based her reminiscence on a six-week visit to the Jacob and Cathinka Otteson home in 1878. As she was soon to marry Rev. O. H. Lee, the stay was intended, in part, to give the young woman a taste of parsonage life. Cathinka Tank Doderline Otteson ran the parsonage and large farm with the help of an adult maid and a fourteen-year-old girl.

The life Marie observed was not uncomfortable. Her description was of an appealing day: it began, for the family, at 8:00 A.M. with a breakfast of eggs, cheese, marmalade, and coffee with cream and ended with wine or chocolate with small cakes followed by evening devotion. Although there were no bathrooms and no furnace, the house had simple, comfortable furnishings that included a piano. The living room, dining room, several sleeping rooms, kitchen, and summer kitchen were a great improvement on that little log house Ingeborg Stub had refused.

Marie's presence also provided a welcome extra set of hands during the Synod's anniversary celebration. The Ottesens and the congregation hosted all the participants. There were one hundred staying at the parsonage with another two hundred for dinner. Mattresses were filled and laid on the attic floor for younger pastors and students; additional mattresses for the young women were placed on the floor of the second floor. Dinner had to be served in the barn. When the festivities had ended and the people gone home, Rev. Otteson apologized to his wife for the hard work and anxiety the event had caused her. Mrs. Otteson's reply revealed the attitude of a pastor's wife who shared in his ministry. "I will recover from the strain and it has been fine for the church and our people whom we both love." However, she advised the future Mrs. Lee about duplicating what she had seen. "Now, Marie, you see how we live in a Norwegian parsonage, but do not try to pattern your parsonage after this one. We are used to it in Norway and could not change, but it is not practical in America."

Marie's visit to the Ottesons' reflects the pattern of close social contact among the dozen clerical families of the Norwegian Synod who arrived between 1844 and 1857. As were the professional families in Norway, these families were intertwined by marriage and old family friendships.[92] There was visiting between the parsonages for pleasure as well as at the time of Synod meetings. The festive gathering at the Spring Prairie parsonage for Christmas 1862 was the subject of one of Linka Preus's sketches.[93] Occasions for visits were anticipated; once over, the time together seemed to have gone by all too quickly. The children of clerical families were sometimes baptized on these occasions. The host pastor and his wife received communion from the visiting clergyman. There was music and amusement as well. Rev. Nils Brandt and Ingeborg Stub gained some fame through the settlement for their singing together with guitar accompaniment. When the Preuses dined with the Duus family they drank a toast to Pastor Duus's parents in "real wine, a novelty in Waupaca County."[94] The children of the families formed lifelong friendships during visits, as recalled by Caroline Koren.

> A great pleasure for us were the long summer visits from the families of the ministers of Spring Prairie, Koshkonong, and Painted Creek. During these visits there were often many in the house, and it was lively both inside and out. We had a long table in the garden, around which we children stood and ate our evening meal, and drank cambric tea from small brown varnished cups.[95]

Indeed, the families of the Norwegian Synod clergymen "felt themselves to be as members of one family."[96]

How much this banding together was the innocent, natural consequence of shared background and common endeavors and how much was a result of class-conscious desire to avoid uncultured contacts is debatable. The evidence is mixed. When J. W. C. Dietrichson decided to look for a second wife, he went to Norway to find her. An early historian of the Norwegian Lutheran churches casts this action in a snobbish mode, suggesting that "though there were many capable homemakers in Wisconsin and Illinois even in those days, it never occurred to this aristocrat that he could marry anyone who was not of his well-defined station and dignity."[97] Caja Munch made her disdain plain in her letters to her parents.

> Everything considered, we do not really miss anything except the company of cultured people instead of these silly peasants who for the most part cannot comprehend at all that we are a step above them and have more requirements. No, they regard themselves maybe as fully as high and always say *Du*, and many such things, which sometimes are really highly ridiculous. . . . For example, many simply call me Caja. Here are not even any cultured Americans.[98]

Her attitude was returned by some of the laity. While he was genuinely respectful of the clergy, Alfred Erickson recalled their tendency to assume and take advantage of their position with disdain.[99] After nearly one hundred years the writer of an anniversary history for Grand Meadow Lutheran preserved the congregation's recollection of Pastor Steen as one whose aristocratic background was the basis of an arrogance that alienated parishioners.

On the other side, H. A. Stub reminded his son of the families who had lived around them in Muskego and commented that their relations were congenial. Indeed, the pastor and his family "often had their most blessed times in going round with these families."[100] Still, he used the less cultured term *kone* to refer to Gunild, Syvert Ingebrigtsen's wife, and the more refined *hustru* to refer to his own wife. Both Linka Preus and Elisabeth Koren wrote fondly of their neighbors, without Caja's condescending tone. Linka's shipboard descriptions of the Norwegian peasants who would become American farmers revealed a slightly romantic view, as did Elisabeth's descriptions of the people she met on her first Christmas in Iowa.

> It pleases and interests me to see and talk to all these different people, our Norwegian farm folk, with whom I have had so little acquaintance up to this time. I find many of them attractive; I like those best who have no city flourish about them, but come up, take me by the hand and say, "Well, we wish you welcome to America!"[101]

No doubt both women had absorbed the attitudes of romantic nationalism current in Norway at mid-century; however, in the United States they lived in day-to-day contact with the people Elisabeth described as "nature's children" and could not avoid the less picturesque elements of farm life and manners.

> . . . it can irk one considerably. . . . On the whole we have to shut our eyes and ears as much as possible to preserve our appetite and good humor when our finer sensibilities are offended by these rustic manners; fortunately, they usually have the opposite effect, however; one glance at each other, and we have a hard time to keep from bursting into laughter.[102]

As the wives of the early faculty of Luther College, Karen Neuberg Larsen and Diderikke Otteson Brandt had frequent contacts with the sons of Norwegian pioneer households. Students remembered the women's kindnesses toward young boys away from home. One recalled that Mrs. Larsen had nursed him and brought him flowers while he was sick in the Halfway Creek parsonage, temporary first home of the college. After the college moved to Decorah, Iowa, the Larsens' home, a suite in the main building, often received visits from fledgling scholars and future pastors. Those who were unable to go home for holidays took part in the Larsen family observances complete with tree trimming.

Mrs. Brandt's contacts with "seminarians" began before Nils Brandt's appointment to Luther. Her daughter related how she contributed to their education.

> Before Luther College was founded, those who were to be educated to become ministers, were sent around to stay at the different ministers' homes and the pastor would teach them whenever they had time. Father was a missionary pastor when we lived at Rock River [1856-65] and was often away for months at a time. Then it became mother's work to teach these young men staying with us. She was well fitted as a teacher, with a thorough knowledge of Norwegian, German, French and English. She even knew the rudiments of Latin which was considered very unusual for a woman of that period.[103]

On the Decorah campus her academic talents were no longer required; she found other ways to contribute to the students' training. With other women from the community she formed a *Lappeforening*, a mending society, which provided new clothing and repaired the old.[104] Like the Larsens', the Brandts' home was open to students over the holidays. Diderikke also was hostess for afternoon coffees, which encouraged cultivation of social refinements along with theological insights. These activities, her good-humored disposition, and freedom from snobbish attitudes earned her the title "College Mother."

This term suggests that parsonages and the women who lived there were playing a role commonly prescribed for nineteenth-century women. They nurtured the young, future leaders of the community by providing tender, loving care; at the same time they transferred their values, both social and religious.[105] Ingeborg Larsen, Rev. Laur. Larsen's second wife, commented on this fact in regard to her kinswoman, Diderikke Brandt.

> . . . the finest thing about her countless acts of kindness lies not in the intrinsic value of her generosity, but in the impression which her thoughtful care made upon the hearts of the young and in the incentive they received to live not for themselves alone but for others.[106]

The *prestefruen* of the early Norwegian Synod were culture carriers, whose "burden" culture consisted of social attitudes and behavior as well as religion.[107]

After the 1870s an increasing number of pastors' wives were "native" Americans: they had been born in the United States of Norwegian parents or had arrived in America as children. Many of them were daughters of pioneer parsonages. Lena Gjertsen and Louise Augusta Hjort accompanied their pastor-headed families across the Atlantic while still children. Louise was five when Pastor Ove Jacob Hjort accepted a call to Waterville, Iowa. Lena was fifteen in 1864 when Pastor J. P. Gjertsen moved to America. Both women became wives of influential churchmen. Louise became Linka Preus's daughter-in-law when she married Pastor C. K. Preus. Lena married Rev. Theodore Dahl, latter president of the United Church; she had a significant role in the organization of the Women's Missionary Federation. Others were daughters of those the pastors served.[108]

In the second generation the original clergy families cemented their relationships through marriages between their children. Two of the Hjorts' daughters married sons of H. A. and Linka Preus. The Ottesons' daughter Didrikka was the first wife of one of the Stubs' sons. The marriages of the Stub, Preus, and Koren daughters widened the circle to include the growing number of pastors trained in the United States. The Brandts' sons both widened and cemented the circle by marrying sisters who were not from a clergy family.[109]

Parsonage life in the late nineteenth century was recorded by Bolette Stub Bergh, Thalette Galby Brandt (Mrs. R. O.), and by Lydia Bredesen Sundby, daughter of Inanda and Adolph Bredesen. The Brandts and the Berghs moved farther west along with the trend of the day; the Bredesens were in Stoughton, Wisconsin, close to the early Dane County settlements. Some of the extreme of frontier conditions were eased; nonetheless, in many ways the life these women presented was similar to that experienced by their parents.

When Bolette Stub Bergh and her husband moved to western Minnesota in the 1870s, their first home was a dugout. Although she did not mention being afraid of Indians, snakes, or insects as had her mother when she arrived in Wisconsin, the roof leaked so badly that Bolette took refuge under a table. She experienced the hazards of grasshoppers and blizzards along with friendly exchanges with her Indian neighbors. She often went along with Pastor Bergh on his preaching tours as her mother had accompanied her father. Sunday school and confirmation instruction were held at the parsonage. If the pastor was absent, his wife "read" with the confirmands. Like many of her contemporaries, Mrs. Bergh had a hand in organizing the congregational women's society.[110]

In 1872 the Berghs moved into a new four-room house called Pascha; the name was given by the neighboring Indians and meant "white heads" or "white people." Only two of the rooms were finished, but it was an improvement over their old dugout and better than the living quarters inhabited by some of their neighbors. One "poor, sick" woman visited Bolette.

> She was so downhearted because she lived in a cellar where the sun never got in. I asked her into the sitting room where the sunlight just streamed in. Oh, how nice she thought it was! I played and sang for her. Then she exclaimed: "Oh, how beautiful; I believe I have come to Heaven!" Poor woman—she turned crazy some years later. It was hard for her to live in a dark cellar.[111]

If the Berghs were spared dismal housing, they did share in the hardships of natural disasters such as blizzards and grasshopper plagues. After the devastation of the latter, Rev. Bergh was paid with forty acres of land rather than cash.

Thalette Galby married R. O. Brandt in 1883; in the wedding sermon Pastor Laur. Larsen warned her not to expect to be first with her husband. "[H]is sacred calling as a pastor was to be first and highest." It was his calling that took them to the Dakotas. Their move was accomplished with the use of a railroad freight car, which allowed them to take along many more household goods than had accompanied immigrants across the Atlantic.

I owned a piano and an organ, earned by teaching school and giving music lessons. Besides outfitting me generously and comfortably as a bride, my mother—then widowed for thirteen years—gave me a sewing machine and a hard coal heater. As there was ample space in the freight car she also sent with us many things which had more or less outgrown their usefulness at home, but were good as new. She thought they "might come in handy" out on the prairies, and they certainly did.[112]

The settlers pressed Thalette to resume teaching school. She, however, felt that her place was at home. The objection was cleverly overcome by setting up a schoolroom in the parsonage attic. The parsonage, the largest house in the area, functioned as a community center. In addition to the school, choir practice, the Christmas tree festival, and Ladies' Aid events were held there. One winter day the women served dinner to 120 people in the twelve-by-twelve-foot kitchen.

Lydia Bredesen Sundby grew up in Christ Lutheran parsonage in Stoughton, Wisconsin, during the final two decades of the nineteenth century. Her memories of it ranged from technological innovations like electrification and installation of a telephone and an indoor bathroom to the natural beauty of the garden and grape arbor where coffee was often served. The interior of the house was elegantly decorated with a cherrywood hall tree, prism-encircled lampshades, and walnut dining room furniture, all gifts from the congregation. The gifts were not without obligations, as Lydia told a Stoughton audience in 1959.

Often when I use the word congregation, I think of how our mother often reminded us, "Now we must all be careful not to mar anything—remember this house is not ours, it belongs to the congregation." For some time I thought congregation was the name of a good man who let us live in his house.[113]

The women who lived in parsonages as wives and daughters longed for the homes they had left behind in Norway, as did women on farms. If there was a contrast between their expectations and what they found in America, gradually they forged new lives with some comforts and some opportunities to use their talents and education within the church. Often the daughters became wives of clergymen. These women provided models of middle-class values and gave their energies to the founding and continued work of women's societies.

Single Women

Among the immigrants there were single women, both women who had not married and those who had been widowed. Some married women were widowed after arrival. Of course, all females born in the United States started out unmarried. The experiences of single women varied. Those who came to America in the company of their relatives were part of a household. Others came alone to join an existing household as a "hired girl" or governess. Some established their own homesteads, either alone or with other women. Many married.

Kari Hagen, a widowed acquaintance of Gro Svendsen, inquired about the prospects for a woman such as herself in Iowa. Through her parents, Gro cautiously advised staying in Norway.

> Tell her I think she would be wise to stay where she is for the time being . . . now that she has not one to provide for her.
> First of all there is the strenuous journey. Then, after she arrives and gets her land, she must hire someone to do all the work because her sons are still too small. And wages are very high. Living in another home with her children would be extremely difficult. She would probably not even be able to have her children with her. There would also be many other problems. I have mentioned just a few. After coming here, she would soon learn that what I say is true. On the other hand, if she could get a faithful companion who would stand by her through all difficulties, it would be worth while for her to come. I do want to say that she must decide for herself.[114]

Some years later she reported that Guri Sando, a widow left with eight small children, received a "great deal" of aid from the community. Gro expected that there would be "no let-up" in the widow's needs.

After Per Hansa's death (reported in the final pages of Rölvaag's *Giants in the Earth*), widowed Beret achieved, in the following two volumes, prosperity of which her husband had only dreamed. Beret, though fictional, was not the only widow who successfully managed a family and a farm. Three widows—Gro Nickols, Hage Lunden, and Turid Lylegrav—proved that self-reliance was possible. At ages forty-six, fifty, and sixty, they and their combined total of eighteen children were among the first Norwegian settlers in Trempeleau County, Wisconsin.[115] In May 1880 the *Fergus Falls Journal* reported that two widows had proved up their claims.

Remarriage was another option for widows. Thurine Oleson's stepmother, Tone, looked after her children and farm for a few years after she was widowed and then married for a second time.

Women who had never married and widows without children could work as a domestic servant or "hired girl" in the home of relatives, of other Norwegians, or of Yankee families. Readers of the *St. Paul Daily Pioneer* in the mid-1860s were told of the arrival of a boat load of immigrants one July and assured that there was "a great preponderance of women among them . . . and most of these young girls." This was important because it "foreshadows a good supply of domestics in years to come."[116] This sort of demand encouraged Norwegian-American young women to continue to hire out, as was a common practice in Norway.[117] In the 1890s 80 percent of the women who worked outside of their own homes were engaged in domestic or personal service.[118]

There were advantages for the workers as well as a demand for their work. Among both the newly arrived and the native born, some women viewed service in a Yankee household as an opportunity to learn something of American ways while earning wages. For others this sort of work was done only because was essential to their family and individual finances. Their recollections of service were unhappy ones.

> . . . it may be added that these servant girls were used or rather abused by their employers as slaves or beasts of burden. A hired girl was janitor, water carrier, clothes washer, floor scrubber, house cleaner, nurse, and in some houses she had to calcimine rooms with lime mixture. Her hours of work were not limited to a certain number of hours. . . . Her bedroom was never heated.[119]

In either case the promise of good wages available for such positions prompted young women to emigrate to America or, once there, to move to the city.

One young woman came from Norway to keep house for her brother in Tumuli, Minnesota, in 1880 and found herself soon a subject for the local newspaper and defendant in the court. Inger Buerd was "with child" when she immigrated; when she gave birth, in her "shame and desperation she destroyed its life" by throwing it in a lake. At the time of her arrest her friends were concerned that she might take her own life as well. In less than a month Inger was found not guilty and "the general sympathy of the public was satisfied."[120]

Opportunities for marriage prompted other women to come to America. Ingeborg Reishus orchestrated a sort of mail-order marriage for a friend. She interested John, an American neighbor, in Siri; he offered to pay her fare to

Wisconsin. Siri, however, was not told of his investment and was under no obligation to him. To the delight of all concerned, John and Siri did marry. "Young, strong, and handsome" bachelor "homestead boys" placed a joint personal ad in 1872 that sought to lure young single women to move farther west, using both sugar and vinegar.

> We urge all the young girls that now live in the older settlements to consider this; to try to picture themselves the unbounded happiness that would be theirs as well as ours by joining us here as our life companions, instead of spending their whole youth working for others until they become cranky old maids with no one to turn to.[121]

The bachelors further assured their readers and potential brides that a Norwegian minister was available to "wed us all in one ceremony, and [to] perform other clerical duties that we may require in the future." How many, if any, women were convinced to move west is unknown.

There were also "homestead girls." *Nordisk Folkeblad* reported in 1869 that Turi Knudsdatter Halvorsgaard, Jorand Olsdatter Enerstvedt, and Gunhild Olsdatter Enerstvedt, all from Nummedal, were each homesteading eighty acres. In addition the reporter noted that Turi had broken and fenced one and a half acres, built a house and a barn, and had two cows and a pig.[122]

In the first decades of the twentieth century other women homesteaded in the Dakotas. In *The Promise of America* Odd Lovoll included an intriguing remnant of their existence: a photograph of Carrie Einerson dated May 11, 1911 with the following inscription.

> Dear Clara, I am sending a photograph of myself in front of my hut. I ought to have sent you a letter, but I have too much to do at the present. Greet your family. Your friend, Carrie.[123]

Mrs. Ella Lindhjem told of two cousins who homesteaded in Velva, North Dakota, in 1901. They each claimed a half section, built an eight-by-eight-foot shack, and proved up in seven years' time. She knew of others who had done the same. Not all of them fared so well, however, as she suggested in a tantalizing but incomplete account.

> Four claimed a section of land, a quarter each, and they built a shack in the very middle of their possessions. Not wanting any interference, they dug a grave and placed flowers on it. On their shack they put up a sign, "Small Pox." The

authorities heard of this and investigated. They found conditions such that the group was ordered off their claim. They were undesirable as citizens.[124]

Mrs. Lindhjem further observed that "improvements removed the joys of real pioneer days, and robbed the wildness of its enchantment." After they had proved up their claims, many women sold them and took up "professions as teachers, dressmakers, etc. A number of girls married and are today farmers' wives."[125]

Many young women born in America worked for a number of years as teachers in congregational or public schools between being a student themselves and marrying.

Marital Relationships

Commentators on Norwegian-American family life have often assumed that the father was the ruler of the household and that the lives of the other members revolved around him. Joan Buckely emphasized this domestic pattern in her study of novelist Martha Ostenso.[126] Surely there were tyrannical men who dominated their wives and children as did the character in Kristofer Janson's controversial short story, "Wives Submit Yourselves to Your Husbands." There were also families in which the husband and wife enjoyed a tender and reciprocal relationship.

Gro Nilsdatter's family opposed her marriage to Ole Svendsen. The first letter in *Frontier Mother* is one she wrote to Ole when it appeared that they would not marry, in deference to her parents. The affection she expressed in that letter continued throughout their shared life in Iowa. Before leaving for the United States, she reassured her family that her choice of husband was a good one.

> . . . you mustn't think for a moment that I regret my choice. I felt then and even more so now that we were destined for each other, and you must never think that I regret not taking any of my other suitors. I knew then that [Ole] loved me deeply and sincerely, and every day in countless ways, I have constant proof of this love. . . . My husband fully understands what sacrifices I made when I left everything most precious to me to go with him into the unknown. Therefore, when I am lonely, he tries to comfort me. With him alone can I share my joys and sorrows, so even when the darkest moods of loneliness come upon me, I feel infinitely better when I have talked with him. . . . As long as my husband is kind to me, I shall never complain.[127]

In the remainder of Gro's letters to her family she frequently commented on Ole's kindness and the development of their relationship, which sustained her through difficult days.

> It is easier to bear one's burden when it is shared. Therefore I am always happy to know that I have him beside me. I can never be too thankful for having such a kind husband. In my quiet moments I often think of how happy I should be if you could observe us as we live and work together day by day, but I hope that you will believe me when I tell you that our love has grown stronger and deeper during these fifteen years that we have lived together.[128]

One of Charles Nord's daughters told a similarly touching story that revealed the tender side of a man known for his loud voice and willingness to boss the whole farm with it. After setting each of his children and hired workers to their day's tasks, he took his wife, Julia, aside and told her that the two of them would hitch up the horses for a drive to Fargo. There they would buy a new coat for her.[129]

Laur. Larsen's daughter told that the family viewed "Father's work [as] the all important thing."[130] However, his letters to his first wife, Karen Neuberg, suggested that she was an important part of his ability to fulfill his duties on behalf of the church. During the years he taught the Norwegian students at Concordia Seminary he was still a young man himself and was often away from home. He wrote to Karen:

> My present ailment is as much an illness of the soul as of the body. To you, my faithful wife, I come begging that you will be the physician of my soul. . . . You know me and you know the commands of God, so you can guide me. And I am willing to be led, for God has humbled me deeply and roused in me the wish to obey Him and serve Him, if only I knew how.[131]

In the midst of the controversy over slavery Karen was visiting the Preuses in Spring Grove; Laur. urged her to return home despite her "disagreeable husband and dreary home."

> God placed you here as my helpmeet, and you have to make the best of it. We are having many difficulties here, and I cannot tell you how much I miss your advice, not only in household affairs, but in more important ways as well.[132]

When he visited Norway in the 1860s, Larsen hinted that he was not completely satisfied with their domestic situation and admitted that he and his work were at fault.

> And I must not think so exclusively of my work. I can't even stand it in the long run, and I wish so much that in our home there might be more time to sit down and visit together and read both the word of God and other things. I am going to try as hard as I can, for I know that you wish this too.[133]

Not all families were as peaceful and cultivated as numerous photographic portraits taken of them having coffee on their lawn in the 1870s would suggest.[134] Fragmentary evidence of uneasy relationships lodged itself in otherwise cheerful accounts. Gro Svendsen filled her letters with tidbits of information about the lives of her Iowa neighbors and news of her friends and relatives in Norway. Some reports were happy: "Will you tell Margit Arnegaard that I have made inquiries about her daughter? She is living in comfort. She married the man she left with."[135] Without giving the context needed to understand the whole situation, Gro also sent fascinating details about less satisfactory relationships.

> [Eli Aadne] hasn't changed in the least since he left home, except that he now wears a beard—a coarse, gray beard. His wife has left him. She is living with another man in a place some two hundred miles to the west.[136]

Although no more complete, Kjersti Raaen's account of the sad situation of a neighbor woman provided some insight into why a woman might have been tempted to run away.

> Last week Sennev Solem was here for several days and didn't want to go home; she said she just couldn't stand it any longer. There must be some awful trouble in her family. The roads are covered with ice and so slippery that you can hardly go anywhere, but Mor had to go with Sennev to Northwood to see a lawyer. After Sennev told her troubles, the lawyer said she could claim all the property and get a divorce from her husband besides, but when he found out she didn't have any money he told her to go home, tend to her housework, and obey her husband.
>
> Sennev has nowhere else to go; she had to do what she was told, but it must be terribly hard. She has to live in a tiny dugout, and her four children are all babies, only a year apart.[137]

The situation in Aagot's home was often unhappy when her father would go into the "shadows," a drinking binge. During one incident he signed a mortgage that burdened the family for many years.

Thalette Brandt recalled an instance in which Pastor R. O. Brandt was called out in the night to intercede between a husband and wife who were camped near the parsonage. The two were quarreling; the man was beating up the woman, who was bruised and moaning. Nonetheless, she took her husband's side when he was threatened with jail. The couple were persuaded to move on, so the outcome of their dispute went unrecorded.[138]

A brief note in the *Fergus Falls Journal* told of a sad ending without the story of the relationship. Mrs. Karen O. Aarhus, age fifty-six, had visited Norway with her husband two years before. While he decided to remain there, she returned to Minnesota, where they had several children. Since then she was described as "at times . . . quite melancholy." On that March morning, she went to the barn to milk and hung herself.[139]

Several "sad" matches in John Oleson's family were discussed more fully by his wife. Of John's grandparents, Thurine said,

> Halvor was known as "the meanest man on earth." He was so jealous, lazy, cruel, and drunken, that he brought Margit nothing but misery. It would have killed an ordinary woman, but Margit took it, and stood it. Not only did she triumph over this miserable marriage . . . [t]he long struggle with Halvor never soured her. It seemed rather to bring out every bit of fineness in her, developed all her clever traits, and made her a diplomat of the first order.[140]

His aunt, Anna, also was married to a man who drank and was lazy. Unlike her mother, Anna did not stand for it. She left once, returned in the hope that he had reformed, and then "one day while he was in town, she took her children and left for good."[141] Anna was last heard of selling Spiritualist literature in California. The widower who married John's sister Julia had children from his first marriage. Julia spoiled the children and disregarded her husband's sense of propriety. When he divorced her, she made a good settlement and stayed on in the same town.[142]

The most notorious instance of disharmony is the case of Oline and B. J. Muus's separation in 1883. It was a delicate situation for the Norwegian Synod, in which her husband was an influential member. Considerable discussion of the case in the church and immigrant press did little to establish agreement about exactly what happened. The formal issue was Oline's right to a sum of money she received as a inheritance from Norway and that Pastor

Muus claimed was his under the Norwegian law. (Both partners were Norwegian citizens.) Mrs. Muus made public accusations of mental and physical cruelty toward herself and her children. Although the charges were not proved, the possibility of their truth was supported by the story of Rev. Muus's refusal to attend to Oline's broken leg or to fetch a doctor from town on the ground that the horses were tired after working all day in the field.[143]

In addition to the civil court proceedings, a congregational meeting was held to determine if Rev. Muus would remain as pastor: the vote was 300 to 1 in his favor. On the basis of their view that a woman should be obedient to her husband, his fellow clergymen accepted him and rejected Oline.[144] Her most vocal supporters were from outside the Norwegian Lutheran community: Kristofer Janson, Unitarian missionary, and Bjørnstjerne Bjørnson, Norwegian author. Neither man's word could anticipate a positive or sympathetic hearing among churchfolk. Bjørnson's description of Oline, likely overdrawn, suggests that even those who sympathized with her situation found it difficult to give their unqualified support due to her personal characteristics.

> God almighty, how he must have struggled with that female, who is all worldliness, indifference, defiance, intelligence, craving for fun, an in her way just as strong as he is. She was so dirty that her underclothing stank, so I had to smoke a cigar to be able to talk with her. She started by pretending to be nice and pious and quiet; but I saw the lay of the land at once and made fun of the Bible and Muus and holiness—and she laughed uproariously and was full of gaiety at once. . . . I think most of the fault lies with him.[145]

Oline was not without more "orthodox" supporters nor was she entirely isolated from the Norwegian Lutheran community. Georg Svedrup and Sven Oftedahl, of the Conference, provided her with some funds. For a while she lived in Minneapolis and made her living as a piano teacher. On one occasion she accompanied a soloist at the bazaar held at Janson's church. Late in the century Oline moved to Fruithurst, Alabama. Many years after it took place, she reflected on her marital disaster in a generous tone.

> The main reason why everything went wrong for us was that, at least in the beginning, we did not understand each other, mostly I believe because of our entirely different understanding of life which in turn grew out of our different characters and from our very different upbringing.
> You know well that when Satan can find a little hiding-place between a married couple, there is no domestic peace, and heart's ease goes out the door; and when love between husband and wife has cooled to an icicle, and respect

and honor have disappeared, what is left then in culture or in spiritual life as a tie?

We both had enough good manners so that we were not on unfriendly terms when people from the congregation were with us, and I never was among those who went to other's people's houses and told everything.[146]

The moderation of this statement rather than the coarseness of Bjørnson's description was reflected in *The Decorah Posten*'s obituary (1922). That reporter noted that Oline had an "optimistic outlook and followed with lively interest everything concerning the Norwegian immigrants and church affairs" and that she had recently completed a piece of needlework as an anniversary gift for Dr. H. G. Stub and his third wife, Anna Skabo Stub.

While Mrs. Muus lived in Minneapolis and associated socially with the Jansons she may have come to know another pastor's wife who was not entirely satisfied with her lot, Valborg Hovind Stub, second wife of Dr. H. G. Stub. She was a professional mezzo-soprano who had received critical praise on a German tour just prior to her marriage in 1884. She moved with Dr. Stub to Minnesota, where he was a professor at Luther Seminary in Robbinsdale. In addition to teaching voice lessons at her downtown Minneapolis studio and editing a collection of songs, Mrs. Stub became friends with Drude Janson and participated in musical evenings at her home. This behavior was not what Dr. Stub's colleagues and their families expected and they "regarded Mrs. Stub as something of a showpiece.[147]

When H. G. Stub received a call to First Lutheran Church in Decorah, Iowa, Valborg returned to Norway. Her absence placed Dr. Stub in an awkward position; he "felt that his position in the ministry was not right . . . [and] had about decided to resign, but thought he better go to Norway and see what could be done."[148] In 1901 she died, either just before or just after his arrival in Norway.

Stories such as Oline Muus's and Valborg Stub's were uncommon. Absence of such incidents in recollections suggest that few Norwegian-Americans were willing to abandon their commitments and risk the shame of a divorce or that, if they did divorce, the shame was great enough to call for silence. Economic constraints likely kept other women than Sennev Solem in unhappy situations. However, the examples of Gro Svendsen and Ingeborg Reishus indicate that many women were satisfied in their marital relationships. Perhaps they were more typical than those who were not.

Conclusions

Within their homes and in their most intimate relationships Norwegian women experienced the process of becoming both American and modern. Immediately they encountered a new environment filled with unfamiliar things and people; some achieved greater prosperity in the ensuing years; many faced increased options. In his study of immigrants from Balestrand, Jon Gjerde described this process of adaptation as a shift from peasant to bourgeoisie. The experiences of the women considered here reinforce his helpful interpretation of the Balestrand group's experience.[149]

Adaptations were most clear in their new physical environment. The landscape was radically unlike what immigrants had left behind. Their move required that they quickly learn to use new resources and unfamiliar equipment. This was the case with regard to many tasks, from cooking and cleaning to field work. The women learned to prepare American foods and their families learned to enjoy them. Their Norwegian clothing wore out and was replaced by American. After their initial exposure to the setting and adaptation to it, women adapted it to their own needs. This was most possible when the family achieved prosperity and with it gained access to options.

The tasks of the wife and mother in the farm household were altered by changes in work, available human labor and mechanical tools, and consequent changes in expectations. The shift of women's activities away from the field was prompted both by affluence and adoption of agricultural production that depended less on haying and animals, both traditional Norwegian "women's work." Arrival of children, hiring of farm workers, and use of machinery also contributed to women's withdrawal from the field.[150] Increased resources allowed purchase of status items such as cookstoves, sewing machines, and pianos, both for labor-saving and luxury, that concentrated female work inside the house and in cultivation of foodstuffs for family consumption.

These material changes were supported by the spread of genteel standards. Although *prestefruen* of the mid-nineteenth century were compelled to stuff their own sausages and do other tasks they would not have been called upon to do in Norway, over time their condition improved. When Ingeborg Stub and Diderikke Brandt immigrated 1840s and 1850s they faced frontier conditions. By the 1870s photographers recorded clergy families having a lovely coffee on the lawns in front of their frame houses. Diderikke infused Luther College students with her standards by inviting them to the Brandt home for Sunday afternoon coffee. When their daughter and daughter-in-law, also pastors' wives, went to the western frontier in the late nineteenth century they were able to take along such things as sewing machines and coal heaters. When Bolette Stub Bergh arrived in Minnesota she lived in a dugout, but only temporarily.

Descriptions of preparations for women's society meetings indicate that parishioners raised their standards of hospitality. In the earliest years the family's belongings had to be removed to make room for the gathering in the small house; guests seated themselves as they could, perching on beds and stools. By the second decade of the twentieth century, preparations included laundering the linens and baking impressive pastries; when the guests arrived they were taken into the best room of the house. These changed standards for entertaining, and one suspects raised standards for day-to-day life as well, required that women devote more of their time to domestic tasks. As a similar trend was also taking place in Norway in the late nineteenth century, these shifts cannot be attributed solely to Americanization, but were in part the consequence of modernization.[151]

Daughters who worked in Yankee homes learned the Yankee ways of doing things and transferred them to their own homes. Young girls went to school where they learned English and American ways along with making friends among Norwegians and learning something of their ethnoreligious heritage. As they matured, the daughters and granddaughters had options that had not been open to their mothers. Some did not marry. Some had lifelong careers in teaching or music, which took them to cities, rather than "hiring out" for a few years before starting a family.

The women studied here adapted their domestic life and closest community but did not make intentionally radical changes beyond the first step of immigrating to the United States. The changes they made were often within their familial and Norwegian Lutheran circles. Their narrative self-descriptions conform to the expectations formed by earlier observations and studies of settlement, intermarriage, and visiting patterns.

The propensity of Scandinavian settlers to cluster together has been portrayed by immigrant novelists and is testified to by the enduring ethnic identity of towns such as Stoughton, Wisconsin, Decorah, Iowa, and Spring Grove, Minnesota. Works by John Rice, Robert Ostergren, and particularly Jon Gjerde suggest that fiction and commonsense impressions about the insularity and self-sufficiency of settlements may be confirmed with careful micro-studies.[152] Gjerde noted that chain migration contributed to the formation of compact communities composed of persons with common origins in Old World regions as well as social and theological affinities. These New World reconstitutions were carried along as Norwegian-Americans moved west to second and third settlement areas.[153]

In his study of assimilation and intermarriage in turn-of-the-century Wisconsin, Richard M. Bernard found that in the late nineteenth century 88 percent of the Norwegian-born and 85 percent of Norwegian-American residents of Wisconsin married within their ethnic group. By 1910 there was gradual expansion, with 70 percent of Norwegian-born and 54 percent of American-born marrying within the group.[154] Nonetheless, rural sociologists in the 1940s found that Norwegian-Americans were still a distinct, self-conscious group.[155] They continued to prefer that their children marry Norwegian-Americans. Nearly half read Norwegian regularly. Many satisfied their needs for social visits and work exchange within their ethnic community. One of the Norwegians included in the study attributed these characteristics to the fact that "up until recently there has always been enough Norwegians to go around."[156]

Changes in how these women regarded themselves as female and how they assessed their relationships are more difficult to discern. The gradual disappearance of the -datter surname, for example, could be interpreted in more than one way. By the 1870s the records of Norway Grove Lutheran in rural Dane County, Wisconsin, mixed -datter names with other naming patterns; by the 1900s the female form of patronymics was gone. This could suggest that women had less sense of themselves as independent persons after marriage and therefore adopted their husband's surname. Because the entire system of naming was in the process of change, this one fact cannot be viewed in isolation. Other Norwegian conventions disappeared: the active patronymic and the linkage of place and name also dropped out.[157] Perhaps women adopted their husband's surname because the two no longer shared a name related to their residence. Again, it should be noted that a similar trend was taking place in Norway.

Courtship and marriage customs also shifted gradually. As Jon Gjerde pointed out, in the United States Norwegian-American women married younger and had more children than in Norway. Throughout the nineteenth century, however, most brides in his sample were in their twenties.[158] Into the twentieth century, women who had teaching careers also married in their midtwenties. Gjerde further noted a decrease in prenuptial conceptions and illegitimate births, which he attributed to increased economic opportunity and new definitions of morality that excluded "night courting."[159] At the same time affective factors came to play a larger part in family relationships.[160]

If contacts outside the community of Norwegian-Americans were limited, as the work of rural sociologists suggests, and similar shifts were taking place in Norway, it must be surmised that the changes that took place in women's homes and families were at least as much a result of a new and modernizing environment as they were as response to American patterns. Some of the significant characteristics of that new environment were the result of arrival in the upper Midwest as it was being settled, developed, and modernized. Norwegian immigrant women and their daughters became modern Norwegian-Americans just as America was also becoming modern.

FOUR

Congregation and Women's Society

The church provided the spiritual and social world in which many immigrant women and their daughters lived. This second, local, religious arena was slightly larger and more public than the household and family. Women's experiences in this sphere varied widely from place to place, from time to time, from woman to woman. Their own accounts revealed the range of those experiences, if not all the details. More than half of Norwegian women did not join Lutheran churches; some of these involved themselves in other churches—Methodist, Baptist, or Unitarian; others ceased to participate in organized religion. Here primary attention is focused on Lutheran women.

The religion of Norwegian-American Lutheran women was not the same as that of their Yankee contemporaries. Unlike much of American Protestantism, it was not Calvinist in background. Indeed, there were nearly constant debates among its clergy and active laity over typically Lutheran points of theology. In such discussions concern for doctrine was emphasized in a manner foreign to the Wesleyan attitude that looked for sympathy of spirit above identity of belief. Norwegian Lutherans did not arrive in the United States until after the pre-Civil War phase of social reform, nor were they active in the Social Gospel movement of the early twentieth century as were "native" women.

Not only was the religion of Norwegian-Lutheran women unlike that of native American Protestant women, it also was significantly different from the types of religion that have recently held the attention of scholars investigating female religious experience. It was neither revivalistic (in the American mode), nor a new religion (such as Christian Science), nor particularly inclined to assign authority on the basis of the spirit (as did Shakers): three sorts of religion that have been considered at length by students of women and religion.[1] Yet the form of women's groups and their activities were quite similar to those in Methodist or Congregational congregations. Thus

Norwegian-American Lutheran women provide an opportunity to compare findings about women and American religion with a different sort of Protestant group.

Norwegian Lutheranism came to the United States as the faith of common people. Neither Norwegian government officials nor leaders of the state church provided pastoral services for immigrants. The first leaders in the United States were lay preachers who conducted worship services for their own and surrounding communities. When neither a Norwegian Lutheran pastor nor a lay preacher was available, some Norwegians went to Yankee congregations; others worshiped in their homes, praying from cherished prayer books, singing familiar hymns, and reading sermons by venerable Lutheran churchmen.

University-trained pastors came to America in the mid-nineteenth century at the request of devoted Lutheran immigrants and the prompting of their own callings. They set about organizing congregations, and whenever one of them passed by as he traveled from the parish that had issued his call he held services. Thus formal worship with the pastor presiding was an infrequent occurrence; a congregation located in the settlement in which a pastor "resided" might not have had his services more than once a month. The parishioners still had to look out for themselves.

Norwegian Lutherans' propensity to discuss, disagree, and divide was proverbial. Away from the constraints of the state church, the partisans of various doctrinal positions, pietistic styles, and moral standards debated one another and formed their own affiliations. Social class and degree of Americanization influenced the debaters' views. Disputes between clergymen and laity split congregations; disagreements among church members and their leaders resulted in the multiplication of synods. Each synod had its own educational institutions, charitable agencies, and periodical.

For these reasons Norwegian Lutheran churches gained a reputation for being doctrinaire, petty, and socially stratified. At their worst, they may have earned that characterization; at their best, however, they served as a primary social institution for thousands of immigrants. In churches immigrants found a familiar setting in which they could speak to people who spoke the same language and saw the world in the same way.

Women's activities in the churches were of five sorts: participation in the life of local congregations, membership in clerical families, membership in women's groups, education in church institutions, and professional service as deaconesses and missionaries.

Congregational Life

No congregations, no church buildings, no pastors awaited the first Norwegian immigrants to the United States. For their religious observances they depended upon their memories of practices at home and their prayer books. Habits of worship in their homes were established and continued after the arrival of clergymen. Circuits of congregations and multiple point parishes spread a pastor's time and service thin until twentieth-century improvements in transportation allowed him to preach at each of his charges weekly. Even by foot, horse, oxen, and wagon pastors covered a heroic distance; in the year beginning with Advent 1861, B. J. Muus traveled 6,900 miles (2,000 in the area of Goodhue and Rice counties and 4,900 beyond).[2]

Perhaps the homely devotions recalled by Martha Hove Hougstad and Mathilde Berg Grevstad were not the equals of a full-blown church service in terms of solemnity or profundity. Nonetheless, by setting Sunday apart from other days by providing some religious activity, they both substituted for a congregational worship service and anticipated one. Both women described events of the 1860s and 1870s. Martha Hougstad, in Worth County, Iowa, explained that the pastor came one week in five. The other four weeks

[w]e would all dress in our Sunday clothes and father would lead the devotion. First we would sing hymns, then he would read prayers from the hymn book, and then he had a book of long sermons by "Johan [sic] Arndt" which he would read very distinctly. This devotion would last for two hours.[3]

During those long two hours the younger children would tiptoe over to their father in order to sneak a peek at the pages and determine how much of Arndt's sermon remained. In the Red River Valley, young Mathilde Berg spent her Sundays in a similar way. She had intense memories of the family's devotions.

On Sundays we had no church to go to, but we had services at home. Father would read the Collect, the Epistle, and the Gospel and we would sing hymns. Then he would read a sermon from "Hofaker's Postille," a book of sermons. Oh, what agony it was to sit through those long sermons. But sit still we must! There was a large picture of Hofaker in the front of the book. One day I scratched out his nose! I don't remember that I was punished for it either.[4]

Surely Martin Luther did not anticipate the conditions of frontier America from his place in sixteenth-century Germany. Nor did he instruct heads of households to do exactly what Martha's and Mathilde's parents did. Nonetheless, these childhood scenes were reminiscent of Luther's admonishment to the head of the household concerning the "minimum of knowledge required of a Christian," which he included in the *Large Catechism*.

Therefore, it is the duty of every head of a household to examine his children and servants at least once a week and ascertain what they have learned of it, and if they do not know it, to keep them faithfully at it.[5]

When the pastor was away preaching and leading worship in other settlements it fell to his wife to conduct a service for her family along with any guests or servants staying in the parsonage. One of Linka Preus's children recalled that her mother would read Luther's sermons aloud on such Sunday mornings. The sermon was

. . . generally rather lengthy, still that did not seem to tire her, as long as it was Luther. Occasionally I sensed that she chose the longer sermon because it developed more fully some problem or question she had been discussing with this or that less orthodox individual, temporarily staying with us.[6]

Caja Munch also took responsibility for a proper observance of Sunday in her household. On Pentecost Sunday she assured her parents that she had spent her morning in appropriate activities.

You should know that first [before writing letters] I have read aloud for my servants the sermon for the festival by my very good friend Hofacker. Otherwise, I never take anything in hand on Sundays except to read in devotional books.[7]

Gro Svendsen made explicit the contrast Caja implied between her observance and that of others, specifically some Yankees. On her way into town to attend church services on Christmas Day she observed "Americans working just as on any other day. . . . It was very disturbing, accustomed as we are to the quiet and peace of the Sabbath."[8] Neither Norwegians nor Yankees were consistent in their Sabbath behavior, however. In New York City Linka observed Yankees who passed the Sabbath in a quiet manner.[9] A young American woman who taught in a Norwegian community observed the tensions surrounding this practice. A new father ran the risk of being excluded from his child's baptismal party by building a shed on Sunday. The next spring the pastor gave his congregation permission to plant on Sunday, after they had come to worship.[10] Although she did not engage in heavy labor on Sunday, Elisabeth Koren's views and behavior were less than solemn. One Sunday afternoon she visited neighbors where she was served "good beer and not-so-good cake."

When a pastor arrived in a settlement a message was sent to the neighbors. They gathered together in the largest cabin, in a barn or schoolhouse, or under a tree for divine worship. Lacking the facilities of an old established congregation, the immigrants made use of what they had. If there was no silver chalice, a beer glass served for one; if there was no paten, a saucer would do. In the absence of a high pulpit, the pastor preached from a tree stump. If there were no altar cloths, a woman loaned her best white tablecloth adorned with distinctive hardanger cutwork. A worship service under the trees left a vivid image in the mind of young Mathilde Berg Grevstad.

> When we arrived at the place where worship was to be held, we found that a table with a white cloth on had been set under a large tree as the center of worship. Planks on chunks of wood served as seats for the congregation. There were quite a few people present, mostly men. I don't remember the sermon at all, but the hymn singing made a deep impression on me.[11]

If the service was held inside, even in the largest of the cabins, it was crowded and stuffy. Caja Munch attended a service with her husband in a small sitting room; sixty-eight persons communed, so there must have been several more crowded in. Pastor Olaus Duus reported that some of his congregation had to stand outside in the entryway, near a window, or on the lawn when the house was not large enough to accommodate them all. After she fainted during the Easter service, Linka Preus brought a chair from home and sat in the shade outside a window rather than go back into the schoolroom where services were held.[12]

Despite the constraints of space, setting, and equipment, worship was meaningful and moved participants. Not long after the Korens came to Iowa Elisabeth remarked upon the "order and dignity" of the crowd that gathered for communion on Epiphany, 1854. The following Ascension Day she described the morning worship in a letter to her father.

> Services were held in the schoolhouse today; I was present, too, though it has rarely been possible for me to attend this winter. Would you believe that the

services in the small houses here make a stronger and more satisfying impression on me than those at home? I do not know why it should be. I think it is the ardent singing of the hymns and the crowded room, whereby the pastor and the congregation come into a much closer and more intimate relation to each other.[13]

On one occasion, Caja Munch was forced to "start them out on the Amens and other things" as there was no one else in the congregation who could sing.[14] Usually a lay assistant, the *klokker*, led the hymns, relying on his own voice or a tuning fork to provide the starting pitch. This respected position was given to a devout and responsible man. The *klokker* in Estherville, Iowa, was "the son of a man from Gol by the name of Mikkel Ruust or Golberg. The son's name is Tollef. He sings well. He is also the sheriff and one of the directors of the public school."[15] The *klokker's* duties sometimes included standing in for an absent pastor by praying with the sick and taking charge of burials.[16]

Since itinerant pastors were not able to make frequent visits to every settlement, they performed the whole range of duties in one day: baptisms, confirmations, weddings, and funerals. Pastor Abraham Jacobson told that of the numerous children were brought for baptism when he traveled in the Dakotas in the 1860s many were as old as three years.[17] Occasionally the parents' marriage was performed only hours before the child's baptism. When a pastor arrived in her home Ingeborg Reishus was determined to forestall this scenario in the case of her neighbor. She took the young woman aside and argued that the expected arrival of a child called for Bergitta and Ivar to marry. Despite a protest from the bride that it was "no fun" to be married that way, the ceremony took place between the morning and afternoon service.[18]

After a few years of meeting informally in temporary quarters, a group of neighbors organized a congregation and united their resources to build a church. Mattea Magdelena Johnson was instrumental in motivating her neighbors in Edgerton, Wisconsin, to take this step.[19] The expense was carried by the members themselves and thus building was slow. Gro Svendsen explained the situation to her family the year she arrived in America.

I said "going to church," but we really have no church. We do expect to have one, however. So far $1,550 has been collected, but a great deal more is needed in order to build. In America money was said to be so plentiful, and may be. But it's hard to get any of it when it's to be used for the common good, for such as teachers' salaries, ministers' salaries, and other expenses connected with the church. The men assigned to collect this money are called trustees. They go about with a list, soliciting from farmers and getting contributions in the same way as we collected the personal property tax and the church tax at home.[20]

The difference, of course, was that there was no church tax in the United States. All the contributions received by the trustees, even those levied by the congregation, were voluntary in the sense that no government agency enforced their payment. And all congregational expenses, including the pastor's salary, were paid by the members themselves, not the government. Consequently, all members might have expected to have a say in what was done, as was the case when Buffalo River congregation decided to build in 1883.

All members walked out into the church yard to pick out the exact size for the building at the close of the meeting. Each member was also asked to give one dollar on the spot for the building fund, however, if anyone did not have a dollar at the time they would be permitted to bring it later. . . . One member immediately asked to be permitted to withdraw his membership. But to offset this, three new members asked to join.[21]

An earlier note that women were specifically asked to be present at a meeting in 1891 about building suggested that it was usually the male members who voted and had a say in how the congregation's money was spent. In many Norwegian Lutheran congregations women were not eligible to vote until the second quarter of the twentieth century.

Contributions were not all in the form of cash. The members of Bear Creek church in Grand Meadow, Minnesota, donated the yield from one acre of land to the congregation's treasury. It was not uncommon for a member to donate land for a graveyard and for the church building. Hegland Lutheran in Hawley, Minnesota, and Drywood Lake Lutheran in Appleton, Minnesota, were built on land given by women. Miss Anna Matters, formerly of Hawley, gave an acre when she heard of the plan to build. In 1893 Miss Anne Lehne donated a plot to Drywood Lake Lutheran.[22]

Materials for the building were also provided by members. Specific assessments varied but the pattern was similar: each household was responsible for a specified number of logs cut to a uniform length or so many suitable stones and loads of sand. Days of labor were also accepted as contributions and recorded as such. Each family unit provided a layer of logs and each single man one log (twenty-five or twenty-seven feet long) to construct Tonseth church in Otter Tail County, Minnesota.[23]

The original furnishings were crude. Seating was made of rough planks laid across stumps or barrels. In *Trefoldighed* (Trinity) Lutheran of Battle Lake, Minnesota, the altar was a grocery box draped with white muslin by the women of the congregation. Until 1906 the altar painting was an embroidered hanging—"a vine covered cross with silver cord on a deep red plush"—skillfully worked by Miss Christine F. Hovren. Few congregations had an organ or piano except for special occasions when a wealthier family among the membership loaded theirs in a wagon and brought it to the church.

The prosperity of the congregation reflected that of its members. In years when the crops were ruined by drought or grasshoppers the pastor's salary was smaller and paid in kind rather than cash. In good years money was available for improvements in God's house as well as the houses of the farm families. Through subscriptions, personal gifts, and the activities of the women's groups money was raised for essentials and luxuries. Miss Kari Helland went around to the members of Lime Creek Church, soliciting a dollar from each place to buy new seats to replace the uncomfortable benches.[24] Congregations made other purchases: an organ, carpet for the main aisle, an altar painting, a font, a pulpit, an altar, or a communion rail.[25] Growing membership prompted additions to the building or erection of a new, larger one. A balcony increased seating; a basement provided a place for women's meetings, dinners, and entertainments.

More members and more income eventually made it possible to support a resident pastor, especially if his services and expenses were shared among two or three congregations. In December of 1865 Gro Svendsen wrote to her parents that the Norwegian Lutherans of Estherville thought themselves fortunate to have had two services that fall. Their congregation had increased from thirteen families to thirty in two years' time. This growth gave her hope that "in time we may be so many that we can have our own pastor." Her wish was fulfilled—after seven years of waiting.

> First I must tell you this bit of news—that we now have a permanent pastor. He came directly from Norway and preached his first sermon on Christmas Day [1872]. His name is H. H. Hande. He was born in Valders and is an exceptionally capable man. He seems to be more concerned with the spiritual distress of his parishioners than with church strife.[26]

As the timing of such changes was keyed to fortunes of church members, they were made earlier in the older eastern settlements, later in the newer ones on the frontier's edge.

The services conducted in church buildings—rustic or fancy—varied according to the synodical affiliations and liturgical inclinations of their pastors and members. From her place on the pastor's family bench, Linka Preus described how Pastor Herman Preus led a worship in the first years of his tenure.

> During the chant the pastor—Herman—steps out in front of the table, which on festival days or on days of Communion services, is supplied with a white table cloth by the minister's wife. After the chants he returns to his seat—a step to the side and a step backward, and he is again by my side. A pulpit hymn is sung, and sung as well as in any other country church. At the singing of the last stanza Herman rises and remains standing, the table now serving as a pulpit.[27]

In many congregations seating was segregated: men on one side, women and children on the other. The Norwegian Synod preferred conventional clerical dress—a long black robe with a pleated white ruff—and used the Norwegian altar book. The dedication of St. John's new building in 1881 prompted the Yankee editor of the *Rice County Journal* to attend that Norwegian Synod congregation and report on it at length.

> And first, let us say, they have a very neat, bright, airy and cheerful church, and on this occasion was well filled. We should say that there were between 300 and 400 people seated, and but very few empty seats.
> The singing was in the choral style, all singing the same part; not . . . as we Yankees sing. The house was filled with melody, but the pieces generally being quite lengthy, it becomes monotonous. . . . The bishop was in full robed canonicals, but the ministers wore only the round plaited ruffles, pictures of which we have seen in books
> . . . as this is a matter of taste we offer no criticism. . . . Possibly Martin Luther in his day wore such a ruffle, and that may be reason enough.
> The way our Scandinavian brethren are seated in church is more Jewish than Christian. The sexes are kept apart, as if they were afraid of each other, or that the "powers that be" were afraid for them.[28]

Wheaton was restrained in his description and displayed an admirable tolerance, even for those practices which seemed odd to him.

Services were long. Members of West Koshkonong church recalled that a hymn was sung during the distribution on Sundays when Communion was conducted. When many people attended, the congregation was known to have finished singing all forty-seven verses and begun again before the distribution was completed.[29] Communion records from the 1870s and 1880s indicated

115

that not everyone who received Communion was a member of the congregation. The proportion of men and women among communicants was close to even.[30]

Without Communion the monthly service at Greenfield Church in Harmony, Minnesota, lasted from two to three hours to accommodate the liturgy, the sermon, and instruction of the young people.

> Ordinarily the sermon took up an hour and a quarter of the time. Catechising the young required from one-half to three quarters of an hour. During Larsen's [1865-1887] and Dreyer's [1887-1904] pastorates it was customary to place the children and young people on the church floor where they were catechised and instructed,—lessons being assigned from time to time. It was an excellent opportunity for the pastor to get in touch with the young. The older people, sitting in the pews were interested listeners.[31]

Thurine Oleson's memories of the church in Winchester, Wisconsin, came from the last quarter of the nineteenth century, after its members were well established. She told of walking to church as the church bell rang and of being instructed to behave herself during the service. The girl must have sat quietly observing her surroundings, as she described them to her daughter in vivid detail.

> The interior of the church was cool and quiet. The light that came through the frosted glass windows did not have the brilliance of outdoor sunshine but a soft, golden hallowed glow instead. From the ceiling hung fancy kerosene lamps. . . . The chancel was divided in two parts with the altar in front of and vestry behind the partition. The *altertavle* (altar painting) in soft reds and blues and greens, was of Christ on the Cross and his Mother. The lower panel was of the Lord's Supper. Beneath that was the altar itself, where the congregation laid the money when offering time came. This altar was covered with a long, white, lace-edged cloth, and on this stood two tall, footed, silver communion goblets. In front of the altar was a raised half-circle of red-carpeted floor, and a railing all around it with a red-carpeted kneeler before it. On this people knelt when they went to communion, when they were confirmed, and when they were married. In front of this railing the coffins were placed during the funerals. On either side of the altar at the back a door led to the sacristy, and over each door an arch of pale blue with a verse of scripture lettered in gold . . . "He that believeth and is baptized shall be saved." The baptismal font . . . was at the front, by the reed organ.

Thurine also remembered the relief she felt in her cramped legs when the *klokker* announced a hymn and everyone stood up to sing. The content of

Pastor Homme's long sermons in "book Norwegian" made less impression on the girl than his appearance.

> . . . the minister appeared as if by magic in the window-high pulpit at the right front, which was called the *predikestol* (preaching chair). It was attached to the wall, and was paneled and curved, with a padded red velvet railing around the top. Pastor Homme was a great stout Martin Lutherish man, in a long black robe, with a starched white ruff coming up to his clean-shaven chin. . . . His keen blue eyes looked over the house from beneath brown brows, and Lena and I sat back in our seats, frozen. Pastor Homme could see things, and we would hear of it afterwards. He grasped the red velvet railing with his great smooth hands, and leaned forward as he preached, searching our eyes with his in earnest pleading and warning.[32]

Except for the *klokker* there were few leadership roles for laypeople in this sort of service. The honor of "carrying the baby" to the baptismal font as one of the four sponsors was an activity that allowed participation by laymen and -women. Often the pastor's wife was called upon to do this. Caja Munch was asked to be godmother so often that she confided to her parents, "Soon I cannot justify doing this anymore, but what am I to do? It is hard to say no."[33] When the Korens' daughter, Henriette, was baptized, one of her sponsors was Guri Skaarlia. Elisabeth was concerned that half the settlement had been offended by Guri's willingness to carry the pastor's child since she ordinarily refused to be a sponsor.[34] Other women were more willing. Mrs. Martha Sorenson, of Ada, carried more children to be baptized than any other member of the congregation. When the church was remodeled in 1910, her gift of the bowl for the new baptismal font was deemed appropriate.[35]

In an emergency, the service of a pastor was not required for a baptism. Both Aagot Raaen and Linka Preus reported urgent baptisms being performed by a layperson. Before her death, Aagot's infant sister, Birgit, was baptized by a neighbor, Gamle Mikkel. Attended by Henriette Neuberg and Thorbjør Møen, a neighbor woman, Linka gave birth to a fragile son.

> A messenger to the Doctor, thirty miles away—a telegram to Herman—all was immediately set in motion—but the Best of Doctors assisted me—"Why, the child is crying!" were, I believe, my first words, and then a grateful mother's thanksgiving. —"All is well with me, but get the baptismal water at once for the tiny creature"—well formed but very, very small. —"Thorbjør and Henriette, baptize the child here at my bed side." With trembling hand and quavering voice, old Thorbjør sprinkled water on the child's head and repeated the words,

"I baptize thee, Carl Christie, in the name of the Father, and of the Son and of the Holy Spirit"—words which Henriette and I repeated in a whisper.[36]

Carl Christie Preus died the next morning. It was assumed that some children baptized in similar circumstances would live; the altar book had a special form to be used in a public ratification of such a baptism.[37]

Since women were not ordained and did not serve as *klokker*, their contributions to the congregation were usually behind the scenes. One congregational historian acknowledged that even after a regular janitor was elected and paid for building the fire, sweeping, and ringing the bell, the "washing and cleaning was, however, done by the women members of the church."[38] In a similar reflection of women's duties at home, at Petri Lutheran in Ada "the ladies of the congregation baked the bread and wafers."[39]

Little was recorded of the sort of informal leadership provided by women to the Haugean revivals in Norway. Most of the women mentioned in a history of the Haugean revival in the United States were honored for their Christian hospitality. Of Mrs. Kari Nyhus it was said, "Without such hospitality and open home and willingness to serve the Haugean movement cannot prosper nor can the local societies."[40] The story of one woman in Muskego was slightly different. Although "she was never encouraged, to say the least, to testify or pray in public after she came to America," in Norway Ingerid Meningen was active in revivals, giving "blessed testimony in private and public." After immigrating to Wisconsin in 1869, she, her husband, and their children joined a Norwegian Synod church: Ingerid became involved in the congregation and in its women's group. Her biographer described her as "representative of many living Christian women" who found themselves in spiritually dead congregations.[41]

Aagot and Kjersti Raaen provided glimpses of Lina Myrold, a young woman who gained notoriety as a revival leader. For a season in 1898 she captured the attention of residents of Newburgh Township with her Bible and guitar. The immediate result was mixed. One family determined to pay back debts to their neighbors that they had neglected for years. But disagreement about the appropriateness of a woman leading a religious meeting caused a rift in the church. (Disputes about the appropriate leadership role for women continued in the Norwegian Lutheran churches and their successors into the late 1900s.) In the Raaen family the lasting influence was limited to knowledge of a few new songs.[42]

Expansion of the musical aspects of worship increased the opportunities for women to make active contributions to the service. Choirs were begun as early as the 1880s, with both male and female voices. When an organ or piano was purchased by an increasingly affluent congregation it was often a daughter of the local church (sometimes of the donor) who played the instrument accompanying both hymns and choir anthems. Anniversary histories honored the choir director and the organist for long and faithful service. The organists of Waterloo Ridge Church received a poetic tribute.

Who serves the church with loyalty,
Who's at her post most faithfully,
Who gives her talents willingly
And plans and works unstintedly?
    The Organist.

For tasks like hers God hath a care;
And He alone can trust her fair.
Therefore, my heart sends up this prayer:
"Dear Lord, bless her with blessings rare—
    The Organist.[43]

Although it may have been the case at Waterloo Ridge that all organists were women, men were not absent from the organ bench and choir loft in other congregations.

Education, both religious and secular, was a concern of even the youngest congregation. Before a community was able to support a public school, and sometimes after, the Lutherans ensured their children's learning by holding their own "Norwegian" school. In the same way that they paid their pastor and built the church, the members of the congregation met the school's expenses with contributions. In Glenville, Minnesota, Round Prairie Lutheran Church the amount of the contribution was suggested: $2.00 from a family; $0.50 from unmarried, confirmed men; and $0.25 from unmarried, confirmed women.[44]

The schedule for such instruction varied from weekly sessions to daily ones over a period of a few weeks to several months. All children—boys and girls—were sent to learn Bible history, hymns, and catechism as well as Norwegian language. In the mid-nineteenth century the position of schoolteacher was commonly combined with that of *klokker* and filled by a man who had been educated as a teacher in Norway. Once the immigrant churches had established seminaries, summer sessions were staffed by young men in the midst of their preparation for a ministerial career. Confirmation class was usually taught by the pastor.

Alternatively, there were Norwegian women who were qualified to teach. Although she cautioned her brother that he might do better to stay in Norway than to immigrate in the hope of securing a teaching position, Gro Svendsen was herself a teacher. In May of 1864 she sent her brother a positive report of her work.

> I've taught school for one and a half months. The pupils come here three times a week, and there are five of them. They were very poor when we began, but they have improved a great deal in this short time. They are obedient, attentive, and eager to learn—quite the opposite of those I had last year. I am very pleased with them, and they and their parents seem to be satisfied with me. I get $12.00 a month, a very good salary for one with so little education.[45]

As pastors' wives were likely to have received some education, they were called upon to teach. *Prestefruen* read with confirmation students while their husbands were away. Diderikke Brandt was remarkable in teaching languages to seminarians. Her daughter-in-law, Thalette Brandt, held school in the parsonage attic.

Although their objections to Yankee schools included the fact that young women were employed as teachers, by the turn of the century the Norwegian-Americans had generally adopted the practice in their parochial schools as well as in whatever Sunday school program they had. Olaf M. Norlie's *School Calendar, 1824-1924* included 3,600 persons connected with Norwegian Lutheran schools. Of those, 41.5 percent were women. Most of the women were born in the United States and many received at least part of their training in Lutheran colleges or normal schools. It was not unusual for them to teach in the public school during the winter term and in the congregational "Norwegian" school during the summer.

Personal Religion

The congregation's activities contributed to the ordering of its members' lives. Although events such as Christmas programs and confirmations are sometimes overlooked by historians and dismissed by churchfolk as superficial, their significance ought not be underestimated. Often these activities provide the structure for a deeply rooted worldview that is taken for granted rather than articulated. The church festivals marked the passing of each year. Christmas celebrations were memorable occasions for adults and children. A large tree was decorated with candles; children learned "pieces" to be recited; they received gifts of apples and hard candy. In the summer mission fests brought the congregation together for a dinner and to hear a visiting missionary speak about the church's work in faraway places like Madagascar, South Africa, and China. Ecclesiastical activities marked the phases of individual lives as well.

A woman's life was punctuated by sacramental and ritual action at each of its major turning points from baptism until burial. Shortly after birth she entered the church through baptism. The significance of the occasion was suggested by the fact that the child was to wear a special white gown. During the years of itinerant pastors, one woman who lived near the church building kept a dress to be lent in the event that the pastor's sudden arrival caught some parents unprepared. Mor Raaen felt it to be a great shame that her children were baptized without such a garment.

The end of childhood and entry into the adult world was signaled by confirmation. All children were confirmed in their midteens, usually between age fourteen and sixteen. First they were prepared by lessons from their pastor or the schoolteacher. Ideally instruction took place on a regular basis over some time, perhaps once a week for a year. If children lived too far away to make the trip for instruction, they stayed with the pastor's family. Other children were coached by their parents or worked their way through the *Catechism* alone as Aagot Raaen did. Gro Svendsen's children reported their progress in letters to their grandparents in Norway. Fourteen-year-old Carl Olson had "completed the Longer Catechism and the Bible History"; his brother Steffen, five years younger, had learned "up to the Second Article in the Longer Catechism" as well as some hymns.[46]

The behavior of a young girl from near Decorah, Iowa, demonstrated the importance she placed on instruction and confirmation. One March day, when Vilhelm was away and Elisabeth was home alone, the girl appeared at the Korens' door.

While I was reading the paper, a girl came in. After she had sat for some time, she asked if there were not to be services today. She had walked twelve miles yesterday from up north under that impression, for she, too, wished to be enrolled for confirmation. She was a grown-up girl and one of those who have been waiting a long time for the pastor.[47]

Confirmation lessons included Bible history, the hymnal, New Testament, the *Catechism*, and the *Explanation*. The last two were learned by heart. In addition to attending classes, confirmation students were lined up in the aisle of the church and quizzed on their lessons.[48] Their knowledge was judged and their grade was noted by their name in the congregation's record book. Except for an occasional star student or an unusually slow one, the marks were distributed evenly between boys and girls.[49]

On the day of confirmation the students dressed in their best clothes to become adult members of the church. Group portraits of confirmation classes showed boys in suits and girls in dark dresses until about the turn of the century, when white dresses began to appear. Some girls wore a spangled Norwegian broach at the collar. Wearing a new plum-colored dress of which she was very proud, Thurine Oleson was confirmed in the early 1880s. That day her "childhood ended"; she recalled it many years later.

> . . . we were placed in rank as the pastor ordered us. Oh, how I wanted to be first! I think I was the only one who knew the two books by heart. . . . He lined us up in the aisle of the church, boys on one side, girls on the other, and walked up and down between us, asking questions. It was a great ordeal for us all.
>
> After the examination, we followed the pastor to the altar. He went inside the rail, and we knelt around it. Starting at the head, he asked us one by one in a solemn voice, "Will you renounce the Devil and all his works, believe that Christ died for your sins, and stand firm in this faith until the end of your days?" We replied, "I do." He then concluded, "Give me your hand, and God your heart," and shook hands with each of us. . . . The next Sunday we took our first communion at that same altar rail, and from then on, we were members of the church.[50]

In Norway many girls would then have hired out. In the United States some continued in school at private academies and colleges. The rise of public high schools in the late years of the century prolonged childhood for more of them. But for many girls, confirmation did mark the end of childhood.

The next major event in their lives was marriage, although it seldom took place for several years. The few teenage brides noted in congregational record books from the 1800s stood out as unusual. Most brides were in their mid-twenties, which was consistent with the Norwegian pattern. In personal recollections surprisingly little was said about weddings. The few times Elisabeth Koren mentioned weddings she described the event taking place with very little festivity, perhaps because of the frontier conditions. The couple came to the parsonage, where the pastor married them and the pastor's wife provided a meal. Pastor Muus sold the couple a leather-bound Bible that served as a wedding certificate; he wrote their names and the date of their wedding on the flyleaf.[51]

Increased prosperity allowed for more extensive preparations and more elaborate celebrations. Kjersti Raaen outfitted herself with linens and other equipment necessary to set up housekeeping in anticipation of her marriage. At her wedding in the 1890s in Lyons County, Minnesota, Barbara Levorsen's mother wore a peacock blue wool dress with deep blue velvet trim and white lace edging; her parents entertained a large crowd of guests for several days. A twenty-dollar gold piece was a gift from the bride's uncle.[52] Bolette Stub Bergh attended Jens Roli and Anne Ogaarden's wedding, conducted by her husband in the winter of 1873. Bolette took part in games of "finding the ring in the flour basin" and "shooting rabbit blind" (a sort of variation on pin the tail on the donkey). But as the evening wore on it became clear that some guests were ready to dance, so the Rev. and Mrs. Bergh were escorted to a neighbor's house. Then the party began.[53] As at confirmation, clothing styles changed. In early years some brides wore traditional Norwegian clothing.[54] A photograph of Cathinka Hjort's marriage to Pastor J. J. Strand in 1897 shows the bride in a white dress, holding a bouquet of flowers, and surrounded by other young women in white.

Marriage was followed by children. This event was potentially marked by a special ritual—churching. The Norwegian altar book prescribed by congregational constitutions included directions. Prior to worship the new mother met the pastor in the sacristy, where he spoke to her briefly. He reminded her to be thankful for God's care in bringing her safely through childbirth and to show her thankfulness by bringing up the child in God's kingdom. Then he blessed her.

> Enter into God's congregation in peace, and thank the Lord thy God, who has done well towards thee. May He strengthen thee further in soul and body, and let thy going in and thy going out, now and always be blessed before his face. Amen.[55]

If the infant had died, the pastor spoke of God's love for the child. Otherwise the woman went directly into the church and the baby was baptized that day.

Marie Anderson observed Pastor Otteson and a group of women in the hall of Koshkonong church and later learned that the women were all new mothers being churched.[56] Her curiosity suggested that she was unfamiliar with the practice. Churching was seldom, if ever, noted in the daily record of services held at each congregation. This fact, together with the lack of references to it in other sources, further indicated that it was not continued for many years in the United States. Instead, her child's baptism became the way a woman's entry into motherhood was marked by the church.

Although there was no ritual for their observance, twenty-fifth and fiftieth anniversary celebrations frequently were held in the church building, attended by congregational members, and served by the women's group. These observances were held by the late nineteenth century, as a photograph of the Aslag Haldorson's golden anniversary taken about 1896 testified.[57] These festivities were noted in minutes and recorded in congregational histories as significant events in the lives of the honored couple and in the life of their church community.

Burial was the final religious event in a woman's earthly existence. Most material dealing with women's deaths was written about them rather than by them. At least one little girl remembered "Fourth of Julys and funerals were the only gala occasions that these early days [1870s and 1880s] provided."[58] The Little Lutheran Biography series included the deathbed scenes of Martha Clausen and others. Their assurance of heaven was emphasized. Martha Clausen and Lena Dahl both requested Communion before they died, the one in the 1840s, the other in the early twentieth century. Kjersti Raaen's death, as described by her sister, was less churchly but no less accepting. To comfort her family she spoke of her sister Birgit, who had died in infancy: "You said Birgit had it good; I will have it good. I will never be sick again. . . . Don't feel bad. You will join me on the other side."[59]

Linka Preus and Gro Svendsen were most inclined to express their personal religious beliefs and emotions when they faced deaths, separations, or loneliness. There were no long expositions of doctrine in Linka's diary and Gro's letters; rather, the two women made brief references to their own responses to leavetaking, childbirth, and the new year.

During her girlhood in Norway and in the first years of her life in Wisconsin, Linka scattered religious comments among descriptions of her daily activities. Her later diary entries were less frequent, filling only a few pages each year. These paragraphs merged into prayer; they were reflections addressed to God to whom she confided all her thoughts.

Thou, my God, art at my side! To Thee will I pour out the burdens and cares of my heart! Of Thee will I seek forgiveness and cry out: Mercy! mercy, for Jesus' sake.[60]

Throughout her diary, Linka was concerned about her own sinfulness, God's gracious care for her and her loved ones, and death; in the later passages her sense of sin was intense. In her self-examinations Linka found herself wanting. After visiting her parents' graves with Herman she considered her desire to be with them as "base selfishness." She asked God's forgiveness for her sinful longings and for aid in running "with patience the race that is set before us." Impatience, unwillingness to accept life as it comes, and insufficient thankfulness for its blessings plagued Linka throughout the next decade and a half.

These emotions were linked to her unwavering anticipation of another life beyond the present, earthly one. She wrote the following sentences in 1850 while waiting departure for America.

This evening I am in a dark mood. Everything seems cheerless and difficult—it seems hard to adjust oneself to life here below. And yet, how dare I utter such thoughts? How then can I hope for a better life, if here below I do not know how to accept life as God sets it before me, without becoming impatient? —O Lord, my God, keep me from such errors, strengthen and sustain me by Thy Spirit, that I may never stray from the path Thou hast chosen for me![61]

Her confidence in God's presence with her in this life was equally firm. Even as she experienced the physical and spiritual isolation of a frontier parsonage Linka cheered herself with reminders of God' nearness—directly and in the persons of her household.

But Linka, how can you say that you are alone? Your God is near. He first and foremost; then you have your little son and your household help. —Indeed, I am not alone, thank God, and hope I shall never be so unfortunate as to be left alone and forsaken in this world. It might, of course, readily happen that I should find myself alone as far as the physical eye is able to see; but as for the spiritual side, how utterly would I despair, were I to have the feeling that I was forsaken by my God.[62]

Despite her certainty of God's loving presence, Linka found it "most distressing . . . that such a mood and yearning for God but seldom possesses

125

me."[63] When such a yearning did come over her, it was often linked to her longing for a dead family member or to her sense of aloneness.

Participation in the Lord's Supper also prompted Linka to reflect on God's faithful forgiveness and her own unworthiness. Although she was refreshed at the table, she found her repentance weak. Before many days passed she had a "feeling of being so empty."[64] This simultaneous experience of joy in God and of a sense of her own sin was in keeping with the Lutheran Reformation maxim: *simul justus et peccator* (at the same time justified and a sinner).

Linka recognized the goodness of her life and was mindful that God was author of the blessings experienced by her family. She faulted herself for a lack of thankfulness for "all the goodness and loving-kindness Thou hast bestowed upon me during the past year." Addressing God as the Father of all mercies, she prayed for "a more loving heart, a more humble heart." She was anxious that her own will conform to the will of God, whom she viewed as the director of all things in "wisdom and goodness."[65] Her desires for her children expressed her notion of life so lived in harmony with God's purposes.

Most earnestly we beseech Thee mightily to aid us that we may so rear [Christian Keyser] and Sina that they shall become good people. When they have run their course here below, may they enter in to Thy joy. If their days here on earth shall be more than a few, may they labor to Thy honor and to the welfare of their fellowmen.[66]

From her childhood death was ever present in Linka's life. Her mother died when she was a young girl; her father died before her marriage; not long after she settled in Wisconsin her grandmother and sister died. Linka recorded her attitude toward death, both the actual death of others and her anticipation of her own. On board ship she considered the possibility that she might die during the Atlantic passage. The thought stirred up fears that Linka attributed to the "sight of the seething sea and the sound of the turbulent winds." She judged her anxiety about death to be false and unfounded. Rather than fear, joy should be the result of considering death, which would join her with God.[67]

Fear of death was the subject of a long passage in 1852. In it Linka contemplated her own death. She judged herself to be "truly a miserable, perverse creature," full of good intentions but without merit. Knowing that she deserved to be "cast into the fiery pit," Linka took comfort in Christ's work on her behalf, which would "permit her to stand before the throne of the Judge." This confidence allowed her to look death in the face without fear.

Instead she viewed death as good since it "comes from Him who alone is good." However, Linka did not take divine graciousness as her right. She implored God,

> Help me to be prepared to stand before Thee! Hinder Thou that I should be like the five foolish virgins, who, when the bridegroom came, had no oil in their lamps! Permit me to love what Thou hast given me on this earth; but nothing, nothing, will I love above Thee. . . . In this endeavor may Thy Spirit strengthen and help my spirit, against the Devil and all his evil designs. . . . All this by the help of Thy Spirit, for the sake of Jesus Christ![68]

Six years later Linka fell into the cellar while she was pregnant. The accident brought on a stillbirth and several weeks of illness. The experience caused her to re-examine her attitude and to discover that she did fear death. She traced her fear to "the joy of living . . . and happiness in the life God has given me."[69] She was near death again when Carl Christie was born. Her desire was to remain with her family, but she prayed, "If it be Thy will, O God, let me die in Jesus' name, and let death become very dear to me, for then I shall love Thee more than all else![70]

The death or near death of members of her family also caused Linka to brood about her willingness to accept life as God gave it. In 1856 her son, Christian Keyser, was very ill. As he lay in a deathlike sleep she "sought to find joy in surrender to the will of God" as Job had done.[71] She also wrote to Elisabeth Koren about the ordeal. The diversity of piety among members of the same church was clear in Elisabeth's response; it revealed a less tortured faith that both acknowledged human sin and relied on God's grace.

> . . . I cannot understand that one can mix joy into one's sorrow at such a time! God has given us our great love for children, this dear heavenly Father will not be angry at our weakness in such a time, that I believe for sure!
> You understand me? I know well that it is a great, great sin that we cannot with humble and believing hearts give back to God the gift he has given us, and with childlike trust to say that God has done it, it is well done—if we will be so unbelieving in our grief—but it seems as if you are reproaching yourself because you do not feel glad when you stood with your dear little child and every moment expected to lose him—I do not understand how anyone can and I do not believe that God is angry with us because we are weak.[72]

Rather than accusing herself, Elisabeth wrote of her thankfulness that God provided friends and family who gave one another "mutual comfort and support." She found this natural and asserted that it could not displease God. Linka seldom referred to the external sources of her views. She merely mentioned that her confirmation instruction took place and that her uncle "addresses to me earnest words concerning my approaching confirmation."[73] One of Linka's prayers, written after her husband's confrontation with a group of Methodists, echoed "orthodox" Lutheran teaching. She gave thanks for her firm conviction "that our Church possesses the one and only saving truth." With God's Word as her defense, she faced the Tempter.

> Jesus Christ is at my side, for His sake alone God forgives my sins, His blood cleanseth us from all guilt. I have no merit, but when I walk here below in faith, hope, and love, make use of the means of grace which He has given me for salvation: the Word, Baptism, the Lord's Supper, then I can calmly look forward to my death, for I shall be saved for Jesus' sake.[74]

Twice she noted that she had been reading Søren Kierkegaard: once on the topic of resolutions and once *Works of Love*. Although she suspected that she did not understand all that she read, she remarked concerning the latter: "I catch some of it, and it seems to adhere to my cranium. I might compare myself to a twirling-stick used in stirring up a velvety butter-pudding: a little butter sticks to it."[75] When Herman was away on a Sunday, Linka read a sermon to the household; she was fond of Luther. On one occasion she copied a passage from a Paul Gerhardt sermon into her diary because she found it "so true and beautiful."[76] Gerhardt's words expressed Linka's attitudes on the transitory nature of human life, the need for repentance, and a Christian way of life. In a negative statement about Yankees, she stated her own views and revealed her intense concern for things within.

> The twittering of the birds that reaches my ear is less pleasing than at home in Norway. Arrayed in great splendor in their gaily colored feathers, it would appear that these birds prize more highly appeal to the eye than the harmony which by way of the ear reaches the heart. It just occurs to me that the birds here are in a certain sense a symbol of the Yankee: externally there may be brilliance, but very little attention—at times none whatever—is paid to that which is within.[77]

The letters Gro Svendsen wrote to her family in Norway were less suited to self-examination than Linka's journal. Gro indicated her religious feelings by interjections of pious formulas rather than in reflective passages. She shared with Linka a profound confidence in God's generous care despite human unworthiness.

> From what I have said you will see that we have not too much wealth, but though we have no material wealth, we have nevertheless possessions of greater worth a quiet and peaceful home with a large flock of children all normal, gifted with health and intelligence, spirited, cheerful, and happy . . . so that I am more than satisfied and thankful to God for all His goodness toward His unworthy children.[78]

Although Gro acknowledged her inability to carry out all her good intentions and took responsibility for the agony she caused her family by immigrating, the sense of sinfulness she displayed was less intense than Linka's. This may have been due to the public nature of her letters.

When confronted with death Gro took a resigned attitude. If she considered her own death, she did not write of it to her parents. Hearing of the death of an old man from her home community in Norway, she observed, "Our Heavenly Father is indeed kind to call him home."[79] Her daughter Sigri died before she reached age two. Although Gro grieved over her loss, it did not disrupt her faith.

> My little girl was a very lovable child, mild-mannered, patient, and considerate. Therefore my bereavement is great; but God, who in his wisdom does all things well, relieved her of all pain and took her home. So even in the midst of the grief and agony of parting we thank God for giving her relief. Would that He could draw us all nearer to Him! He took her, who was so dear to all of us, home in order to draw our thoughts closer to Him. With my sisters and brothers I, too, have one of mine who has gone to intercede for us at the throne of mercy. We must not let them pray in vain. May we all be united with them beyond death and the grave![80]

Death was a passing into another life; it provided an occasion to be thankful for God's love rather than to question it.

This was Gro's attitude toward all sorts of hardships. "My health is not always of the best," she wrote to her parents, "but so far God has spared me from any prolonged illness, and so I feel that I cannot complain. Rather I should thank God for His infinite goodness."[81] From bad crops to poor health, difficulties provided a reminder of God's kindness.

Before immigrating Gro had been led to expect that the people in America were very pious and "more devout." She met only one woman whom she judged to be "sincerely religious." As for the others, she wrote, "I don't think people are any worse, but they are certainly not any better."[82] In her descriptions of the pastors who offered their services to the settlers, Gro revealed the characteristics she judged important. She commented that Clausen was a good preacher. "He is a good and conscientious man and works to the best of his ability for things temporal and spiritual. So far as I can tell, he is a sound Lutheran."[83] She appeared pleased that Pastor Hande, their first resident minister, seemed to be "more concerned with the spiritual distress of his parishioners than with church strife and politics."[84] He was followed by Pastor Hoelseth. Gro was less satisfied with him. In her estimation he lacked "the keen mind so necessary in this place and in these times."[85] In these brief comments, Gro displayed the Norwegian Lutheran fusion of orthodoxy and piety. While she was attuned to doctrine and peppered her correspondence with religious comments, she was impatient with doctrinal disputes and political maneuverings which intruded on faith.

While Linka and Gro took comfort and courage from their faith, Karine Neuberg struggled with hers. Karine's sister, Karen, was married to Pastor Laur. Larsen, one of the young leaders of the Norwegian Synod. Both Karine and Henriette, a third sister, came to the United States under the protection of their brother-in-law. They moved in the close social circle of the early clerical families. When Karine seemed to "lose her faith" and refused to attend Communion she received counsel from Pastor Preus as well as Larsen. Their method of reading to her from the sixteenth-century Lutheran Confessions demonstrated their concern, but may have lacked sensitivity to the existential issues.

After a flirtation with Episcopalianism, Karine returned to the Lutheran fold. The cause of her return cannot, however, be firmly identified as the pastors' reading to her from the Augsburg Confession. It might as well have been a realization of her need for the small community centered in the church from which "conversion" would have alienated her. Or her marriage to Dr. Magelsen, an active Lutheran layman, may have prompted her to keep her peace about her questions. Karine had few options aside from marriage or a position as a governess in one of the parsonages. As a single woman from the Norwegian elite she could not strike out on her own. Marriage gave Karine a place in the community.[86]

Of the thousands of women who did leave the Lutheran churches, Lutheran sources said little, of course. Rasmus B. Anderson and his siblings took paths that typified the options available to Norwegians. Abel became a pastor in the Norwegian Synod; Cecelia and Dina married Lutheran clergymen, Pastors Styrk Reque and T. A. Torgerson. Rasmus moved in and out of the Lutheran synods, agreeing and arguing with first one and then the other. Martha and Elizabeth became Methodists under the influence of Norwegian-speaking preachers. Elizabeth defended her conversion, answering her own question: "Why forsake the Lutheran Church?"

> Because I was afraid to trust my spiritual welfare to the guidance of any one of the Lutheran ministers I ever knew . . . [furthermore] God has honored the Methodist Church by helping it to be the means of my conversion and I am going to honor the Methodist Church by giving my support. All this will not, of course, satisfy you as a theologian. Nothing but my being able to prove that there is something wrong in the Lutheran doctrine would vindicate my right.[87]

She confessed that her time was taken up more with household affairs and care of four children than with theology. The time she had she devoted to prayer and reading the Bible.

Admitting that reading the Norwegian New Testament over and over was the first reading "worth mentioning" that she did, Mrs. Harry Ranger made a different decision for her children in the final years of the nineteenth century. As soon as they were old enough to go to Sunday school she took them to the Congregational Church instead of Ringsaker Lutheran because the Congregationalists spoke English.[88]

Unitarian minister Kristofer Janson complained that young men from his congregation returned to Lutheran churches when they married Lutheran women. Among his own contacts were both women who adhered to Lutheran teachings and those who wandered far from it. When Louise Bentzen was hired as a teacher for the Janson children she had already cultivated her powers as a medium. Because little of her life prior to her entry into the household was preserved, it is impossible to know if she once held more conventional beliefs.[89] At the opposite extreme, an unnamed old woman brought a copy of Luther's *Catechism* with her to one of Janson's downtown Minneapolis lectures. After the program she confronted him with the book, demanding to know if he intended to conform to it. She responded to his predictably negative reply with a warning that she would call a curse down on his efforts.[90]

131

This woman was perhaps unusual in her bold approach. She was, nonetheless, typical in her devotion to her religion. Many other women also found meaning and solace in their faith. They may not have been overly concerned with nuances of doctrine and polity within Norwegian Lutheranism, but they displayed a piety, "a settled disposition, a persistent attitude toward God," which was informed and in keeping with the "brief and simple . . . statement of Christian teaching" found in Luther's *Small Catechism*.[91]

Women's Groups

As early as the 1860s the women of the Norwegian Lutheran churches began to form groups to support the local congregation and the mission of the larger church.[92] As their meetings were often informal, complete records were not always kept in the early years. The records that were kept were usually sketchy financial ones. One of the first groups was the *hjelpeforening* established by Diderikke Brandt in 1865 to aid the students at Luther College. Although the *kvindeforening* (women's society) was seldom formed until the congregation was several years old, it was usually the first group organized within the congregation. The general purposes expressed by these women's groups, both at their founding and in retrospect, were inevitably those stated by the women of Vang Lutheran: to "meet in true Christian love and fellowship to further the Lord's work in this locality and also strive to do their bit for foreign missions."[93] When English began to be used, the groups were called Ladies' Aid.

The impulse to organize came from a variety of sources. At Ness Lutheran of Elbow Lake, Minnesota, there were women who had been involved in such a group in Norway where the first *kvindeforening* in support of missions was organized by Mrs. Gustava Kielland in 1840. They felt the need for a group of their own. Exposure to groups in other congregations was the source of the idea at East Freeborn Lutheran; Mrs. Margit Henry "caught the inspiration" during a visit near Madison, where there was already a *kvindeforening*.

Sometimes one woman called her neighbors together. Nellie Johnson Houkom told about her mother's role in starting a group in the 1870s.

> Mother read much and had been out a good deal and she saw no reason why there should not be a women's society there. So she consulted with a good friend and the pastor being in sympathy it was decided to organize.[94]

In another settlement there was a great deal of talk about a women's group before one was finally formed at the invitation of Mrs. William Johnson in June of 1884. There had been a wedding at the Johnsons' and all the leftover food prompted her to ask the women to return the next day. The ten who came founded the Ladies' Aid. If the women of the town had not been involved with such a group before, the pastor was instrumental in organizing the women's group. Frequently his wife was also involved.

Not all clergymen were sympathetic to the idea; opposition to women's groups came from pastors and others. When women of Bethel Lutheran in Madison formed a group over his objections, their pastor, Herman Preus, accused them of being nothing more than "gossip societies." Mrs. Schmidt was elected president in 1879; less than a decade later her husband, Professor Schmidt, became a leader in the Anti-Missourian Brotherhood and thus one of Preus's opponents.[95] H. A. Preus prevented a women's group from being established at Spring Prairie until 1877, when his daughter-in-law, Louise Hjort, came to live in the parsonage with her husband, Rev. Christian Keyser Preus. The elder Preus appeared to be reconciled to the idea of women's groups by 1889, when he requested that the South Aid be organized to benefit the Children's Home in Madison.[96]

Mrs. M. O. Wee, wife of a Hauge Synod pastor, and four other women founded a women's society. When they did, "anonymous letters" addressed to Pastor Wee were put under the parsonage door, asking him to stop the women from organizing.[97] The founders of the women's groups of Red Oak Grove in the 1870s encountered some resistance. Although the intensity of opposition was played down, it was still remembered when a history was written for the congregation's seventy-fifth anniversary in the 1930s.

> There was never any strong opposition to this organization [the South Division of the Ladies' Aid]. Of course some were not permitted to belong to it for various reasons, but the society continued to grow until it included nearly every woman living south of the church.
>
> Sentiment for the [North Division] in the beginning was not very popular. One woman stated that she had a difficult time attending meetings as her father looked upon the meetings as a *sladre forening* (gossip society).[98]

In another area people made fun of the women by making a pun on *kvindeforening*, calling it the *kvindeforstyrellse* or *kvindeforviring*—the women's confusion.[99]

Concern for being viewed as a "gossip society" may have kept women from noting the social benefits of their meetings. Or that may not have been a conscious factor in their decisions to organize. The women of Ness Lutheran in Elbow Lake did recognize their need for "social fellowship" as a reason to began their *kvindeforening*.[100] However, even if they were not sought out, the members received personal benefits from their meetings. Belle Nelson was a charter member of a women's society organized in 1884. She recalled the importance of the group to its members. "Besides their homes and families . . . the main interest of the women was their church and their aid. Their money went for missions. I am sure it did good there and it also did them good to work for missions."[101] In one of the oldest congregations, East Koshkonong, "the aid was an event because it was the only voice that the ladies had in making decisions."[102] The daughter of one founder judged that ". . . the *kvindeforening* was a new adventure—a Godsend. It was an opening up and a broadening of their lives."[103] It provided something of value to its members, which evoked great loyalty. An elderly woman from Westby, Wisconsin, told Lydia Sundby, "I'm 78; have raised seven children and missed only three meetings."[104]

Generally all adult women in the congregation were considered members of *kvindeforening* as soon as they married and set up housekeeping. One member recalled that this was so "as long as they came once in a while." Not to take part was to exclude oneself from the community. Family problems made it impossible for Aagot Raaen's mother to attend; nonetheless, the other women seemed to look down on her for her absence. Lists of charter members included some single women—both widows and those who had never married. Occasionally a single woman would serve as an officer.

Photographs of early meetings show that the men and children of the congregation attended the Ladies' Aid. Although they were unlikely to participate in the working part of the meeting, they enjoyed the social contact and the meal. Mrs. K. J. Hanson answered the question, "did men attend?"

> Yes, for it was not considered fitting for a woman to lead in devotion so the men often served in that capacity and in one case, at least, a man acted as president for years. The story is told of one man when asked why his wife didn't come that he replied, "Aa, hun er hjemme or kjöre höi." (Oh, she is at home hauling hay.)[105]

In other areas the men came only when rain kept them out of the fields.

But even if other husbands, brothers, and sons were not present, the male pastor frequently attended the women's meeting to conduct the devotion. In some cases he also served as an officer of the group. He was not the only man to do so. At Rollag Church in Hawley, Minnesota, Herbran Erickson was the treasurer because no woman was willing to take on the job. After eleven years he refused to continue, saying, "I consider the women perfectly capable of caring for the office themselves."[106]

Each local *kvindeforening* established its own pattern of meetings and projects. Commonly they gathered every two weeks or once a month in one of the member's homes. Wearing long white aprons over their dresses, women walked the several miles to their hostess's house, knitting as they went. Miss Karen Alfsen of Little Cedar Lutheran was fortunate to own a sewing machine in the 1880s; she loaded it and several of her neighbors in a wagon and drove them to the meetings.[107] When the meeting was held at a farm, the town members were treated to a ride in the hayrack.[108] The investment of time required to get to the meeting may have determined that it would last all day. Proximity and difficulty of transportation led to the organization of more than one group: the North Aid and the South Aid.

In the pioneer years the hostess had to carry many of her family's belongings, including the beds, outdoors to make room for the guests in her small cabin. When a frame house afforded more room and the meeting was only for an afternoon, hosting the *kvindeforening* still required preparation. Looking back to her childhood, from 1937, Winifred Langum Remington described a meeting at her mother's house.

The tremendous domestic upheaval. Everything in the house cleaned, scrubbed and polished. Clean, tucked and ruffled pillow shams, clean bed spreads, clean "splashers," embroidered with water lilies and the ubiquitous duck, on the wash stand, fresh tidies on the chairs. The tall silver cake stand polished to the nth degree, the long heavy linen table cloth laid in readiness.

And then such doings in the kitchen, and we youngsters rushing home from school to see if the hired girl had saved the frosting dish and some little ball doughnuts and standing with ever ready fingers for drops or crumbs or the papers removed from cake bottoms.

Then the great day! At noon time we were rushed into clean dresses and our Sunday shoes and sternly instructed to remember to be "lady like." After an afternoon at school that dragged out interminably, the dash home—in at the kitchen door and shyly edging into the front room with the hope that some of the guests had brought their babies.[109]

The day-long meetings of the nineteenth century were taken up with hand-work, a devotion, and meals. In the first years Norwegian was spoken without question; later English could be used at the discretion of the hostess. By the 1930s English was in general use in many women's societies. The transition was usually gradual. At St. John's of Northfield the change came in 1919 when the group nominated as secretary a women who was "not Norwegian." Over her protests that she could neither write nor speak Norwegian she was elected and the language issue settled.[110] Materials from the national Women's Missionary Federation were printed in both languages. In 1920 English was adopted as the official language of the national organization.

Anything from knitting stockings to piecing a quilt was done as handwork. The materials were secured in various ways: the members provided their own or they paid for them out of their treasury and delegated one member to purchase them. Each month members deposited their dues, from five to twenty-five cents, in the treasury. Women who were unable to attend meetings could still work on the common projects and sometimes were assessed dues. The work was not without conflict. The women of Spring Prairie ceased making quilts after criticism of one woman's skills prompted her to leave the group.[111] Once a year their finished mittens, shirts, and aprons were sold at an auction, with the proceeds returned to the women's treasury to be distributed to their projects.

The devotional segment of the day was very like an abbreviated version of home worship services. Some groups arranged their meeting day so that the pastor could attend. If he was present, he read a Scripture passage, commented upon it, led the women in singing a hymn, and prayed with them. Without the pastor the devotion was still held; it was nearly the same except that the president or one of the members led it. One or two women in the group who displayed particular ability were called upon to do so. Mrs. Christopherson and Mrs. Moe were frequently the devotion leaders for Red Oak Grove, South Division.[112] Mrs. Jens Rudh, the first president of the Swan Lake Mission Society, was known for her "convincing sermonettes at Ladies' Aids and elsewhere."[113] All the members joined in praying the Lord's Prayer in unison.[114] In keeping with the mission focus of many *kvindeforening*, their programs included a reading from a mission publication such as *Mission Bladet*. At Rock Valle the women subscribed to *Santhal Missionaeren*, from an independent Norwegian mission in India; one of them read it to the others as they worked.

Day-long meetings required that at least one meal, and often two, be served. When the North Aid of Crow River organized in 1897, the menu for their meetings was specified: "two kinds of bread, one kind of cake and cookies or doughnuts and coffee."[115] This was a modest meal compared to those served in later years; one anniversary history described them as "real dinners" that included turkey, *lefse*, and other Norwegian dishes.[116] After "the society all but choked itself to death on food, having no place to go because the lunch had been too burdensome," rules were made limiting the number and kinds of dishes that could be served at a meeting.[117] Serving more than "bread and butter with meat or cheese, one kind of cake, and one kind of sauce" to the *kvindeforening* of Comstock Lutheran resulted in a one-dollar fine to be paid into the treasury.[118] At least one woman was cheerfully willing to pay the penalty for the opportunity to provide a more impressive meal.

At mealtime, the men of the congregation appeared to eat and to collect their womenfolk. Until about the turn of the century all meals were served at a table, sit-down style. If there were more diners than chairs, they ate in shifts. The switch to a "plate lunch" was noted in histories of local groups, suggesting that the women perceived it to be a significant change. Within the next decade in many areas another change was brought about by the construction of a basement under the church. Meetings were held there rather than in the members' homes.

In addition to regular work meetings, the women's groups sponsored activities for the entire congregation. In summer or autumn an auction was held, in conjunction with a dinner, to raise money for the women's projects. The women's handwork brought good prices, usually above market value. In 1890 the women at Rock Valle made $71.98 at their auction. The dinner was sometimes free, to attract customers for the women's handwork and other times part of the money-making venture. In addition to quilts, mittens, and shirts, other items, such as apples and oranges, were sold. A visit by a missionary, home on furlough, turned the event into a mission fest such as were held by the women of Rock Valle in the 1890s.

To see and to hear a missionary in those days was like a breath from another world. Dinner would usually be served out in the open by a long table seating 40 to 50 people and free to anyone from far and near who was so kind as to attend the auctions. Coffee—lots of it by the boilerful—was boiled on the farm-house kitchen stove and carried out to and around the table in large coffee pots. "Var so god, en kop til" [If you will be so kind, a cup here] were words often heard. It did also happen at times that the wind would whirl and play around and disarrange the set tables and spice the food with a little of "this" and "that" or bring a few innocent rain-drops. However, the day would usually turn out fine. "Lord, bless this day for us" were silent prayers in the hearts of many. After the sale, a hymn was sung by the audience and the apostolic blessing spoken by the pastor and the crowd would be treated to free coffee and a bite to eat before leaving for their homes.[119]

Dinners were also held without an auction. The *Fergus Falls Journal* announced that a dinner would be served by the Southern Ladies' Aid Society of the Svederup church. The cost was twenty cents and everyone was welcome.[120] The dinner menus ranged from Norwegian favorites like *lutefisk* to fried chicken or oyster stew. At St. John's of Northfield the women served American fare at their earliest meals; it was not until 1898 that they first provided Norwegian food. In less than a decade the affair became so popular that "large numbers of servers dressed in the fantastic garb of Norway" fed 600 people 300 pounds of *lutefisk* and 700 pounds of meatballs. They cleared $200 for their efforts.[121] In these ways the women raised significant sums, which they contributed to the local congregation and the larger church.

In at least two congregations the women demonstrated that Herbran Erickson was correct in his judgment that they were capable of providing their own treasurer. The women of Highland parish lent money to the local farmers at 10 percent interest. "It was not a high rate then, as compared with what the banks demanded." When the church was built in 1892, the women were able to contribute $700.00. The financial report of Reque Lutheran, near Albert Lea, indicated that in 1889 the women had $41.17 in their treasury and $58.00 lent out at the same rate.[122]

The recipients of the funds raised by women's societies varied from place to place and over time. Half of the funds from the women of Petri Lutheran went to their parochial school; half to foreign missions. This was a common ratio of local expenses and other causes. Desire for a church building prompted the women of Emmons Lutheran and those of St. Paul's in Preston to organize their groups. (In Preston the congregation had been holding services in the county jail.) The same may have been the case at St. John's in Elbow Lake; formed in 1894, the women's group there was one of the few founded prior to the congregation. After the church was built, women of the congregation continued to contribute to its expenses. They paid part of the teacher's salary, purchased equipment—pews, an organ, an altar painting—and paid for adding a basement or building a parsonage.[123] A congregation in Hitterdahl received its church bell as a gift from the women. On one side of the bell was an inscription: *"Buffalo River Menighed's Kvindeforening satte mig her At tolke i sorg og tale is glaede."* (The Buffalo River Congregation's Women's Society put me here to express sorrow and to speak gladness.)[124]

The money for the mission of the larger church was dispersed among education, mission, and charity, with the three activities blending together. The *kvindeforening* members favored specific projects with which they had some personal contact. Money was sent to individual missionaries with whom the women corresponded or to support one child in a mission school. Missions staffed by a son or daughter of the congregation received special attention. Mission fest speakers and reports in church periodicals established connections and kept them current. During their first fifty years (1897-1947) the North Ladies' Aid of Crow River contributed to almost twenty causes "besides the regular projects." [125] This range of gifts from the very local to far abroad was typical, as was the mix of types of institutions. Financial contributions linked the women of a local congregation to the work of the church at large, or the work of the particular Norwegian Lutheran group to which their congregation was linked.

The women seldom contributed to projects not connected with the Norwegian Lutheran community. Exceptions appeared when World War I forced women to look beyond their ethnoreligious group and to forge alliances. The war mandated less elaborate lunches at meetings and prompted cooperation in relief work. In Austin, Minnesota, the women of Bear Creek Lutheran Church worked with the local Red Cross.[126] The Ladies' Aid of Central Lutheran in Edgerton, Wisconsin, purchased $200.00 worth of Liberty Loan bonds, sent cards to soldiers, donated a service flag to the congregation, and adopted two war orphans.[127]

Kvindeforening were begun at the local level; their membership included all the women in the congregation or those who lived in a generally defined geographic area such as "south of the church." Over the years this organizational scheme was altered by improvements in transportation, changes in the church's resources, and shifts in the congregational demography. Easier movement and greater resources encouraged consolidation of regional groups into one that met in the basement of the church. Members still took turns hosting one another, using their newly acquired and freshly equipped church kitchen to prepare and serve lunch. In some congregations the unified group met less often, while the smaller groups continued to meet in homes.

Pigeforening, girls' societies, were formed as the daughters of the women's society reached adolescence. Their aims were nearly identical to their mothers'.

139

The *pigeforening* of Waterloo Ridge was founded in 1895, sixteen years after the *kvindeforening*, with three stated objectives:

1. To render help to our own Church and community.
2. To extend our help outside our own Church and community to benevolent institutions.
3. For the benefaction of our own self, literally, to improve our minds, our character and our Ladyship and in other words, to make us more God-like and better fitted for good society.[128]

At their monthly meetings the girls worked at improving themselves by practicing their fancywork and having a devotion. The proceeds from the sale of their handwork was added to the income made at ice cream socials and oyster dinners to fulfill the first and second objectives of the group. They adopted "a heathen girl at the mission station at Tananarivo, Madagascar, whose name was Ratsivoro Naro." In 1897 the girls purchased for their own congregation an altar painting that served as "a constant reminder of Christ's Triumph over death and sin."

The Waterloo Ridge girls' society held its final meeting in 1909 and then merged with the Young People's Society. In its end as in its activities, the group was typical. In other congregations a series of young women's groups were formed as each generation of girls reached the age to join. Long-standing groups changed names through the years. The *pigeforening* of Hamar Lutheran, Rothsay, Minnesota, became the Sewing Club in 1924 and later became the Dorcas Society.[129] The Bethlehem Lutheran Busy Bees affiliated with the national Lutheran Daughters of the Reformation and took a new name, the Gleaners.

As their organization changed so did the activities of Ladies' Aids. The Trefoldighed Ladies' Aid of Battle Lake, Minnesota, stopped sewing and holding sales as early as 1898 when Dorothea Koefod married their pastor, Rev. Norman. They continued to meet in one another's homes. Devotions were led by Pastor or Mrs. Norman. Lunch was served. And a donation was collected from each woman in attendance. The Tabitha Society was organized specifically to look after the material needs of the church.

The move away from money-making to study was slow and never complete. After 1904 the women of Bethlehem Lutheran in Fergus Falls no longer sewed at their meetings; however, they continued to donate items for the sale.[130] Even groups devoted solely to study tended to continue to make contributions to their congregation, missions, and charities. The national

Women's Missionary Federation encouraged free will offerings over other forms of fund-raising.[131]

Differentiation on the basis of activities also took place in other congregations. In small congregations the membership of the groups devoted to different purposes was nearly identical. Age and marital and professional status were other bases for differentiating groups. Young mothers' groups and professional women's groups were instituted in some town churches in the 1940s. At Trinity Lutheran in Minneapolis there was a Norwegian circle composed of the older women of the congregation into the 1940s.

In the same years in which local groups were becoming increasingly specialized, there were movements to unite them into synod-based federations. The first extracongregational groups were the work of pastors' wives who knew one another and had the personal contacts and freedom of movement necessary to organize. Within the Hauge Synod inspiration for the group came from Mary Nelson Wee, wife of Pastor M. O. Wee. She proposed the idea of an organization for "all the women, and especially the pastors' wives of the church" to Mrs. Hannah Rønning. With Mrs. Rønning's encouragement, Mary Wee, Olive Hodnefield, Ida Grossoth, Mrs. J. A. Quello, and Mrs. Lars Harrisville formed the *Missionduen* (Mission Dove) in June of 1901. Among the group's projects was a common prayer hour held each Friday from 6:00-7:00 P.M.[132] At first Mission Dove membership was restricted to wives of pastors, teachers in Christian schools, and female missionaries.[133]

Not long after the birth of the Mission Dove the women of the Norwegian Synod met at the Synod's 1903 jubilee celebration and organized *Prestekone*. Mrs. Adolf Bredesen presided over the meeting, with Mrs. R. O. Brandt elected as secretary. Two years later Mrs. C. K. Preus was elected president. While Inanda Bredesen was of the elder generation of *prestefruen*, Thalette Brandt and Louise Hjort Preus were the second generation; their families held strikingly different attitudes toward women's societies. Brandt's mother-in-law, Diderikke Brandt, was responsible for the organization of one of the earliest local women's groups. Preus' father-in-law, Herman Preus, had opposed formation of women's groups in congregations he served.

The educational institutions of the Norwegian Synod were the principal recipients of aid from the *Prestekone*. This was in keeping with the pioneer work of Diderikke Brandt. A special fund was established to provide financial assistance to needy students (all male). Money was raised to purchase a bronze statue of Luther (a copy of the Worms monument) for Luther College in

Decorah. The women donated a marble copy of Thorvaldson's Christ to Luther Seminary on Hamline Ave. in St. Paul.[134]

In the year that the Norwegian Synod organized, the United Church also moved toward a federation of women's societies. At the church's 1903 annual meeting in Duluth a group of women, which included pastors' wives, pledged themselves to contribute five cents to missions every week; this "mite" was beyond their usual giving. Formal organization waited a few years until the 1911 annual meeting in St. Paul. The convention approved the constitution submitted by a committee of three men and three women. (The constitutional committee had been elected during a prior meeting at the request of women interested in missions.) That afternoon the women gathered at the United Church Seminary to elect officers and begin their work. Rebekka Oline (Lena) Gjertsen Dahl, wife of the United Church president, was elected president.

Lena Dahl had been considering a women's mission federation since 1898. Mrs. Th. Eggen recalled hearing Lena propose the idea to Pastor J. N. Kildahl during a family visit. According to Regina Eggen's account, Mrs. Dahl said,

> Friends, there is something brewing in my mind—something new among our people. Mr. Dahl is the only one I have mentioned it to. He thinks it would be a fine thing. I feel that our women should begin to plan for a mission federation. What other church denominations are doing, we can do with the Grace of God. What will our pastors think about it and how will our women take it? Now I wish you pastors will give me your candid opinion on this question.[135]

The pastors were supportive and Mrs. Dahl promoted her idea gradually as she continued to work with the young people of the church and edit a paper for them. When her husband was elected president of the United Church, the Dahls moved to Minneapolis, where she recruited a few other women to assist her in writing letters and mailing out tracts. After women at the 1903 meeting pledged their extra nickel to missions, she urged other pastors' wives to distribute mission boxes in the women's societies of their congregations so that mission giving would be extended into the homes.

As its president, Mrs. Dahl launched the newly formed Women's Missionary Federation into an ambitious building project to provide houses for missionaries in the United States on furlough. Within four years four cottages were built and furnished. The titles to the houses were later transferred to the United Church without encumbrances.[136] The WMF gave substantial financial support to the Hydro Therapeutic department at the Deaconess Home and

Hospital in Chicago ($3,557.34); the Sinyang, China, girl's school ($2,300); and to the Klashon, China, Hospital for an X-ray machine. In addition the federation promoted missions by encouraging local women's societies to form special mission circles. The executive board members and a few other women donated their time and work to send out tracts and pamphlets.

Women of the Lutheran Free Church organized in 1916 at the annual convention in Willmar, Minnesota. The 150 women present elected five officers: Miss Ragna Sverdrup, daughter of the influential professor, served as treasurer. Projects supported by the federation were similar to those pursued by the women of the United Church: a mission cottage; distribution of pamphlets; publication of *Mission Hilsen*, a small paper; and financial contributions to the work of female missionaries.

Each of these groups represented a different one of the Norwegian Lutheran synods. Loyalties to churches were notoriously deep and feelings were fierce when issues flared. Women were not among those who debated at conferences and in newspapers. However, they could not have escaped some awareness of the conflicts, whatever their level of interest or personal opinions. While Linka Preus thanked God for her confidence that "our church" had the one truth, Gro Svendsen had little interest in "church strife and politics." Mrs. Mary Wee came from a United Church family and married a pastor in the Hauge Synod. In their first parish she was asked not to mention her former affiliation. Her mother accepted the situation, remarking, "Well, it might have been worse if he had been a Methodist."[137] In local women's groups synodical tensions could surface, and they did. Rival loyalties to United Lutheran Church and Bethel Lutheran in Underwood, Minnesota, brought about a split in the *Nordens Kvindeforening*.[138]

In 1917 the United Church, the Hauge Synod, and the Norwegian Synod joined to form the Norwegian Lutheran Church of America. The women of the *Synodens Prestefrueforening* (Norwegian Synod), *Missionduen* (Hauge Synod), and *Kvindernes Missionsforbund* (United Church) also united their work. At a meeting held in the Palm Room of the St. Paul Hotel they organized the Women's Missionary Federation of the NLCA. The objectives stated by the new group in its constitution were in line with the purposes of its predecessors.

To create interest in and stimulate love for the great cause of missions, to unite, if possible, all women's societies within The Norwegian Lutheran Church in harmonious cooperation for missions; to promote the organization of separate

143

mission societies and children's societies wherever it is found practicable; to disseminate knowledge of missions in general and of the Missions of the Norwegian Lutheran Church in particular.

All aspects of the church's work, "including charities, Christian Education, and Pensions," were part of the women's interpretation of mission. To carry out their purpose, the women elected Lena Dahl president and authorized the wives of the district presidents to organize the federation at that level and to plan for circuit level groups.[139]

As there had been opposition to local women's groups, there was also opposition to linking the local groups. The federation was described as a "church within a church" and viewed as a threat to the unity of the entire church. Clara Rygh, who served as general secretary of the federation in the 1920s, saw the leaders' family connections as valuable in overcoming this sort of opposition to the federation. All the officers and many committee members elected by the WMF in 1917 were wives of prominent churchmen.[140] These women were, by Rygh's estimation, "high-minded . . . [and] well aware of the opposition that would be met and the necessity of proceeding slowly and carefully."[141] They were able to lend the federation their own status and respectability. Delia Ylvisaker (the federation's second president), for example, sought out the advice and support of her former Sunday school teacher, Dr. J. K. Kildahl, and her former pastor, Th. Eggen, thus winning their support for the women's group.[142]

Loyal members of the congregational *kvindeforening* saw no need for a federation, which they perceived as a threat to their self-sufficiency and autonomy. A letter to Katharina Blilie from Mrs. Amanda Ekem Sundstad related fears among Iowa women that the federation was a movement to usurp the pastoral office.

> I definitely assured them first that we had no intention of interfering in any way with the pastor's function. Some said that they had heard that women wanted to preach now. Of course I assured them that this was all wrong. Not a single person I had met—and I knew all those at headquarters—had even mentioned such a possibility.[143]

Mrs. Sundstad also told her audience that local groups would be encouraged to continue their work. Lydia Bredesen Sundby, daughter of the first president of the *Prestekone*, was elected president of the Madison Circuit of the WMF. In her efforts to organize the federation at that level she discovered that while some women did not object to the federation, neither did they care to become a part of it. One woman told her, "I'd like to be with you, but I do not like the joining."[144]

President Lena Dahl wrote a pamphlet to promote the federation, answering objections and outlining its work. She emphasized the Women's Federation's place within the "regular channels of the Church" as an auxiliary to the Board of Foreign Missions and the Board of Charities on which the president and secretary of the WMF served as advisory members. Mrs. Dahl was an advocate of organization, system, and uniformity; she urged the organization of the federation in four layers—national, district, circuit, and local—which duplicated those used by the NLCA, assuring her readers that the women's societies would offer the church "almost unlimited resources." They would "bring the great household in order. . . [as] the Church expects of its daughters."[145]

The federation's support to missions was three-pronged: prayer, education, and fund-raising. It carried out an ambitious program of education through its literature committee, which published information about the missions of the church in both Norwegian and English. In addition to pamphlets, they produced programs for Sunday school classes and mission groups. To support the smooth running of district, circuit, and local societies, constitutions and a book on parliamentary rules were made available by the national federation.

Fund-raising for the projects of the national group was achieved through the use of mission boxes (printed in Norwegian or English) in homes, sale of life memberships and in memoriam memberships, and an annual contribution from local groups at the assessed rate of ten cents per member. Local groups were urged to channel all their funds through the national treasury and thence through the general fund of the NLCA; this provided evidence of the "magnitude" and success of the Women's Missionary Federation work. Judged by financial standards, the work was successful. Eight thousand mission boxes were prepared for distribution in 1919. A special appeal to meet the Board of Foreign Missions' deficit brought in $6,397.73.[146]

Officers of the Women's Federation used their funds for projects directed to women. They sent Christmas greetings to "all our women missionaries and also to women preparing for service in the mission fields" in 1920.[147] Educational materials highlighted women's work. Program topics distributed to local groups encompassed woman's place in the Temple, in the Apostolic church, in the Reformation, in missions, and in the present church. The Literature Committee issued biographies of several women in the Little Lutheran Biography series and in *Some Marthas and Marys of the N.L.C.A.*

Mrs. Oscar Hellestad's appeal on behalf of an Industrial School for Chinese women and girls elicited a positive response.

> The Committee strongly feels that the Federation's special duty and call lies in just this line of work; to help especially the heathen *women* in efforts to christianize their home life. It has been strongly brought out in recent missionary lectures that the christianized father was always hampered, and his efforts very often brought to naught, by the heathen influence and superstitions of the *women* in his family and clan.[148]

This sense of special obligation toward "heathen" women was common among Protestant women's missionary organizations of the period.

During World War I there were discussions about the federation taking up war work in connection with the Red Cross. Mrs. Hove reported that "rather than do nothing," the women of Luther Seminary in St. Paul had joined a Red Cross group that had neither ethnic nor denominational affiliations—"an American unit." A less noble motivation lurked in President Lena Dahl's comments on the desirability of organizing Lutheran women in the Twin Cities; she remarked, "Also that the Catholic women are organized and receiving credit for their work whereas the Lutheran women, lacking an organization, get none."[149]

The minutes of WMF board meetings recorded the tensions and struggles within the federation and in the alliance between the women and the boards of the church; these difficulties were not aired in promotional materials. The close acquaintance and family relationships between the leaders of the WMF and the NLCA did not prevent difficulties in their working relationships. It was only after the women inquired of the members of the Board of Foreign Mission as to their views of the federation's position that they received their advisory seats in 1918. Discussions between WMF officers and those of the boards of the NLCA continued. Later that year Lena Dahl and Anna Skabo Stub met with Rev. Birklund and Dr. Stub; in 1920 Mrs. Dahl and Mrs. N. Flaten met with various secretaries again regarding the relation of WMF to the boards.

Operating through the regular channels of the church reduced the women's autonomy and slowed their actions. Purchase of the first missionary furlough cottages had been quickly accomplished by Lena Dahl, and by her account it was nearly a miracle. Minutes of the Norwegian Lutheran Church of America's Board of Trustees for 1919 revealed that the procedure was considerably complicated. Mrs. Dahl alerted the secretary of the Foreign Mission Board that a house was available in Northfield; the Foreign Mission Board acted to recommend purchase to the trustees; the trustees voted "that the purchase of the above property by the Women's Missionary Federation, as recommended by the Foreign Mission Board be approved."[150]

Ongoing problems with accounting procedures and in relations with Augsburg Publishing House prompted Inga Bøckman to attempt to resign in March of 1918.[151] While the women were probably all too familiar with the details of the difficulties, they did not include them in their minutes. The same month a committee was formed to confer with the editors of the *Lutheraneren*, the church paper, in an effort to secure four pages every two months for the federation's use.[152]

The literature committee faced the frustrations of limited funds. Mrs. Wee reported on the problems at the January 1919 board meeting. Pamphlets published by the federation were not paying for themselves; there were difficulties in securing space in *Lutheraneren* when it was needed and their request for a special page had been denied. She asked the board, "Is the work of the Literary Committee to be a mission work, or is it to work in such a way as *not* to incur expenses on the Federation?" If the purpose was mission, she requested that money be allocated for the committee's use and that they be given "free hands."[153] The arrangement with the official church papers continued to be unsatisfactory and in 1920 the women resolved to established their own paper.[154]

In 1919 the federation resolved to hire Miss Mathilde Rasmussen as field secretary.[155] Although this resolution passed, there is no evidence that it was carried out. (Rasmussen did serve as first vice president for five years, 1923-28.) If it had been it would have moved the women another step toward an organization that resembled the larger church in form. In addition to centralization of leadership and standardization of program, they had a paid specialist in the city. It is little wonder that some members in local societies felt that their familiar ways were threatened by the federation.

Conclusions

Although they were excluded from leadership, women participated in the founding and ongoing life of Norwegian Lutheran churches. They were active worshipers who took part in the sacraments and rituals of their church. Each woman was baptized and confirmed. Most children had two female and two male sponsors. Women partook of the Lord's Supper, for which they often supplied the elements. Through women's societies, women purchased the equipment for worship: pews, altar, communion ware, etc. By singing in choirs and playing the organ women contributed to the musical aspects of worship.

Aside from the pastor, the *klokker*, and a few officers, men's participation in the congregations was very similar to women's. They were baptized and confirmed; they worshiped and sang. Men, however, had the possibility of taking on leadership. Those men who did not become pastors could serve as officers or delegates to intercongregational meetings. In their own congregation, they could vote. Perhaps these two differences contributed to a third—until the twentieth century men did not form men's groups and then only in a few congregations and without the same level of activity and success of women's groups.

Women, who were not allowed to vote, hold office, serve as delegates, or be ordained, formed their own arena of activity, *kvindeforening*. Their stated purpose was to support the work of the church, to further God's kingdom. The financial needs of the local parish were frequently the motivation for establishing a "Ladies' Aid." Once the group was organized it was the women's channel of local influence; their financial contributions enabled them to decide that there would be a parochial schoolteacher, which altar painting would hang in the church, or that it was time to dig a basement under the building. Their dollars also voted for the ongoing work of missionaries in China, Madagascar, and Alaska and for the continued ministry of orphanages, schools, and hospitals in the United States.

The money raised and contributed by women helped to build and maintain the Norwegian Lutheran churches and their affiliated institutions. In this way women took part in the financial transitions from a tax-supported state church to a member-supported American denomination. The Norwegian church and government did not make provisions for the immigrants' religious needs. Nor would any American group provide Norwegian Lutheran services. Therefore, a new pattern of voluntary stewardship was essential if the newcomers were to have a familiar church that used their language, ritual, and hymnody.

A dual pattern of stewardship was developed. Expenses were met by contributions to the general treasury and by funds raised by women's groups. Although this system was a financial success, its implicit notion of membership and responsibility had less fortunate consequences. Rather than all members sharing a unified sense of responsibility for the whole work of the church, women were excluded from direct decision making and their "extra" financial support functioned as their voice and vote. While this arrangement did provide the women with some influence, it absolved men from responsibility for certain aspects of the church's life. Further, women's influence and access to decision making were limited by their ability to purchase them. Their domestic skills were made use of at the same time that members of the congregation and the surrounding community were urged to pay above market prices for the women's products. This system encouraged covertly manipulated support, not stewardship.

The short-term consequences for the women themselves were positive. The church was built up and its ministry expanded; the female members had the satisfaction of sharing responsibility for that achievement despite their auxiliary status. Through their own societies, women were able to use their distinctly "female" domestic skills to produce income and thus to give tangible economic support to their church. The fact that this method of funding was adopted suggested that the necessity of voluntary financing was coupled with a slight crack in the household unit of economic production. While the unit did not break up, an unarticulated awareness of women's noncash contributions in the form of domestic labor was encouraged by conversion of that labor into cash at *kvindeforening* auctions and dinners.

Establishment of women's societies demonstrated further that the members had a sense of themselves as women, separate and distinct from men, and that they had a need for social interaction and mutual support. Despite male attendance and even service as officers, the groups were named *kvindeforening*, emphasizing their female membership. Meetings were a forum for exchange of information, an opportunity to admire one another's skills, and an occasion to share in religious activity that was sometimes led by the women themselves.

At the same time, women's groups were one factor in immigrant women's adaptation to a new environment and thereby a factor in the gradual formation of a Norwegian-American and finally an American identity. At first the local groups retained Norwegian language and food habits, even as they forged a new behavior. Over time—several decades—Yankee dishes appeared at Norwegian Lutheran church dinners and English crept into Ladies' Aid meetings. The shift in name was another indication of adaptation. Although the recipients of the women's generosity were almost without exception Norwegian Lutheran, the form of fund-raising and support to missions and charities was quite like that followed by other Protestant women's groups in the United States.[156]

149

The process of Americanization and modernization was accelerated when local groups affiliated with a national organization that produced standardized educational materials and increased contacts between local members via meetings and publications. Both the organization and its publications were led by wives of clergymen who had contacts beyond Norwegian Lutheranism. After the 1917 merger the Women's Missionary Federation moved toward more organization, more centralization, and more standardization, all rationalized characteristics of modernization.

Confusion about membership and responsibility produced by local *kvindeforening* was duplicated at the national level by the Women's Missionary Federation. To some the WMF appeared to be a women's church within the larger church; these critics failed to see that outside of the worshiping congregation, the larger church was a men's church. The women made themselves essential to the NLCA by their financial support. Their success in this effort assured them of influence, but only indirectly, as an auxiliary, not as full members of the governing boards. While the WMF increased women's visibility within the church and assured them of a place, it also isolated them in their own organization and perpetuated a division within the NLCA as in congregations.

The value of women's groups to their members and to the church was ambiguous. The financial benefits to the church and the personal benefits to the women were countered by divisions within the church symbolized by a dual system of contributions and budgets and by women's isolation in auxiliary groups. The results of this pattern of stewardship and decision making were neither intentional nor anticipated. The expressed purpose of the women's societies, local and national, was support for the church's work.

Whatever side effects their work produced, the women's primary motivation can be interpreted as an active appropriation of Luther's explanation of "Thy will be done," the third petition of the Lord's Prayer, which they had memorized as adolescents. "The good and gracious will of God is surely done without our prayer, but we ask in this prayer that it may be done also among us."[157] This purpose remained constant through shifts in activities and structure. Individually women also manifested this motivation. It was seen in Gro Svendsen's willingness to write letters for her neighbors, in Ingeborg Reishus's generous response to a family infected with the pox, and in Linka Preus's prayers for her children. The implicit understanding of "us" gradually expanded. Missionaries were sent out to foreign lands. The enlarged

Norwegian Lutheran church was formed through mergers, and by the 1980s it included persons of other ethnic backgrounds and religious temperaments.

FIVE

School and Ministry

Women provided significant ministry within their churches despite the fact that women were not ordained into the ministry of word and sacrament in Norwegian-American Lutheran churches until 1970 and they were often unable to vote in congregational meetings until the twentieth century.[1] While the local churches would have been greatly impoverished without women's talents, time, and money, women's contributions were not limited to their home parish or their own organizations. Norwegian-American Lutheran women moved beyond the arena of their homes and families and that of congregations and women's societies into the larger, extralocal church as students and teachers in the churches' educational institutions and as professionals who ministered to and for their community as teachers, deaconesses, and missionaries.

In these activities the female members of Norwegian-American Lutheran churches were not unlike other American Protestant women.[2] Teaching, nursing, and missionizing were regarded as continuations of women's domestic roles. A mother was responsible for teaching her children and often took care of her family and others in times of illness; it was a short step to doing these same things in new settings. On the mission field women were expected to address themselves to their "heathen sisters" and their children. There too their primary activities were to be continuations of their domestic work.

These expansions of women's conventional roles provided options to wife- and motherhood either as it had been experienced in Norway or as it was encountered in Yankee ideals. However short the step from teaching one's own children, nursing one's own family, and praying with one's own women's society to teaching, nursing, and praying in other settings, it was a step that changed the actions. Frequently teachers, deaconesses, and missionaries were unmarried. Training for the various responsibilities of these positions provided women with additional knowledge and specialized skills. This took them to new places, American cities and foreign nations, and introduced them to new people, some like themselves and some quite different. Perhaps they did their work out of love and gospel motivations, but they also received a paycheck—no matter that it may have been very small.

Norwegian-American women, both those recently arrived as adults and those born in the United States, were educated at schools operated by various manifestations of their Lutheran churches. There they were trained both for wife- and motherhood and for service in professions. In addition to training the students for their future careers, either conventional or unconventional, Lutheran institutions provided contacts with American culture. Some women were employed as teachers and were examples of professional women.

The professions of teacher, deaconess, and missionary (and wife of missionary) were not formally regarded as being in the same category with that of the ordained pastor. They were, nonetheless, forms of ministry that were carried out in the context of the church. Through the work of these women the church nurtured the religious and ethnic heritage of its children, provided medical and social services to its members and neighbors, and witnessed to the truth of the universal gospel in faraway lands. Local congregational historians were aware of the special status of women who served in these ways, particularly as missionaries and deaconesses, and included them as "daughters of the congregation" along with the "sons" who were pastors.

Education

Norwegian immigrants had the reputation of being far more literate than many other national groups. A conventional linkage of religion and education in Norway contributed to this situation. It also encouraged immigrants to work out a system of "Norwegian" or parish schools. In them both girls and boys received religious instruction along with Norwegian language and culture.

In the United States elementary education was not enough. Church leaders, both lay and clergy, recognized the need to provide additional educational opportunities within the church. Training for would-be pastors was undertaken early in the Halfway Creek Parsonage in 1861; the faculty of two and the handful of students moved to Decorah, Iowa, the following year to open Luther College. The young school curriculum was patterned after the classical training that pastors of the Norwegian Synod had received in Norway. Its primary purpose was the preparation of young men for entry into theological seminary (usually at Concordia Seminary of the Lutheran Church-Missouri Synod in St. Louis) and thence into the ordained ministry.

No provision was made for educating the sisters of these male students. A few girls, among them Lulla Hjort and Sina Preus, were given "crumbs from the table" in an informal school, *Comitia Dumriana*. In this "community of dunces" they studied German, music, and handwork. Under the supervision of Luther College professors, but not in Luther College classes, they also studied English and history. Diderikke Brandt housed the girls in the already crowded Brandt home, one more act of generosity that made her deserving of the title College Mother. Several of this handful of unofficial students married official Luther College students.[3] Lulla's mother, Christiane Otteson Hjort, also conducted an informal school for girls so "that they might learn a variety of thing of which they might otherwise remain in ignorance."[4]

Rasmus Anderson's ill-fated effort to form a Norwegian educational association had the salutary result of prompting the foundation of numerous academies by the Norwegian Synod, other church organizations, and private parties. Those who applied to the academies for admission were expected to be

at least fourteen years of age, be able to read Norwegian readily, write moderately well, and with some experience in handwriting, be able to cipher to the scale of four and possess about as much Christian experience as a well prepared confirmant. It is additionally desirable that they know some English. Their pastors must give assurances that they have moderate gifts for learning and have both a good record morally as well as promise of progress in an institution where Christian discipline is practiced.[5]

Over seventy-five were in operation for larger or shorter periods of time with more or less success.[6] A few, such as St. Olaf School, developed into colleges and were operated far into the twentieth century. These offered girls an opportunity to receive instruction comparable to high school. When academies expanded into colleges they were coeducational; the colleges founded to train pastors, Luther and Augsburg, were not.[7] Two other sorts of educational institutions operated by the churches were open to girls: normal schools and ladies' seminaries.

St. Olaf College

St. Olaf College began as an alternative to the common schools in the late 1860s. Rev. B. J. Muus hired Norwegian teachers for his children, Birgitte,

Nils, and Jens; a few other children from the congregation also attended school in the parsonage. Muus was encouraged in his desire to found a school by the outcome of a meeting called in 1874 in Madison, Wisconsin, to organize a Scandinavian Lutheran Education Society. Disagreements with Rasmus Anderson and John A. Johnson prompted Rev. H. A. Preus and a large number of the 300 participants to withdraw. The dissident majority reconvened to devise their own plan, which endorsed establishment of academies to provide high school level education to children of the churches who had been confirmed. Preus's views in support of academies had been printed in *Kirelig maanedstidende* some years earlier:

> With the establishment of several such schools higher education may became a general advantage rather than a privilege of a few and out of a due consideration for the place woman occupies as sister but especially as wife and mother, we should consider providing our girls with an opportunity for more enlightenment than is generally the case now. As to whether we should propose coeducation, that is another matter which we do not propose to settle now.[8]

Although Preus was clearly unconvinced that coeducation was the best way to include girls in this educational scheme, girls were enrolled in the academies from their first sessions. His own suggestion included establishment of a school for girls in Red Wing, Minnesota.

Muus recruited several lay leaders from the Goodhue and Rice County settlements as convinced supporters and financial backers for his proposed school. Northfield businessman Harald Thorson agreed to supply five acres of land and a cash gift if such an institution were located in the town on the Cannon River. Reaction from the Norwegian Synod clergy was positive but passive. They did not volunteer any aid; some were undoubtedly concerned that adding another school to the appeals made to congregations and members would reduce the amount given in support of Luther College. (Muus himself was a major advocate of Luther College and had raised hundreds of dollars for it among his parishioners.) Despite this seeming foot-dragging by Muus's ministerial colleagues, he and his local collaborators continued their efforts.

On July 6, 1874, St. Olaf School was incorporated; in January 1875 it began operation. The two frame buildings in downtown Northfield hardly suggested the imposing campus of limestone buildings that would later be built on a hill across the river. Nor did the three dozen students and the two teachers (Rev. Thorbjørn N. Mohn and L. S. Reque) give any secure promise of the generations of students and faculty who would come and the achievements they would make. Too many schools failed in the years of St. Olaf's growth for its success to have been assured.

Three characteristics contributed to that success: identification with the well-defined Norwegian Lutheran community; commitment to general, practical education for all its students, not just those called to ordained pastoral ministry; and coeducation. These were stated in the articles of incorporation and in promotional materials in such a way that the school attracted a constituency that shared the same characteristics, and thus the tradition of the College was shaped by them.

> Articles of Incorporation, 1874: The general purpose of the corporation is for the advancement in education of pupils from fifteen years of age and upwards as a college, preserve the pupils in the true Christian faith, and nothing taught in contravention with the Symbolum Apostolicum, Nicenum, and Anthanasianum; the Unaltered Confession delivered to the Emperor, Charles the Fifth, at Augsburg in Germany, in the year of our Lord, 1530; and the Small Catechism of Luther.

> Promotional leaflet, 1880s: Young men and women of Scandinavian parentage who desire a thorough, practical education will find it to their advantage to enter an institution in which they may be permitted to begin where their acquired education is cut off. . . . The school is up to the times and thoroughly American in spirit.

> Students of either sex admitted, provided they are fourteen years of age, or more, and presents a certificate from some reliable person (as a rule, from their pastor) to the effect that they are persons of good moral character, and endowed with capabilities to learn.[9]

Students reported that they selected St. Olaf because it was Christian, because their parents supported the United Church, and because of familial connections with the faculty or students.[10]

Marie Aaker's name headed the list of students in the first class enrolled at St. Olaf School. She was also listed as the first graduate of the academy division. Girls were a significant part of the academy student body throughout the entire existence of that department and were present on the St. Olaf campus from its establishment on Manitou Heights in 1876.

For the first few years the whole college community, or at least representatives of every part, shared living quarters in the first campus building, which later came to be known as Old Main. President Mohn's family and that of other faculty members had apartments on the first floor; girls had rooms on the first floor; and boys occupied the third floor. Ever frugal, Mr. Thorson arranged for the lumber from the two frame buildings downtown to be transported up the hill where it was used to construct Ladies' Hall. Here too a faculty family lived with the students, as did a preceptress. (The second preceptress was Lina Koren, daughter of Vilhelm and Elisabeth.) Some students lived with local families and in rooming houses such as the one run by Johan and Nikoline Kildahl. The long walk up the hill, if nothing else, made this arrangement less than ideal. It was necessary because Ladies' Hall was never large enough to provide rooms for all the female students. Twenty-two of the one hundred thirty-six girls enrolled in the college and academy departments in 1906 lived in Ladies' Hall.[11] The building was also inadequate judged by structural criteria. There was no running water, and the building was poorly located.

Campaigns to replace Ladies' Hall were finally successful in 1912. The prolonged struggle for and construction of Old Mohn Hall was also a struggle for the continuation of coeducation at St. Olaf.[12] Student comments on the topic were recorded in the newspaper and the annual. An unnamed writer appealed to the religious purposes of the College in support of its female students in the college annual:

> Should we not guard the young women of our church with the same solicitude [as we do the young men]? Truly our church can no more sacrifice its young women than its men to religious indifferentism. If we recognize the necessity of giving those who are to be the fathers in our church a Christian education and discipline, do we not admit that those who are to be its future mothers have the same imperative need? Or, can not a mother's influence be favorably compared with a father's?[13]

Two years later another student defended the need for a new women's residence with more references to the domestic and maternal nature of the female soul.

> In the first place, girls ought to have a home of their own. Instinctively they love home. The very sound of the word strikes a responsive chord in their souls. With them the home ideal is the most prominent, the great center around which everything else gathers. . . . The girls too, would exert a wonderful influence upon each other, mutually developing love, sympathy, kindness, and regard for others. . . . And we must not forget our long wished for and long-planned on cooking department, our ideal kitchen. . . . No girl has a complete or sufficient education who has not mastered the art of cooking.[14]

Much earlier, in 1885, President Mohn had assured one of his correspondents that the experience at St. Olaf demonstrated that coeducation did not lead to undesirable excesses; rather, it was in keeping with the way things were in families.[15]

Student life in the early years was well regulated. The day began at 6:30 A.M. when the wake-up bell signaled that breakfast would be served in forty-five minutes. Class commenced at 8:00 A.M. Any time not devoted to prayers and meals was for study. Course work included math, geography, penmanship, literature, and music conducted in English and religion and history in Norwegian. Lights out came promptly at 10:00 P.M. Forbidden activities included drinking, dancing, gambling, playing cards, and using tobacco or foul language.

Despite the rules and close schedule, students found time for fun. Petra Hagen, a student in the last years of the century, reported to her diary on the evening activities in Ladies' Hall. She described one autumn gathering. "After devotion we had a big time as usual, eating apples, telling funny stories; Miss Johnson answered us by making all sorts of funny faces. It's a wonder what a good time a lot of girls can have together." Another student from the first decade of the new century wrote the following on the page of her diary headed "Dances and Teas": "Had this page been entitled, 'Dances, Coffees,' I could have written more, for I am a 'kaffekjaring' and not an English woman, who loves tea."[16] The girls' behavior was subjected to female standards. They were told by the preceptress that it was "unladylike" to throw apple peelings around in the parlor and were not allowed to attend a political torchlight rally in Northfield with their male classmates.

Contacts between boys and girls were subject to institutional guidance. If a young girl was to be escorted home by one of her male classmates, she first had to secure permission from the preceptress; he sought the same from President Mohn. Sexually segregated dining was maintained into the 1890s.[17] Efforts were made to keep the boys' behavior in line as well. Petra was present when President Mohn lectured them about an upcoming social gathering, instructing them to stay clear of the girls' door. "[President Mohn said,] the boys should keep away from the 'North Door.' He said among other things that it was their 'brute nature' that drew them there and it was the same thing that prompted us to let them see us home."[18] She was pleased that on the evening in question the girls took the initiative and went out the boys' door. There were other evidences that the students were not docile in their acceptance of rules. An anonymous student editorialized on the need for more opportunities for social gatherings.

> That fact that this is not a matrimonial institution has been thoroughly implanted in our minds. The wisdom of this policy is not questioned, but we believe that the underground current demanding more frequent recreations or social gatherings, which breaks out every time we are refused such privileges, has some cause for existence. . . . Something more [than dining hall and chapel receptions] is necessary for the proper development of the social qualities of a person.[19]

Although St. Olaf was not matrimonial in purpose, it did provide the setting for romances that culminated in weddings.

Religion was not neglected. There were devotions every day at the school and Sunday worship at St. John's Lutheran in addition to religion classes. Petra and some of her friends ventured out to an American revival meeting one evening.

> We went in the Norwegian church but changed our mind and went to the revival meetings at the Congregational church. . . . The pipe-organ they have is just grand. The singing was also good. But on the whole we were disgusted with the whole business and went out just as the main sermon was to begin.[20]

Extracurricular Bible classes were held and a YWCA group was organized in 1909 but not affiliated with the national association.

Other social groups were formed. *Utile Dulci*, a literary society for academy girls, was organized in 1889. This group strove to combine the "useful with the sweet." It gave a tea to raise money for an American flag, hosted an oyster dinner to raise funds for the new ladies' dormitory, and each member gave $0.25 to help furnish the parlor in the boys' residence. These activities were in addition to their Saturday evening literary meetings, where "instead of the more masculine accomplishments of debating and impromptu speaking, essay-writing, sketches and music have been given more prominence."[21]

Minerva was organized for female students in the college and the upper levels of the academy a few years later. Its aim was "through declamations, readings, and written matter, such as essays and book reviews . . . to develop their powers of delivery and abilities for graceful literary expression, as well as give a close acquaintance with the best production of classical and modern literature."[22] With its new name, Phi Kappa Phi, the group published a cookbook to help finance the new female dormitory (they raised $1,000). The contents and organization of the book suggest that its compilers retained their Norwegian heritage while acquiring American tastes and skills. Norwegian foods such as *lefse, lutefisk, primost,* and *fattigmans bakkels* were segregated in a twenty-page Norwegian Department at the back of the book. All these would have been familiar to their grandmothers; baking powder biscuits, macaroni and cheese, escalloped cauliflower, pineapple preserves, and banana cake, however, would have been innovations in a pioneer household. Before long a large membership dictated the need for another female society and Phi Kappa Phi split into two; the "daughter" group took the name Delta Chi.

Some groups admitted both girls and boys. *Normanna* was devoted to the promotion of the Norwegian language. Its male members gave admittance to their female classmates after 1890 because "by their constant attendance and interest shown they made their influence felt."[23] Girls also added their voices to the famous St. Olaf choir and took part in the whole music program of the school, which was expanded by the establishment of a school of music in 1904.

St. Olaf achieved Muus's goal of college status in 1889. Between that year and 1903 six women graduated with the B.A. degree. (There were 132 male graduates.)[24] Each one was the only woman in her class. Recalling her student days, Georgina Dieson described the confusion of looking for a classroom and the experience of attending a Greek class in which she was, of course, the only girl. As Dieson had come from a high school class composed of "eight bright girls and two rather insignificant boys," she was shocked by the situation.[25] Under the title "Only One," she gave expression to her attitude toward the situation in the 1904 *Viking.* "Still she can not help but wish that there were, but one more girl in her class. . . . [But s]he knows that she is a pioneer in a good cause."

While still a student, Agnes Mellby, class of 1893, wrote on the topic "Women and Professions" for the student paper. She noted the opening of "nearly all fields" to women and the "ample chances of becoming independent." Mellby observed that women seemed to take advantage of those opportunities out of necessity rather than choice. She suggested that the fault fell upon those who had early influence over children. They imbued boys "with professional ideals from early childhood" but seldom encouraged girls "to develop [their] capabilities and become useful."[26]

Of the first six B.A. alumnae five used their capabilities as teachers; four returned to St. Olaf as faculty members. Four of the women married. The two who remained single had careers in church work: Agnes Mellby at St. Olaf and

Agnes Kittelsby at St. Olaf and on the Chinese mission field. By 1914 there were almost ninety female B.A. graduates. Eight earned advanced degrees, four were in social work, three were missionaries to China, two were R.N.s, two were in the insurance business, and one was a foreign broadcast editor. Over 50 percent married.[27]

Many girls who attended St. Olaf did not graduate. In the early years it was not unusual for a student to come for a term or two without earning a degree. During their student days the girls came under the influence of the adult women of the community: wives of faculty, the preceptresses, and female members of the faculty.

Mrs. Mohn, Mrs. Ytterboe, and Mrs. Thea Midboe Felland, wives of early faculty, were all remembered fondly for their "wholesome influence." They lived on campus, where they had frequent and intimate contacts with students. The Fellands lived in old Ladies' Hall with their four children and Thea's sister, a student in the Academy division. Emma Quie Bonhus, a former student, described Mrs. Felland's influence by example and precept.

> . . . despite finicky taste and diligent habits the slender, trim-looking lady was no drudge. Fond of wearing pin-check gingham dresses with starched white collar and cuffs, she would top the outfit with a sailor hat when she took the baby out in its carriage, or went on other errands. The blue eyes were always kind and sincere, just as the voice that spoke to us was full of friendly interest. From her we learned Queen Alexandra's excellent maxim: "Be thankful for what you have; ask for what you want; never grumble."[28]

In 1909 the faculty wives and female faculty organized themselves into the Women's Social League, "to foster good fellowship and social intercourse amongst its members [and] in college circles."[29] The first activity was a coffee for the members of Phi Kappa Phi and several music students. In subsequent months other girls were entertained, as were the wives of church officials from St. Paul. Members served a reception at commencement.

Among the female faculty there were soon St. Olaf graduates who returned there to teach out of devotion to their alma mater. Agnes Mellby was hired in the 1890s and served as both preceptress and teacher. In *The Viking* of 1904 a student wrote of Mellby's positive contributions to the school.

> Kind and sympathetic of mind, with a heart filled with noble Christian feelings, her influence is refreshing and ennobling. As preceptress she exerts her beneficent influence upon the young ladies, a power that will in the future manifest itself in the development of noble womanly traits.[30]

Undoubtedly, she did these things; however, the cost to her was not small. It was loyalty to their school and its community that prompted St. Olaf graduates to teach there despite salaries lower than their male colleagues' and lower than they might have commanded elsewhere. Clara Hegg came in 1910 for only $700.00 per year when she had hoped for $900.00, because she wanted to teach *there*.[31]

Female faculty were often single and thus without the immediate emotional and professional support of a family. The closeness of the college faculty may have been some compensation in the earliest years. (For Mellby, the women's society of the church was another possible source of support; she served as secretary pro tem of the Women's Missionary Federation in its first year.) After a decade of teaching Miss Mellby was discouraged. She wrote to President Kildahl expressing her response to the plans for the coming academic year.

> I suppose that means that I shall have to teach odds and ends in the sub-classes, and I am not very happy in the prospect. That work will not be at all satisfactory and I know that my natural abilities will not help me. The special qualities required are those a drillmaster and a disciplinarian, which I consider my weakest points. Furthermore, beginning my tenth year, it is rather hard to start at the bottom again . . . I should like in the future to get into some department where I would be secure against so much change. Having to experiment in different branches each year does not give one a fair chance.[32]

Despite her sense of futility, Mellby stayed on and pushed for a female faculty. She reminded the president that the entire faculty needed to support its female members and urged engagement of a teacher "who has been either at a woman's college or in some Boston school."[33]

Agnes Larson, class of 1916, was just such a person. She and her sisters, Henrietta and Nora, were all St. Olaf graduates who went on for advanced degrees in their fields.[34] Agnes returned to teach at St. Olaf in 1922. She was given leave to complete her graduate work at Radcliffe. Although she was offered positions at eastern women's colleges upon receiving her Ph.D., she went back to Northfield because it "was the place where I wished to give my services. These were my people and this was my church."[35] During her thirty-four years as professor she had contact with some 4,000 students. Through those years she, like Mellby, was not always entirely satisfied. For example, in 1942 she wrote to the college president, "I get weary of these people who stress only the fact that we educate ministers in our church schools. The church would be sadly lacking if we didn't have a few lay people too who did things."[36]

Among the laywomen who were doing things were the numerous successors of the *kvindeforening*, such as St. Olaf graduate Agnes Kittelsby, on foreign mission fields, and Agnes Larson's colleague on the St. Olaf faculty, Karen Larsen, daughter of Luther College's first president. St. Olaf College contributed to these women's work by providing them with "a thorough, practical education" that both eased their contacts outside of their ethnic and religious community by teaching them English and American customs and bound them to it through the ties of personal friendships and institutional loyalties. The college recognized and memorialized Agnes Mellby, Agnes Kittelsby, and Agnes Larson by naming residence halls after them.

Lutheran Ladies' Seminary

A decade and a half passed between Rev. H. A. Preus's initial suggestion that the Norwegian Synod establish a school for girls and the formation of the Lutheran Ladies' Seminary corporation in 1889. Building on the eighteen acres of Red Wing bluff land was delayed when money was diverted to repair damages caused by a fire at the boys' college, Luther in Decorah. The seminary opened the doors of its imposing three-and-a-half-story, red brick, gothic building in November 1894 to a class of forty young women; another seventeen joined them before the year was out. In the next quarter of a century hundreds of students spent a few months to several years there, learning to be "ladies." In the final years of its operation Lutheran Ladies' Seminary (LLS) was accredited as a college by the state of Minnesota. It was, however, never turned over to the Norwegian Synod as had originally been planned; nor did the newly formed Norwegian Lutheran Church in America accept the institution. When the main buildings burned the night before graduation in 1920, the school's active history came to an end.

The stated aim of the seminary was to provide a "thorough and liberal education [and] also to furnish a practical course . . . and above all to imbue the student with a true Christian spirit."[37] As Todd Walsh pointed out, the Lutheran Seminary had much in common with other women's seminaries of its time, specifically a school such as Rockford Seminary, well known for its famous graduate, Jane Addams.[38] The founders, President Allen, and the staff of the Red Wing school were anxious to provide their students with a top-quality education that was both liberal and practical, would educate mind and body, and would contribute to their Christian growth. From its beginning there were some who hoped for the transition into a college, which took place in 1912.

At the same time the curriculum was designed to prepare young women to take up their conventional domestic role. This was stated in the 1919-1920 catalogue.

> The founder of this institution . . . realized, as we do, that the welfare of our homes depends in the highest degree upon what type of woman is making them. Thrifty, neat, and well-trained home-makers create thrifty and well-ordered households. Intelligent, educated and cultured mothers and wives understand how to make the homes centers of noble interests and elevating influences. Pious, spiritually enlightened and devout Christian women are the most zealous guardians of earnest faith, pure morals and unselfish activities.[39]

The possibility of some graduates becoming teachers or businesswomen was not mentioned in the purpose and aim but was suggested by the course offerings. The original departments of study were preparatory (high school), seminary and classical, normal, business (actually secretarial), art, elocution, and conservatory of music. Domestic science was added. Instruction was provided in academic subjects, artistic skills, and housekeeping.

Every part of the day gave opportunities for learning of some sort. The faculty ate with the students in the dining room equipped with a large carved mahogany buffet and china painted by students. Tables were set with white linen cloths. Breaches of etiquette were corrected by notes placed under the offender's dinner plate. In his baccalaureate sermon Rev. J. R. Baumann impressed upon his auditors the religious significance of each of their activities.

> What is the good of reading? Is it not a means by which we learn to know what we have never seen or heard. To this the Savior refers when he says: "Search the scriptures; for in them ye think ye have eternal life." (John 3:39). What is the good of cooking? Is it not the crystallization of the thought: "What shall we eat?" (Mt. 6:31), formed by proper proportion of the nourishment of our frail body.[40]

When she arrived at the "well-equipped, high grade school for girls . . . with scholastic advantages equal to the best schools in the East," the LLS student brought along items indicative of the sorts of activities that would occupy her in the coming months. She had a dictionary and a Bible for use in her required

165

religion and other literary courses, a suit for drills in physical culture class, a large apron to protect her cotton dresses when in domestic science labs, and napkins and a ring for proper dining.[41] Students in the four-year seminary and classical departments, the heart of the seminary curriculum, took a large variety of courses in subjects such as Bible (in Norwegian or English), Augsburg Confession, physical geography, zoology, arithmetic, United States and English history, drawing, and optionally Latin, German, or Greek. The 1884 catalogue listed housekeeping and needlework as "obligatory throughout the whole course." Students were also required to attend chapel exercises and "divine services in the Lutheran Church with which the school is in connection [Trinity, Norwegian Synod], unless parents or guardians request that they attend a church of a different denomination."[42] By the 1910s physical culture included basketball, tennis, bowling, and "free, light, and aesthetic gymnastics."

Growth of the music program into the Conservatory of Music led to the construction of Music Hall, a three-story brick structure in the collegiate-gothic style. It housed a 450-seat auditorium with two concert pianos and a pipe organ, thirty-six practice rooms, and the gymnasium. All students participated in the chorus and sang in its two annual concerts. The seminary octet directed by Jacob Lauritz Hjort went on tour, providing entertainment to the school's friends and soliciting support. Recitals and concerts by students and guest artists were well attended by the local residents and even by parties traveling to Red Wing from the Twin Cities for the events. Dr. Bernard F. Laukandt, appointed director of the conservatory in 1907, built the program's reputation. His recruitment efforts among German-Americans strengthened the entire institution through increased enrollments.[43]

Domestic science was an important component of the school's program. In its classes girls learned skills that they all would be able to use, anyplace they went. In the cooking department, for example, they mastered the art of setting a table, serving, and preparation of dishes such as hollandaise sauce, layer cake, and stuffed eggs. Among the student body there were strong advocates of the societal value of such training. Miss Esther Lien read her essay, "The Value of Domestic Education," on Class Day in 1911. A local newspaper summarized Lien's presentation, which

> discussed the economic changes that had taken place in the past few years and the necessity that every girl should have a scientific training in woman's greatest mission—housekeeping. She placed emphasis on this particular branch and believed that the awakening of the nation to its great and imperative value meant much for its future prosperity and happiness.[44]

Cooking and cleaning were not, however, considered sufficient skills for a woman. Even students in the domestic science department took two literary courses along with Bible, which was required in every department. Martha Reishus recalled that this came about through the initiative of a board member who

> noticed that many of the Home Ec. graduates would marry ministers, and he suggested that it would be very profitable for them to "take up" some literary subjects too. "Saa de kan komme op til sin stand." [So that she could come up to his level or position.][45]

The ladies of the seminary lived a well-regulated life. The 1919 catalogue stated that, "Only such rules as are necessary for the well-being of the students and for the best interest of the school as a Christian school-home, will be made, but these rules will be strictly enforced."[46] Among the rules made through the years were the following:

> Rooms must be orderly by 7:45 every morning. Sweeping from the floors must be deposited in baskets provided for that purpose.
> No visiting, talking, laughing, playing, or loitering in the halls will be allowed during the hours set apart for study and recitations, that is, from 7:45 to 12:05 A.M. and from 2:15 to 4:55 and 7:00 to 9:30 P.M.
> Leaning out of and talking from windows is a sign of ill-breeding.
> Students are not allowed to read dime novel and other pernicious literature and are advised to consult the teachers in regard to reading matter.
> Visitors may be received by the students during the school days from one to two o'clock P.M. and from five to six o'clock and on Saturday afternoons. Gentlemen are not permitted to visit students except upon written permission from parents or guardian.
> Students are advised not to have correspondents outside their home circle as much letter writing consumes valuable time and draws the student's mind from her studies.

Other rules were directed toward achievement of a balanced life.

> Students are *absolutely* forbidden to study during free hours, that is, from 12:05 to 2:15 P.M. and from 4:55 to 7:00 P.M. Students are expected to be out of doors during the free hours, if weather permits.
> Students are permitted to visit each other and to come together to sing and play.[47]

167

Whether in response to the rules or out of the natural high spirits of youth, the students found ways to "come together" for a variety of entertainments. Organized extracurricular groups included the Laurean and Lamba Sigma Literary Societies; *Vaarliv*, a Norwegian society; the Crescendo Club; and the Grieg Glee Club. Students published *Cresset*, in which were "found articles contributed by the pupils, reports of lectures delivered, concerts given, and an account of everything else worthy of note that happens at the school."[48] Alumnae were encouraged to subscribe. The staff exchanged their periodical with their male counterparts at Luther College. Occasional comments appeared in the *Cresset* concerning the quality and content of the older *Chips*.[49]

Besides going to church each Sunday with chaperones "fore and aft," the young women were permitted to go downtown once a week. They patronized the local merchants, including Boxrud and Hjermstad Company and both Kuhn's and Bender's drugstores, which served ice cream and "specialized in 'dates.' " Martha Reishus reflected, "It would be interesting to know how many romances began there!" She recalled that the Hauge Synod's book department dealing in religious literature and school supplies was another place where romances sometimes began.[50]

Each class was organized upon arrival and planned activities for itself and the others: picnics, an annual boat trip on the Mississippi, teas, costume parties, and the like were recorded in photographs and memory books. After Easter the senior students began to wear their caps and gowns. Throughout that year there were traditions to be carried on; each class chose colors and a motto to be placed on their class pin.[51] An unusual ceremony had its beginning in the generosity of the Indians in the area, who gave the seminary a peace pipe just prior to graduation in 1895 "in recognition of the burial site that existed where the seminary stood."[52] Each year the senior class attached ribbons in the colors of the junior class and passed it on to their younger colleagues with a poem:

> Now come today you juniors,
> put away all thought of struggle
> for behind you leave the memory
> of unkindness we have done
> you, the juniors, and we the seniors
> are about to say "Farewell." . . .
> —and this our parting wish
> "The Grace of Heaven—before, behind thee

and on every hand enwheel thee round,"
Farewell, dear juniors.[53]

The graduating class also wrote a class will and prophecy.
Josephine Riveland, class of 1911, cast the prophecy in the form of a letter
written after her class's five-year reunion. The range of futures predicted
indicated that not all the students of LLS expected to settle down to fill
"woman's greatest mission—housekeeping." Clara Allen (daughter of the
president) and Grace Eaton had been on a concert tour of the western cities.
Emma Brandt was "as smiling and happy looking as ever, for she is now a
'prestefru' gladly performing her many duties as such." Emma Nelson,
Josephine Solberg, and Emma Bartke were all back at LLS—one as domestic
science teacher, one as dressmaking teacher, and the other as nurse. Agnes
Flaskerud and Agnes Kalhein worked in partnership "in the slums of Chicago.
Agnes Kalhein is rescuing the boys from vice and Agnes Flaskerud is teaching
them politeness. They are surely worthy successors of Jane Addams." Nora
Hjermstad had traded in her motor car for her own biplane. Other classmates
were employed as a detective for the Secret Service and as society columnist
for the St. Paul *Pioneer Press*. Elise Smedal had a career as a renowned
lecturer with "Equality of the Sexes" and "Co-education" as her principal
topics.[54]

In 1910 an alumnae association was organized to "preserve an interest in the
seminary and to promote its welfare."[55] It continued to meet into the 1960s.
Although there were approximately 500 graduates of the school's various
programs, an enrollment list for its entire years of operation contains nearly
700 names. Among those young women who attended LLS were several who
were connected by birth or marriage with some of the leadership families of
the Norwegian Lutheran churches.[56] The subsequent activities of the former
students were not indicated, but a few were prominent. Martha Reishus
Langemo was the author of *The Rag Rug*, a major source for this project.
Lydia Bredesen Sundby was president of the Eastern District of the Lutheran
Women's Missionary Federation and its third general president. Amanda
Rasmussen returned to the seminary to teach art; after study at the University
of Wisconsin, Elizabeth Clauson returned to teach mathematics and history.

The school was declining in the 1910s due in part to the strains of war, in
part to changes in leadership, and in part to organizational shifts brought
about by the formation of the Norwegian Lutheran Church in America in
1917. From its formation, the corporation that owned the seminary had

intended to turn it over to the Norwegian Synod, the body with which it was aligned. However, the newly formed church did not accept the school's affiliation; rather, its Board of Education recommended that an endowment be established for its support.[57]

Twice in the 1919-1920 academic year the seminary was subject to fire. The first, in December, was contained and repairs were made while the students were on Christmas break. The second took place the night before June graduation;[58] both the main building and the Music Hall were declared total losses at a cost far above the insurance coverage. Local businesspeople and President Hoff made unsuccessful efforts to raise the funds needed to begin anew. The Board of Trustees put the question of rebuilding to the Synod. After two years the decision was made not to rebuild the Lutheran Ladies' Seminary.

The Luther College alumni association granted honorary membership to the members of its sister institution and the alumnae group disbanded. A few ruins of the buildings remain on the bluff. As the ladies die, the memories of what might have been a fine Lutheran college for women also die. The school was not even mentioned in *Lutheran Higher Education in North America*, published in 1985.[59] The fate of the women's schools it did consider suggested, however, that the Red Wing school was typical in its brief life. Only Marion College for Women survived through the 1920s, and it closed in 1967.[60]

The legacy of the Lutheran Ladies' Seminary was primarily through its students and their influence upon their families, their churches, and in other arenas. The seminary provided its students with a "thorough and liberal education" supported by a practical course designed to "imbue the student with a true Christian spirit." The lives of graduates such as Lydia Bredesen Sundby, Bessie Fries Gullixson, Emma Brandt Naeseth, and Idella Haugen Preus displayed its success. Like St. Olaf College, the Ladies' Seminary exposed its students to American culture and cultivated their participation in it while binding them to their own Norwegian-American, Lutheran subculture.

The Lutheran Normal School

A third sort of education was offered to young Norwegian-American women at the coeducational normal schools operated by the Norwegian Lutheran bodies. The primary purpose of these institutions was to provide teachers for elementary schools both parochial and public. The annual catalogue of the Lutheran Normal School (LNS) in Madison, Minnesota, stated its reason for being: "It aims to give to young men and women an education on a Christian foundation, and to qualify them as teachers in the schools of the church and in the public schools."[61] The LNS was founded and operated by the United Norwegian Lutheran Church, not by a special association. It carried out its purpose from 1892 until declining enrollment and economic depression forced its closure in 1932.

At its first convention in 1890 the United Church delegates authorized establishment of a normal school. Within two years a site had been selected and construction of the first building was begun on the ten acres donated by a Madison farmer, Gunder P. Kjosness. The three-story brick structure housed a chapel, classrooms, and student rooms: girls on the second floor, boys on the third. The success of the school and growing enrollment required construction of a second dormitory, which housed sixty students in 1899 and Lokensgaard Hall in 1914, with room for eighty-six girls. At a cost of $30,000.00 the latter had modern facilities—steam heat and electric lights—and provided a new dining hall for 200 persons.[62] The school reached its peak enrollment in 1916.

Students were attracted to Madison by its church connection, by its ethnic connection, and by its program preparing teachers. Some took their entire training at LNS; others attended several institutions. Tilda Jorstad, class of 1895, recalled her path to the Normal School.

I lived in Goodhue County, Minnesota. The nearest church school was St. Olaf College where I attended its academy in the school year 1891-92. Then my father thought it was best for me not to finish a college course, but rather attend a small school such as the St. Ansgar Academy which was located in St. Ansgar, Iowa. So, I went there for a few terms. There I could get the necessary education for teaching in rural and parochial school in less time.

By this time the newly built Lutheran Normal School, for students who wished to become teachers in the elementary and parochial schools had begun its work in Madison, Minnesota. This school seemed to be the right one for me, and I decided to transfer my school credits and enrolled there, arriving in Madison on January 1, 1895.

I had enough credits from St. Olaf and St. Ansgar to allow me to register for study in the senior class and hoped to graduate in June of that year. I was the only student in the senior class, if it could be called a class.[63]

Less than half of those who attended LNS graduated.

From its first year LNS offered both preparatory and normal courses to its students. The former was attractive to recent immigrants whose age would cause them to feel uncomfortable and out of place in a public school. Among the eleven female students who had careers as foreign missionaries, six came to the United States in their late teens or early twenties. At LNS these students were given the opportunity to learn English while pursuing their other studies in Norwegian and with students who shared their ethnic identity. The names of the students who attended LNS during its four decades indicate that nearly all of them were Norwegian in background even if they were not immigrants themselves.[64]

The curriculum offered by the Normal School varied in details over its existence but remained similar in general intent. Every program required some study of Norwegian and religion; the courses offered in religion included Bible history, church history, symbolics, exegesis, and catechetics. Additionally, students received instruction in topics such as U.S. and general history, arithmetic, elocution, geography, didactics, vocal music, and physiology. Until 1913 graduates of the normal course were required to be examined by the appropriate state agency prior to certification for teaching. In that year a model school was begun, bringing LNS into compliance with Minnesota state requirements. Consequently, graduates qualified for a First Grade public school certificate in Minnesota without further examination. This situation continued until the normal department was discontinued in 1926 due to the difficulty in meeting the rising state standards.[65]

Two programs were offered in addition to the preparatory department and the normal course. A special program, held by Norwegian Lutheran congregations during summer months, was instituted in 1902 to prepare teachers for the parochial schools. The one-year program placed emphasis on religion, Norwegian, and music. It was later expanded to a two-year program. By 1914 a four-year high school course also was available.[66]

As at other schools student life was enriched by activities outside the classroom and chapel. Each year the school held two series of lectures. One was devoted to standard missionary topics highlighting various fields of work and the journeys of the apostle Paul. The other was wide-ranging. During the first two decades, topics included Luther and the Reformation, Gustavus Adolphus, Phrenology, Etiquette (by Miss Thina Biorn, a member of the faculty and the only female lecturer), Yellowstone Park, Reminiscences of the Civil War, Temperance (on several occasions), Savonarola, Freedom in Christ, and Greek Architecture and Sculpture, in addition to the more expected religious topics.[67]

The organizations available at LNS were typical of those at other schools. Every student was assigned to either the Amphictyonic or the Hyperion literary society. These groups met every third week for talks, musical programs, and readings. The debate societies, Columbia and Castalia, were organized by sex. Only male students participated in the Senate, which was a model of the United States legislative body. After 1903 there was a Norwegian society, *Det Norske Selskab*, meeting weekly. The professional goals of the majority of students were recognized by the *Laererforeningen*, the teachers' society, devoted to discussion of topics related to their future task, "particularly as it could apply to parochial school teaching."[68] Two groups cultivated interest in the church's mission work: the mission society founded in 1892 and the girls' mission society, which later affiliated with the Lutheran Daughters of the Reformation. On Thursday evenings prayer meetings were held for the edification of students and teachers. The physical aspects of education were not neglected. Boys had football, basketball, and baseball; girls had basketball, calisthenics, and tennis.

Most of the students lived on campus. The accommodations improved as each new building was added. When Marie Gumpolen, class of 1902, arrived there was only Old Main.

All of . . . the other students, were strangers to me, except Ole Kjeldergaard, Albert Nestande, and Martin Pederson from my home community at Fairfax, Minnesota.

My room [shared with Martine Hanson] in the southwest corner was furnished with a bed, mattress, a table, two chairs, a bookcase, towels, washbowl, broom and dustpan. Across the corridor were two large class rooms. In the basement were the furnace, the janitor's quarters, and a large dining room. Near the furnace a deep cistern was located from which the students pumped rain water into their pitchers. On the north side of the Main building there was a well, but it did not give good water. Therefore, drinking water was hauled in barrels from the city.

In 1899 the boys' dorm was built; there were rooms for girls in the south half and an apartment for Professor Ole Lokensgaard on the first floor. According to Marie, Lokensgaard acted as a supervisor of the dormitory. "If the lamp lights were burning at ten o'clock n the evening he would tiptoe through the corridors and bang on the door of the room where the light shone through the transom."[69]

Petra Bly was a student in the mid-1910s. She shared a room in Lokensgaard Hall; it was provided with a built-in clothes closet, two single beds, desks, and chairs. There was no longer any need for water pitchers and washbowls, as each floor was equipped with "modern washrooms." The students brought along other items, such as dresser scarves and window curtains, and were responsible for cleaning. Their day began at 6:30, when the morning bell was rung. Meals were provided by the boarding club and taken together. "The menus were planned by a committee. The meals were plain but nutritious and substantial. . . . Table prayers were always given before and after meals, led by one of the men students in charge of the dining room. The girls took turns waiting on tables. Several girls earned part of their expenses by washing and ironing table-cloths."[70] In the evenings, Petra recalled, students sometimes gathered in one another's rooms to share "goodies" received from home. In this breach of school regulations they were like their counterparts at St. Olaf College or the Lutheran Ladies' Seminary.

Throughout the day there were other opportunities to socialize. Students who shared a similar religious and ethnic background formed friendships.

There was a family-like mingling of the boys and girls during the meal hours, choir practice, and the short free period on campus after supper. Dating would usually be two or three couples at a time. This may have been an economy measure if it involved the renting of a livery rig to go somewhere on a Sunday or a Monday when there were not classes. . . . Many of these co-educational friendships developed into courtships and marriages. The homes thus established have been happy and stable because of the compatibility and similar cultural backgrounds of husband and wife.[71]

In this way, as well as by providing teachers, the Normal School contributed to stability and continuance of the Norwegian Lutheran community that founded and supported it.

In accord with the school's purpose, many of its graduates spent at least a few years working as teachers in parochial or public schools. However, 40 percent pursued other careers.[72] Male graduates went into law, medicine, and ordained ministry. Female graduates also worked in medicine and ministry. Among the 558 female graduates were 36 nurses and one physician, Nellie Pederson Holman, who earned her M.D. at the University of Minnesota in 1918. She also served as a missionary in China. Ten other women who attended LNS were missionaries in China or Madagascar. One of them, Inga Dvergsness, was a deaconess.

Like St. Olaf College and the Lutheran Ladies' Seminary, the Normal School in Madison had the Norwegian-American Lutheran community as its primary constituency, and providing a godly, practical education to the youth of that group was its primary goal. It too mediated contacts between "general" American life and its students' Norwegian-American communities through bilingual instruction and by the composition and activities of the community. This was particularly so for those older students who had recently arrived in the United States. At the same time the school forged enduring personal relationships among students and trained them for professions that reinforced their connections with their religious and ethnic communities.

Women's education was supported with assurances that the students would not cease to be woman or to carry out their expected tasks. At St. Olaf and LLS, the two schools providing college education and the greatest variety of options for unconventional roles, there were laudatory statements made about women's "greatest mission" as wives and mothers. The curriculum of all three schools, however, provided young women with training to expand their conventional roles as wives and mothers into careers in teaching, on the mission field, or even outside the church. Building on the foundation begun at these schools, they could take up medicine or music. Among their teachers they had models of women whose lives included a profession.

Ministry

Teachers

Initially Norwegians in the United States reproduced the educational pattern they knew from Norway. Men specially trained to teach (likely in Norway) or pastors were sought to conduct schools for children. Olaf M. Norlie compiled a biographical dictionary of teachers in the Norwegian Lutheran schools in the 1920s. The data he collected indicated that by the turn of the century young, American-born women were teaching in parochial and public schools.[73] Many of these young women received their training in the three schools discussed or others like them, such as Concordia College or the Normal School in Sioux Falls.[74]

These women had extremely varied careers. Not quite half taught only in Lutheran settings. All the others had some position with a public institution. Some affiliated with another denomination or gave private lessons. Most taught in more than one type of school. Frequently they were employed by common schools or parochial schools, but some women also taught in high schools, academies, normal schools, ladies' seminaries, and Lutheran colleges.[75] Many women eventually returned to their hometowns to teach in the local schools.

The variety and similarity of careers was illustrated by the specifics women reported to Norlie for his *School Calendar*. Matilda Agneberg's career was typical of the most simple pattern.[76] She was born in 1879 in Pigeon Falls, Wisconsin. At age sixteen she completed high school in Whitehall, Wisconsin. Following her graduation in 1895 Matilda taught in the Whitehall common school for four years. In 1899 she went to the Normal School in Madison, Minnesota; as she stayed two years it is reasonable to assume that she took the parochial or normal course. With her newly acquired training Miss Agneberg returned to teach in the Whitehall common school for the years 1901-1903. In the following three years she taught in the parochial schools of Whitehall and Pigeon Falls, Wisconsin, and Norman and Polk counties, Minnesota, and in the common schools of Polk county. At age twenty-eight she married Iver Johnson and moved to Beltrami, Minnesota. It was usual for a woman to stop teaching when she married.[77] Indeed, it appeared that for some women teaching between finishing their education and marrying took the place of the Norwegian custom of "hiring out" between confirmation and marriage. Throughout her life Matilda was a member of a Norwegian Lutheran congregation, first in Pigeon Falls and then in Beltrami.

Sophie Bergh followed a similar path.[78] She was born in 1877 to Rev. J. A. and Bergitha Bergh in Fergus Falls, Minnesota.[79] For one year, 1893-1894, she attended Lutherville Ladies' Seminary in Lutherville, Maryland, but she finished her high school at Beloit High School in 1896. Sophie then enrolled at St. Olaf College, where she spent four years and presumably earned a degree in 1901, although she did not report it. Milwaukee Normal School provided her with an additional year of training before she became preceptress at Augustana College in 1903. During her three-year tenure Miss Bergh also taught English, pedagogy, and history. In 1906, at age twenty-eight, she married Rev. J. R. Larvik and withdrew from teaching.[80] The couple moved to Alberta where Sophie resumed teaching English for one year at Camrose (Lutheran) College. She also served as organist in the various congregations to which she belonged and as an officer in the Ladies' Aid.

Clara Bergan's life took a slightly different course.[81] She was born in 1886 in Olmstead County, Minnesota. At age sixteen she completed high school and went to St. Olaf College for one year. A move to the West Coast followed and Clara continued her college work first at Spokane (Lutheran) College and then at University of Washington; she received a B.A. in 1911. Her first job was at Columbia (Lutheran) College in Everett, Washington, where she taught English and German until 1913. That year, at age twenty-seven, Clara married H. G. Fatland. Mrs. Fatland attended the American School of Home Economics in Chicago for one year and taught Latin, algebra, and domestic science at Camrose College from 1916-18. After Mr. Fatland died in 1920 she returned to the United States. In 1921-1922 she taught English at the Lutheran Normal School in Madison. The following year Clara went to Central Wisconsin (Lutheran) College to teach German. Like Matilda Agneberg Johnson and Sophie Bergh Larvik, Clara Bergan Fatland was a member of Norwegian Lutheran congregations; she listed five different ones between 1900 and 1921 but none after then. She also served as a Sunday school teacher and edited the church newspapers.

Theresa Genevieve Bjørneby went farther from her Norwegian-Lutheran beginnings than did the other three women.[82] She was born in 1891 in Grafton, North Dakota. Like Bergan she moved west, graduating from high school in Flathead, Montana, and then attended Spokane College, 1908-1912. In her final year at Spokane Theresa was an instructor in German as well as a student. After one year of study she received an A.B. from St. Olaf in 1913. She returned to Montana, where she taught from 1913-1920: first grade school in Devon and Dunkirk and then high school in Kalispell. In 1920 Miss Bjørneby left teaching and took a job in the art department of the Glidden Company in Chicago. Two years later she moved to Los Angeles, where she was employed as a designer in an art shop. She did not report any church memberships.

In her two autobiographical volumes, *Grass of the Earth* and *Measure of My Days*, Aagot Raaen provided a richer portrayal of a teacher's career than can be gleaned from the biographical data of Norlie's dictionary. Aagot had not been to public school for more than a few weeks; with determination she received her training in bits and pieces at Concordia College in Moorhead and at Mayville Normal School.

Although expenses were low, her resources were less so; she lived frugally, eating wheat mush with bread and butter, and studying late. Her diligent study paid off when she passed the North Dakota state examinations and was given a second-grade certificate that allowed her to teach for a year at the school in her home district and one nearby. In the year she spent teaching

Aagot was able to save money to return to the Normal School. Her experiences in the time away had given Aagot confidence to ask questions and increased her already high motivation. When she graduated she was one of the three students who read their essays at commencement.

Although she would have a lifetime certification after her year of teaching, Aagot's desire for learning was not ended. She managed to get a year of study at the University of Minnesota as a freshman before family responsibilities drew her back home, where her annual routine was set: six months at the home school, spring term at a nearby school, and six weeks at a parochial school. As she described it, Aagot's daily activity was simple but exhausting.

> [She] arose long before dawn, built the fire and ate a hurried breakfast. In the bitter cold and snow she set out for a three-mile hike to the Erstad school, where she had to build another fire to warm the school room by eight o'clock, when shivering children began to arrive. Twenty eager children made work what it should be, pleasure. During the noon recess Aagot wanted to plan work for the following day, but when the younger children begged her to join them in snow battles against the five big boys, she always yielded. When school was called in the afternoon the pupils insisted that Aagot read aloud for fifteen minutes; they always reported the important points the following day and thus much history and literature were learned without much effort.[83]

After the children had prayed together, been bundled into their coats, and sent home, there was still work for the teacher. She carried ashes out and new fuel in, swept the floor, and washed the blackboards before her three-mile walk home. Some nights she spent in the schoolhouse, sleeping in a hammock. In her view, Aagot was "living a good life"; she had "an endless amount of constructive work [that] left no time for self-analysis and no thought for self-pity."

Aagot was never satisfied to stay too long at one thing. After some years at rural schools in Newburgh Township she took a position at Oak Grove High School for Girls, a Lutheran school. In addition to teaching her classes, Miss Raaen observed the teaching methods of her colleagues in the Fargo city schools. She saved carefully to fund trips to St. Louis and the West Coast and Europe. Six years after her term at the University of Minnesota, Aagot went to Madison to study at the University of Wisconsin. When she finally earned her degree, she had studied for three months in rural schools, twelve months at Concordia, four years at Mayville Normal School, one year at the University of Minnesota, and three semesters and summer session at Madison.[84] She taught for a year in Washington state. In 1916 Miss Raaen returned to North Dakota to make a successful campaign for superintendent of schools in Steel County; she held that position until 1923. Later in her career she taught in Hawaii for several years.

Matilda Agneberg, Sophie Berg, Clara Bergan, Theresa Genevieve Bjørneby, and Aagot Raaen were only five of the Norwegian-American women who became teachers. Although undoubtedly an exaggeration, Eva Thortvedt's remark that "of course every girl more or less had their goal to be a teacher" held some truth.[85] Many other women benefited from and contributed to the schools of their communities. They gave their students access to their dual heritage as both Norwegians and Americans. By using Norwegian they continued the students' knowledge of that language. By teaching them from the *Catechism* in summer school they contributed to the students' understanding of their religious heritage. By teaching in English about American history, science, and nature they contributed to their students' ability to participate in their American community. In these and other ways the female teachers of the various Norwegian-American Lutheran schools took part in the ministry of their churches.

Deaconesses

Deaconess work was a possible professional ministry for Norwegian Lutheran women. The aim of deaconess work was to further the mission of the church, especially with regard to service. Sister Ingeborg Sponland, an early leader of Norwegian Lutheran deaconess work in the United States, described that work in *My Reasonable Service*:

> The deaconess must be determined to follow the will of God and serve men whether they be high or low, rich or poor, black or white. All are precious souls in the sight of the Lord. The ultimate aim of all deaconess work is to minister to man's soul.

Sponland linked the deaconesses' work with that of the whole church; it was not limited to works of charity. Rather, the deaconesses shared in the total mission.

> Therefore deaconesses are trained for both physical and spiritual work. As members of the church they strive to win souls for the Lord Jesus Christ. . . .

179

The opportunity to work among the sick, helping to alleviate pain, is only a small part of her work. The avenues of service for the Lord are numerous, and investing her life in His service because she is constrained by the Lord brings dividends a hundred-fold.[86]

Hospitals, schools, foreign missions, social work, and congregations all benefited from the labor of deaconesses despite their small number and the Norwegian-Americans' unfamiliarity with deaconesses.

The diaconate has a long, but disjointed, history in the Christian church, with its beginning in the events recorded in the Acts of the Apostles.[87] In those early years both women and men were engaged in this ministry of loving service. Gradually the office of deacon was defined as a part of the clerical hierarchy; the distinction between deaconesses and the "widows" was not clear. Both groups of women cared for sick and poor women, instructed female catechumens, and assisted in the baptism of women. In the early medieval period female deaconesses disappeared from the western church.[88] Monastic houses provided a specialized religious life for women but did not allow them to move about ministering to their neighbors' needs. Women's efforts to live in noncloistered communities and to work among the poor and needy met with official resistance.[89]

The female diaconate was revived among German Protestants through the efforts of Pastor Theodore Fliedner and his wife Fredericke in 1836. Their work began with a cottage that served as a home to freed female prisoners. The Kaiserswerth community expanded its activities to include care of the sick and education of neglected children and to train deaconesses for care of the needy, teaching, or parish work.[90] From Kaiserswerth deaconess work spread among European and American Protestant churches. It was introduced into Norway in the 1860s with Sister Catinka Gulberg, who had received her training at Kaiserswerth, as superior of the newly founded motherhouse in Oslo.[91]

Norwegians, such as Sisters Elizabeth Fedde and Ingeborg Sponland, were instrumental in the development of deaconesses work among Norwegian-American Lutherans. Elizabeth Fedde trained under the direction of Sister Gulberg. In 1883 Sister Elizabeth came to the United States in answer to a call from the pastor at the Seamen's Mission in Brooklyn. One of her first tasks was to organize a women's society to support her work. There was plenty to keep her busy. "It was not long until the Sister acted in the capacity of midwife, doctor, minister, as well as scrub woman, nurse, night nurse, charity dispenser and in many other capacities."[92]

Five years after her arrival in New York, Fedde took a trip to the Midwest. During her visit in Minneapolis she met leaders in the Norwegian-American community who were interested in extending deaconess work into their city. Despite financial setbacks this was accomplished with the aid of Fedde and later with the resident direction of Sister Ingeborg Sponland.

Sponland also trained in Oslo. After five years of training and work in hospitals, she was consecrated in 1886 on the day that the new motherhouse cornerstone was laid. In her autobiography, Sponland discussed the significance of consecration.

> Consecration means the dedicating of oneself to the Lord's work. A consecration service has a great significance to a deaconess. To the deaconess probationer it is as impressive and solemn an occasion as ordination is to a theological candidate for the ministry. The deaconess does not make a vow at consecration. The promise she makes on her consecration day is a promise to the Lord that she will be faithful in the calling He has given her. Hers is a life calling, but if for some reason the deaconess chooses to leave the diaconate, she is free to do so after going through the regular procedure of resignation.[93]

Following this she continued her hospital work in several Norwegian cities. When she came to the United States in 1891 the trip was intended to be a yearlong visit. The Board of Trustees for the Minneapolis deaconesses prevailed upon her to take charge as sister superior. She accepted and the visit extended for the remainder of her life.

Soon after Sister Ingeborg assumed her duties in the small community composed of Sisters Gunda Torsen, Jensine Erickson, Christie Olson, and Lena Nilsen, she discovered that Norwegian-Americans did not understand the calling and work of deaconesses and that the church was preoccupied with internal struggles. (This was shortly after the Predestinarian controversy and the formation of the United Church.) Many people equated deaconesses with nurses and treated them as "cheap servants." The demands placed on deaconesses went beyond those called for by their office, as illustrated by the case of one parish sister.

> Her duties were to take part in the congregation's activities, visit the members, teach Sunday school, as well as organize and direct the summer parish school. She was also to do enough private nursing to pay her own salary. This was to be work outside the congregation, for members were to have her free. The result

was that nursing became the main thing, chiefly among members of the congregation. . . . The Sister . . . became a sort of maid-of-all-work . . . contracted tuberculosis and was disabled for many years.[94]

Some clergymen were indifferent to deaconesses; others were openly opposed to them, or any "women's activity in the church except to serve suppers and keep the church clean." These men thought that all "spiritual" work should be reserved for the pastor.[95] The Norwegian Lutheran churches' failure to appreciate the possibilities of diaconal ministry and thus to support it plagued Sponland's career at the Minneapolis and Chicago motherhouses and much of the deaconesses' work; finally, it contributed to the demise of the movement in the mid-twentieth century.[96]

In the years of their activity the Norwegian-American Lutheran deaconesses had various relationships with the churches. Initially the work in Brooklyn, Minneapolis, and Chicago (1896) was begun without official affiliations, although the members of each house's Board of Trustees were drawn from the churches. The Chicago house and its hospital became the property of the United Norwegian Lutheran Church in 1904; following the 1917 mergers, the Brooklyn community associated with the Evangelical Lutheran Church and the Minneapolis community with the Lutheran Free Church.[97] Each national church body treated the deaconesses in a slightly different but generally inadequately supportive way. Susan Everson attributed this lack of support to the churches' failure to understand the role of the deaconess in the church and the boards' related tendency to limit the deaconesses' autonomy in a manner that inhibited their ability to carry out their ministry.[98] The frequency and intensity of conflicts over money, initiation of projects, and internal leadership appeared to increase in the second quarter of the twentieth century. For example, when the Chicago community chose a successor to Sister Superior Ingeborg Sponland in 1936 they were surprised to discover that the Board had overruled their decision.[99]

Conflict and misunderstanding were not the only characteristics of deaconess and church relations. Professor Sverdrup, Reverend H. B. Kildahl, and other clergymen were advocates of the women's work. Sponland noted that during her tenure as sister superior in Chicago, Kildahl "represented [them] nobly at the church conventions, fighting for the institution, its aims, its principle, its work, its need."[100]

The women of the churches were also supporters of deaconess work from Sister Elizabeth Fedde's first organization of a women's society in Brooklyn.

Each time the ownership or supervision of a house was transferred this sort of group had to be reorganized. The Women's Missionary Federation of the Evangelical Lutheran Church made significant financial contributions to the deaconesses. In 1929 it instituted a program department with a dual purpose:

> First, to acquaint our people with the Deaconess work, a vital part of our Church work.
>
> Secondly, to do all in our power to find young women who will consecrate their lives in service as Christian Deaconesses, thus to increase the number of deaconesses, and meet the demands placed on the Church by the Savior.[101]

Both of these activities were needed as the work of the deaconesses was not well known and their numbers were small even several decades after Sister Elizabeth arrived in Brooklyn.

There were American-born women who entered the diaconate. Perhaps the best known was Sister Anna Huseth. She was born in 1892 in Kenyon, Minnesota, where she was confirmed in Holden Church and attended high school. With a commitment to "do some work of Christian service," she continued her education with three years of study at St. Olaf College, six months at the University of Minnesota school of medicine, and the nurses' school at the Chicago Deaconess Hospital.

In 1919, the year of her consecration, Sister Anna went to Brevig, Alaska, where she took the position of matron at the Eskimo orphanage. The following year she moved to the village of Igloo farther out on the Seward Peninsula. The rowdiness and deceit of white male traders had created "a real need for a white woman [as a missionary]—against whom there was not built-up antagonism." The Minnesota woman found much work to be done.

> There is not much time for leisure in this village. Sunday I conduct service in the morning, also Sunday school and Bible class; then service in the evening again. Monday is my day of rest—more or less. Sometimes it is a pretty busy day. Tuesday I wash clothes and make calls in the village and any number of other things. On Wednesday I have the Women's Club, and Thursday evening prayer meeting. Then I have a boys' choir and girls' class in personal hygiene. To keep house and run a mission keeps one person going pretty fast all day and sometimes part of the night. But I enjoy it immensely.[102]

In addition to her "mission" work, Sister Anna was known as a fine dog-sled runner and found time to pick, mount, and classify fifty varieties of Alaskan flowers. Photographs of her in trousers and a fur parka show the face of a woman who loved her work and the people with whom she lived.

Few in number and often without adequate support, deaconesses nonetheless made important contributions to the mission of the Norwegian Lutheran churches through their work in many fields. As early as 1896 Laura Eng was sent by her Eau Claire, Wisconsin, parish to train in the Brooklyn motherhouse and return to them as a parish worker.[103] Sisters Flora Moe and Martha Bakke were involved in home missions in Chicago. Moe, together with Pastor Ellestad, organized Emmaus Lutheran, which was later made a part of United Lutheran of Oak Park. Bakke was responsible for the Milwaukee Avenue Mission, from which Bethany Church came.[104] In the 1930s they were active in "hospitals, children's homes, old peoples' homes, Magdalene asylums, prisons, juvenile courts, kindergartens, day nurseries; work among the feeble-minded, epileptics, and unmarried mothers; homefinding work; work in the congregations, on the home and foreign mission fields."[105] The deaconesses themselves regarded their work as a "vocation of service which they viewed not as sacrifice but fulfillment."[106]

In the United States it was often members of Norwegian-American Lutheran churches who benefited from the deaconesses' care. Newcomers from Norway received aid in finding work and establishing themselves. In their ministry the deaconesses also expanded the definition of the "us" among whom God's will was prayed to be done. This was made explicit in the eleventh annual report of the Brooklyn sisterhood. There, service to those outside the Norwegian-American Lutheran community was described as duty owed "to the community and country in which we live. If we share the blessings of our adopted land, it is certainly our duty to help carry its burdens and to shrink from no responsibility resting upon us."[107] Despite criticism, the sisters at the Chicago hospital refused to limit their service to Norwegians or Lutherans. They insisted on answering the needs of all their neighbors in an area that was increasing in ethnic and religious diversity. Sister Ingeborg defended their action.

> To us as deaconesses truth cries out that all human beings have a soul which has been bought by the blood of Jesus Christ for the Kingdom of heaven. There can be no discrimination as to nationality or creed when it comes to serving our Master. He served all humanity and bids us to follow in His footsteps. In modifying our methods of approach so as to be able to serve people of various nationalities and creeds we gain a broader vision and a deeper sympathy and understanding—a compassion and love for souls that are without Christ.[108]

Her statement echoed the New Testament message that God is no respecter of persons and anticipated the late twentieth-century Lutheran churches' concern for inclusiveness.

Women of the Norwegian-American Lutheran churches who became deaconesses participated in the ministry of the church. Their hospitals provided training for women who wished to be nurses but not deaconesses. Some of their number served as missionaries in distant places such as China, Madagascar, and Alaska. In the United States they, like teachers but to a lesser degree, had Norwegian Lutherans as their major audience. Often the tasks they performed were similar to those women did in their homes and congregations: they nursed, they taught children, they attended to the needs of the poor.

Deaconesses were, however, professional church workers whose commitment to their careers was perceived to preclude their becoming wives and mothers. This fact perhaps suggested to their early twentieth-century contemporaries that they were not merely expanding women's usual roles or taking a temporary position before assuming those roles as was expected of teachers.[109] Rather, it may have appeared that deaconesses rejected their conventional place as women. Whether this was seen as a radical notion or a sacrifice, it likely contributed to misunderstandings of the diaconate and to the small number of women who entered into that ministry. By the early 1960s, when a merger created the American Lutheran Church, this option of female professional ministry had nearly disappeared from the Norwegian-American Lutheran churches.

Missionaries

Mission work is the greatest and most important work the church has to do. To preach the gospel to all nations, and to bring them in to fellowship with Jesus Christ is not a problem solved in a day. . . . You are invited to help in this endeavor, dear friend, to insure its successful accomplishment. It is your duty as a Christian, a holy duty, imposed on every one who confesses the name of Jesus.[110]

Thus began a leaflet issued by the WMF of the United Church in the early years of the twentieth century. The women of the church were encouraged to be "co-workers" with God through their prayers and financial contributions to both foreign and home missions. There was work to be done and workers willing and ready to be sent: this was evidence that their earlier prayers had

185

been answered. Among the missionaries sent to Africa and Asia by the several Norwegian-American Lutheran church bodies were women: married women, single women, nurses, teachers, and deaconesses.

In this appeal to women for prayers and money and in the female staffing of missions, the Norwegian-American Lutherans were like their Yankee neighbors and their Norwegian relatives.[111] The pattern was typical among American Protestant groups that had been active on various fields since the early 1800s. The work was supported in large part by the extra gifts of women in female mission societies, from small local groups or large national boards.[112] These women felt a special burden for their "heathen sisters" who had none of the advantages given to women by a Christian society. They were particularly moved by stories of foot-binding and female infanticide in China and Indian suttee. To provide missionaries to carry the gospel to their sisters American women raised money at sales and through contribution of their own mites;[113] they publicized the missionaries' work through their periodicals, at meetings, and in their correspondence; they prayed for its success; and in the second half of the nineteenth century they formed their own sending agencies.[114]

The relationship between the women's societies and their denominational mission groups was problematic. There were disagreements over finances and the assignment of decision-making authority. Some denominational boards absorbed the women's missionary groups, perhaps in the hope of gaining control over their seemingly abundant money or perhaps in an effort to unify and streamline "duplicated" efforts.[115]

As discussed in Chapter Four, Norwegian-American women's groups were also enthusiastic supporters of foreign missions from their earliest days. Often the local *kvindeforening* donated a substantial portion of its treasury to that cause either through a Norwegian missionary society or the work of their Norwegian-American church, or directly to an individual they knew personally. When the local groups linked themselves into federations they continued to be generous contributors to missions. The leadership articulated a special concern for work among women. Like their counterparts in other denominations, they too had some difficulties with "their" church regarding the relationship of the WMF and the NLCA mission board.

Initially, American protestant groups such as the Congregationalists' American Board of Commissioners for Foreign Missions (ABCFM) called married men to be missionaries. The men were sent abroad to do the church's work of evangelism and their wives were sent to make a home and look after the men. When children were born, American wives had the added task of looking after them. In addition, some wives were actively engaged in linguistic endeavors and other mission activities. This double load made it nearly impossible for married women to do the special work that they perceived was needed among the women around them. Consequently, after 1850 both the women's sending agencies and the general boards began to call single women as missionaries. This strategy met two needs: It secured female workers to labor among the women of the missionized country and it provided a professional role for women within the church just as they were gaining opportunities for education but not for employment in the United States. By the early 1900s women outnumbered men on the foreign mission field.

Norwegian missionary groups sent both married and single persons to their various fields. This was also true of those sent by Norwegian-American groups that began their labors only in the last decade of the 1800s, after the ABCFM and various female societies had begun to sponsor single women. Among the women were those who had been educated at schools like St. Olaf and the Lutheran Normal School. Some of the single women were deaconesses. As for other Protestant women, the mission field provided Norwegian-American Lutheran women with the opportunity to participate in their churches' ministry as professionals.

In earlier decades Norwegians had considered the United States a mission field. Many of the pastors who came in the first years regarded their call in this way despite the fact that they came to minister to Norwegians rather than to evangelize the "heathen." Norwegian-American interest in evangelism abroad was sparked by personal contact with visiting missionaries from the Norwegian Mission Society in the 1880s and further stirred at several intersynodical gatherings.[116]

The primary fields in which Norwegian-American Lutherans had mission stations were Madagascar and China. Two men were sent to Madagascar by the Conference in the late 1880s; they served under the auspices of the Norwegian Missionary Society. That group divided its field with the United Church in 1892. The area was further parceled when the United Church shared its portion with the Lutheran Free Church. Work in China was begun in 1890 by an independent group, the Norwegian Lutheran China Mission Society, composed of members of the Hauge Synod and others. The Hauge Synod soon launched its own mission; the China Mission Society's work was taken over by the United Church in 1903. The Norwegian Synod was the latecomer; it began its Chinese mission in 1912. As mergers took place in

North America, the churches also merged their mission work.[117] Through the work of the Norwegian Schreuder Mission there was contact with and participation in South African evangelization.[118] Alaska was also viewed as a foreign mission.

Individual women were stimulated to consider mission work in various ways, beginning in their girlhoods. Even before the Norwegian-American churches established their own stations and sent out their own workers, missionaries and their labors were very much a part of the life of congregations through mission publications, mission fests, and visits from missionaries. The genesis of Anna Rønning Hompland's commitment to China was described by her sister Tilda.

> My sister's call to be a missionary in China happened in our home. My father was a very sincere Christian. He loved the China Mission and read aloud from a magazine called '*Kinamissionaren*' and always during devotions prayed that one of his children would go to China as a missionary. Anna told me many times that it was at the age of twelve that she was sure she would go to China.[119]

Anna's call was reinforced during her education at the Normal School in Madison and St. Olaf and during a year of nurses' training at the Chicago Deaconesses Hospital. She went to China in 1914. Another LNS student, Elise Holland Tverberg, recalled that her call to missionary service began in her girlhood and matured through her experiences at LNS. Her account highlighted the important role the *kvindeforening* played in supporting missions by encouraging women to answer the call to go to foreign lands.

> I have early childhood memories of accompanying my mother to Ladies Aid and hearing her read mission stories for Madagascar while the others were working for the mission. This seed sown in my young heart was nourished and naturally grew with the years. At the LNS we were met daily by the Word of God in chapel, in class room, Sunday School Bible class and in Sunday afternoon Mission Society. Maybe those of us who were more mature and were called on to contribute a few remarks based on a scripture passage received the greatest benefit to the hidden longings to carry the Gospel to those near by or to the uttermost part of the world. . . . I had the privilege of hearing Anna Lee, a Normalite, speak in chapel about her life and witnessing in China.[120]

Elise and her husband worked in Madagascar from 1914 until 1946. Her sister and brother-in-law were also missionaries there. This situation was typical;

frequently familial relationships were part of the contacts between the field and North America. Several members of a family often served in the same country. The ministry carried out by women in China and Madagascar included work with women and children, but it was not limited to those audiences. One of the first to go to Madagascar was Nellie Dahl. As a young girl Nellie vowed to God that she would become a missionary if God spared her ill sister's life. Before she made good on her promise she studied at St. Olaf, the universities of Idaho and Minnesota, Luther Seminary, and the Chicago Deaconesses Hospital. Perhaps the fact that her mother's sister had been in Madagascar as a missionary with a Norwegian society influenced Nellie to go there in 1905.[121]

The respect with which she came to be regarded by her colleagues was revealed in an anecdote. When discussing women's work in the mission, one male missionary said that as many deaconesses as could be sent he would find work for. The other asked, "Have you forgotten Nellie Dahl?" "No replied the other, but there are not many like her."[122] Much of her work was linguistic. She wrote a Malagasy language textbook and translated both Norwegian and English texts into Malagasy as well as writing lyrics for songs. In the 1920s Miss Dahl was the editor of the *Messenger*, a periodical published by the American Lutheran missionaries. As did most of her colleagues, when she was on furlough she traveled to many congregations and other church meetings to speak about the missionary work in Madagascar.[123]

By 1923 there were six deaconesses, to whom Nellie Dahl had been so favorably compared, serving in Madagascar. Disease had forced others to leave. Sister Jørgine Mjøvik contracted tuberculosis and returned to Chicago after five years' service. She brought with her Marie Magdalene, a young Malagasy women, to be trained to continue Sister Jørgine's work. Sister Caroline Thompson, a native of St. Ansgar, Iowa, attended Highland Park College in Des Moines and St. Olaf prior to her consecration.[124] In Madagascar she worked at the girls' asylum in St. Luce, the boys' asylum in Fort Dauphin, and as a *bibelkvinde* (Bible woman) at the station in Tsivorn. Perhaps it was the tragedy of her death in a shipwreck that prompted the WMF to produce a tract recounting the story of her life and thus publicized both missions and deaconesses.

Astrid Pernilla Dahl Awes graduated from Moorhead State's five-year advanced English course by alternating teaching in local schools and attending classes. In 1917 she and her husband went to Manasoa, Madagascar, where her sister was head of the boys' school. In addition to her domestic

189

responsibilities for her own household, Mrs. Awes had many responsibilities within the mission. She

> had charge of the native women's sewing circle; looked after the welfare of the many school boys that were housed and fed at the station; taught the native pastors' and teachers' wives to read; tried to learn the art of preparing the many new dishes peculiar to the products of this tropical climate.[125]

The weight of these activities was crushing to Astrid's general health and nervous system. In an effort to repair the damage she was sent to South Africa, where she spent two and a half years. During that time she completed a correspondence course with the University of Chicago, taught in mission schools, and visited other mission stations. Although her health improved, it was still not up to the climate of Madagascar, so she and her husband returned to the United States.

Norwegian-American women also ministered to the Chinese. Thea Rønning was the first; she, her brother Rev. Halvor Rønning, and Hannah Rorem (the future wife of Halvor) were sent by the China Mission Society in 1891.[126] As she was born in Norway and immigrated to Minnesota in 1887, only four years prior to going to China, Thea's American self-identity may have been weak. In a speech thanking the Hauge Synod congregation in Faribault for their kindnesses to her she referred to herself as a Norwegian and to them as Americans; in China, however, she called America her home.[127] At the Hauge Synod's annual meeting in 1891 Thea spoke of her desire to go to China and of the special needs of Chinese women.[128] She continued to voice this concern throughout her career.

The three new laborers traveled to China with Pastor Nestegaard, who was sent by the Norwegians. Upon their arrived in Hankow they were met by other Norwegians, who had prepared a welcome. On the wall of the dining room was a red lettered greeting sign in both Norwegian and Chinese. Before they had adjusted to the odors and other unfamiliar conditions they were busy at their language studies.

Despite her frequent illness, Thea plunged into her work and reported on it to supporters in the United States. This sort of "publicity" correspondence was essential to the continued well-being of missions. She wrote to a girls' mission society about conditions in Hankow.

> You would be amazed. The streets are narrow and crowded, we must walk single file. Many are blind, crippled, etc., the air is so bad it cannot be described.

On the way home from prayer meeting, we had to pass through a crowd at a theater. People began to scream "foreign devils, foreign devils" but we thought of Jesus. The poor heathen! Pray that the wind of Pentecost will convert them.[129]

Other women arrived to help at the mission. Olava Hodnefjeld and Thea cooperated at a school for girls. Giving careful attention to the particular difficulties of female students, Thea described the school in a letter printed in the Hauge Synod's periodical.

We have forty girls in our girls' school. It was late that we got the school and few girls came. We couldn't find a woman teacher, that goes against Chinese custom. . . . One cent a day buys coal for their feet which hurt because they are so ruined. They often sit and hold them up and weep. Poor children! They believe they should do so and set great honor upon having the smallest feet. When we talk to the parents about this, they say it is our custom and we cannot overthrow it. When will the Chinese wake up and see how dumb they are?

The missionary women also went into the homes of their students and talked with their mothers.

Now we have started to make house calls and then we really discover need. We talk to the women and children about God. It is so new they cannot fathom it, but God's Spirit has power and can open the heathen heart.[130]

Being unmarried did not exempt Miss Rønning from conventional "women's work." When Mrs. Netland died in 1893, the care of the Netland children fell to her. Despite this extra load, single women received a salary $50.00 less than single men. The Mission Society did, rather surprisingly, authorize funds to hire a domestic servant for Thea and Olava so that they could devote more time to language study.[131]

There were several marriages among the mission personnel. Halvor Rønning and Hannah Rorem were married shortly after their arrival in China. After his first wife's death, Sigvald Netland married Oline Hermanson. In 1896 Thea and C. W. Landahl were married. Together they and Miss Hodnefjeld went to start a new station in Taipingtien.[132] The work flourished, but only two years later Thea contracted meningitis and died within two days. Although her career was brief, Thea Rønning Landahl was memorialized as a woman "first in her field" by the WMF in *Some Marthas and Marys of the N.L.C.A.*

Agnes Margaret Kittelsby was honored in the same way for her nine years in China with the United Church Board of Foreign Missions.[133] Agnes was American born. She spent her early childhood near Decorah, Iowa, with Vilhelm Koren as her pastor. When she was twelve, her mother died and Agnes went to live in the home of her brother-in-law, St. Olaf professor H. T. Ytterboe. As might be expected, the girl attended both the academy and the college departments at St. Olaf, graduating in 1900.

Her teaching career began at St. Ansgar Seminary and continued at Waldorf College. When Agnes Mellby was given a yearlong leave from her position as preceptress at St. Olaf, Miss Kittelsby filled in. After a short stay at Augustana College in South Dakota she was given a permanent position teaching English literature at St. Olaf in 1907.

In Northfield she read that the mission board was looking for someone to run the American School for missionary children in Kikungshan but judged herself to be underqualified. The board thought otherwise, and the call was extended to her; in 1914 she assumed her duties.

> She had to be the executive and administrative head as well as teacher. She was called upon to be mother and counsellor to this large group of boys and girls, ranging in age from seven or eight up through high school years. She was the supervisor of both work and play activities, as also of their worship, and the whole range of their daily life. And she not only supervised, but entered heartily into it all, including the play.[134]

As was not uncommon among missionaries, this heavy responsibility broke Agnes' health. She died at age forty-five in Hankow.

During her trip around the world in 1926 Sister Ingeborg Sponland visited the missions in China and several of the twelve deaconesses serving there. In Fancheng she saw the high school in which Olava Hodnefjeld had worked. Sister Inga Dvergsness, a former LNS student, took her to Sinyang. There she "met many of the missionaries as well as Chinese, both in church and social life." Summing up her impression of the Chinese missions Sister Ingeborg emphasized the difficulty and slowness of the work. She paid special tribute to the missionary wife.

> She is first and foremost to be a wife and mother and hers is a tremendous privilege as well as responsibility. For in a heathen land she has problems bringing up her family which no American mother can fully appreciate. She must be ready to entertain guests at any hour of the day or night, to shoulder responsibilities when her husband is out on errands of mercy, to encourage and

cheer her helpmeet under the most trying conditions, to part with her children at an early age to send them to school.[135]

Sister Ingeborg did not ignore the sacrifices made and dangers faced by single women either. All in all she was favorably impressed by what she saw.

On the mission field women participated in the ministry of their church in a visible and essential way. Although their audience was usually composed of persons other than Norwegian-Americans, through correspondence and visits they were in close contact with that group. They were accountable to their churches for their ministry, both to the boards that called them and to the various women's societies that supported them with letters, prayers, gifts, and money.

These women often saw their special mission to be to women and children; their work of nursing, teaching, and praying was thus a transfer of their conventional roles from the home onto the mission field. As it was transposed it was also altered. Female missionaries expanded the conventional female roles. Some had expert training in religion, teaching, or medicine (both nurses and physicians) from church or secular schools. As Bible women, worship leaders, or publicists they took on tasks that very likely they would not have been given in the United States.

For the single women in China and Madagascar there was the possibility of marriage. There were, however, women who remained unmarried throughout their career, devoting "their full time and energy to the winning of souls for Christ."[136] If their singleness was viewed as a sacrifice, they were also admired for their work. The ambiguity of this perception may have confused some girls; it would also have allowed others to consider the possibility of a fulfilling life that did not include being a wife and mother.

Conclusions

Women were active participants in the educational institutions of the Norwegian-American Lutheran churches and workers in the ministry of those churches. Through parochial schools and three types of secondary schools—colleges, ladies' seminaries, and normal schools—the churches provided girls with opportunities for education that affected them in several ways. Through the use of the Norwegian language either as a means of instruction or as a subject of study and through religious instruction and worship, these schools reinforced their students' religious and ethnic identity. Friendships and personal loyalties formed during school years further linked them to that community. Knowledge and skills acquired at St. Olaf, the Lutheran Ladies' Seminary, the Lutheran Normal School, or other similar institutions equipped young women to be contributing members of their families, congregations, and women's societies as well as to embark on careers either within the church or beyond it.

By teaching English, perhaps by teaching in English, and by teaching about American history and culture, these schools exposed their students to their American identity. Among the student body and the faculty there were occasional Yankees and persons whose Americanization had proceeded at various rates. This too mediated the girls' contact with things American, enabling them to go beyond the Norwegian-American community without demanding that it be left behind.

While the influence of education in these schools was conservative, linking young women to their familial communities and returning them to conventional female roles as wives and mothers, it had the potential to be expansive as well. Even mediated contact with American culture may have been the road some women took out of the Norwegian-American community and out of the Lutheran churches, although those women have not been treated here. Those students who returned to their familial homes, married, and had children did so with broadened horizons: they had lived in another place, they had friends in other parts of the country, they had learned to learn, perhaps they had had a career as a teacher, and thus their perspective was also changed. Some expanded upon the conventional roles in short-term careers before they married; others had lifelong careers and lives that did not include a husband and children.

Undoubtedly many women pursued careers that were personally satisfying and also an expression of their Christian vocation but were not recognized by the churches. There were also women whose professions contributed to the ministry of the Norwegian-Lutheran churches. Teachers in church schools, deaconesses, and missionaries are specifically included in this category. Women in these ministries were accountable to the churches or to church institutions for their work and frequently the church was the primary audience of their work. Although they were not ordained, deaconesses were consecrated and both deaconesses and missionaries used the vocabulary of being called to their work.

This work included a wide range of responsibilities that usually stopped short of those tasks unique to and definitive of the Lutheran pastoral office—preaching of the gospel and administration of the sacraments. There were, however, exceptions. When broadly interpreted, preaching the gospel includes teaching, which women in all three groups did. Parish sisters helped start congregations; on the mission field women led worship. In dire circumstances nurses and missionaries baptized. But the validity of these women's ministry did not rest on similarities of their activities to those of the pastoral office. Their work as teachers, deaconess, and missionaries both publicly and professionally advanced the church's mission and contributed to "God's will being done" among their own community and beyond.

SIX

Conclusion:
On Ethnicity, Religion,
and Gender

I have examined Norwegian-American Lutheran women in the period from the mid-nineteenth to the early twentieth century, both immigrants to the upper Midwest and their American-born daughters and granddaughters. My portrayal of these women's experiences focuses upon ethnicity, religion, and gender as these three factors influence one another and as they affect the women's adaptation to the United States. My choice of materials and persons has held the ethnic and religious variables relatively stable. The women I have included are primarily those who identified strongly with the Norwegian-American Lutheran church and participated in its worship and women's societies. Consequently, it is not surprising that the influence of that community and of its institutions upon *these* women was generally positive. Within the communities defined by the Norwegian Lutheran churches these women became Norwegian-Americans and recast their expectations of their church and of themselves as women. The factors of ethnicity, religion, and gender intertwined as a braid; in the various arenas of life first one factor and then another was most apparent, but all were present.

The family was composed of people who shared a common heritage of ethnicity and religion. Therefore, one would expect gender, which was not shared by all members, to be a significant element in individual identity within the arena of home and family. Although women recorded few abstract reflections about the importance of femaleness to their self-identity, they did note changes in their work and thus in their role within their homes. The material adaptations women made to the needs and resources of the American environment contributed to the "Americanization" of the whole family.

Unfortunately, the sources and the process of these adaptations and innovations are nearly impossible to rediscover.

The origin of shifts in diet and clothing, for example, are difficult to pinpoint. It is possible that hired girls brought some foods with them from their Yankee employers into their own homes. Other changes, such as heavy use of pork in the mid-1800s, were a reaction to availability. Still others were made possible by new technology, such as cookstoves with ovens, which enabled women to bake yeast breads. Daughters at schools such as the Lutheran Ladies' Seminary were exposed to new foods. Ladies' Aid meetings provided opportunities for women to display their culinary skills and innovations. Perhaps some women also took part in more formal competitions at county fairs.

A similar set of circumstances contributed to adoption of American dress. Initially some women wrote home complaining about the shoddy quality of American-made fabrics; but later exposure to the fashions and climate of their new country combined with the availability of cash to purchase factory-woven material encouraged women to exchange their Norwegian woolens for American cotton dresses. It should be noted, however, that at the same time the *bunad*, Norwegian regional dress, was being altered in its native context. The "traditional" costume had been in a constant process of adaptation; a uniform style for each region was adopted only after the *bunad* was no longer common for everyday use. Thus, as with loss of the active *-datter* patronymic, parallel modernization was taking place in Norway and the United States.

As the women contributed to the process of material modernization and Americanization in their families, it was within those families that the women's own modernization and Americanization took place. With the loss of peasant patterns of labor and household relationships came different options. In the United States, where the old work exchange and social groups did not exist, the importance of the family for both material and social support increased. On the other hand, a young couple did not have to wait for the parents to retire before they married; they could strike out on their own. Teaching and nursing provided women with alternatives to hiring out before they married or made possible an alternative to marriage. On farms and in parsonages there appeared to be a slight leveling of class distinctions. Pastors' families began in the same frontier conditions as their parishioners. In the years after the Civil War the community prospered and there was a return to something of their Norwegian status, with hired workers to help run the parsonage. While some second- and third-generation marriages reinforced the old world connections between the clergy families, others expanded the circle to include the children of more ordinary immigrants and settlers. Eventually the pastors' wives kept their own houses just as their neighbors did. As their farm families prospered, farm women adopted increasingly genteel standards for their own behavior and moved their primary labor from the fields into the house. While the most refined clergy family and the most impoverished farm family remained far apart, the *alume* (common people) and the *conditioneret* (people of quality) moved closer together in the United States.

Norwegian Lutheran congregations were composed of people who shared an ethnic identity, but many Norwegian-Americans chose not to join Lutheran churches. Those who chose to belong selected between several different synods. This suggests that in the arena of the church, religion distinguished between members of various groups and gender distinguished among members of one group as in the family.

Women, however, displayed less pronounced conflicts between various types of Norwegian Lutheranism than those seen among male leaders. The instances in which internal disputes were mentioned by women were few. The tone of those remarks conveyed little of the intensity and contentiousness usually associated with the debates. Rather, women made matter-of-fact statements about the consequences. One woman recalled that as a girl she was not allowed to play with a child whose parents were on "the wrong side." Disagreement caused one *kvindeforening* to split. Mary Nelson's mother put things in perspective when her United Church daughter married a Hauge Synod clergyman, M. O. Wee. She observed that it could have been worse if he had been a Methodist.[1]

Women's freedom from preoccupation with the nuances of polity and doctrine did not signal disinterest in religion. Religion was very important to many of the women considered here. In the first generation they comforted themselves and their loved ones in Norway with the prospect of reunion in heaven. From Elisabeth Koren, the wife of one of the earliest Norwegian Synod pastors, to Petra Hagen, a young student at St. Olaf, they shared a devotion to their Norwegian Lutheranism and regarded it as superior to the religions they saw around them.

A congregation provided women with a community outside their family and its rituals marked the passing of the stages of their lives. They were baptized as infants and they were instructed as children in the gospel as understood by Lutherans. Their confirmation as members of the church signaled the onset of adulthood. Their marriages were celebrated in the church. Likely the major

199

anniversaries of that ceremony were celebrated there as well. The members of the congregation shared in joyous and sorrowful events as had the members of the *bedlag* in Norway. In times of grief women were consoled by their faith and when their own death came the church gave them a start on life in yet another new home.

Norwegian-American Lutheran women also had their own women's organizations. These groups were founded to support and advance the ministry of the church; they also supported their members both as individuals and as members of the Norwegian Lutheran community. In the 1870s and 1880s when the first *kvindeforening* were organized, they gave women an opportunity to socialize, to display and share their skills as homemakers, to learn about their religion, and to worship together as well as to produce financial support for the church. To the extent that meetings were a kind of work exchange to fulfill a common obligation and make work more enjoyable they replaced Norwegian social conventions such as *dugnad* and *bytesarbeid*.

These social and work functions could have been carried out in groups that were neither Lutheran nor Norwegian. Linking them with the ethnoreligious community strengthened it and gave women a place and a role in churches that did not allow them formal positions of leadership. Through their societies, both local and federated, women helped to move their church from a tax-supported state church to a voluntary denomination. Their prayers, their knowledge, and their financial gifts supported the church's ministry and often determined which aspects of it would prosper even when they were not allowed to vote in congregational meetings. Women used their influence and their money to support projects and people they knew and that aided Norwegian-American Lutherans: orphanages, old people's homes, hospitals, schools, foreign missions. In these ways women took actions that advanced their prayer that "God's will be done also among us."

Beyond its local manifestation, the church had educational institutions that played an important role in women's sense of themselves as Norwegian, Lutheran, and female. In schools such as the Ladies' Seminary in Red Wing, the Normal School in Madison, and St. Olaf College the educational setting was Norwegian and Lutheran in its human composition and in its commitments. Most of the faculty and student body were members of Lutheran churches. The curriculum included instruction in Norwegian as well as in Lutheran religious teachings. This forged links between students and that community.

At the same time these schools provided special training and offered mediated exposure to general American culture. Both training and exposure fostered contacts beyond the community defined by Norwegian Lutheranism. Students learned about English-language literature and American history along with music, math, and science. Female students acquired skills that led them into careers in education, publishing, medicine, and other fields. Some used their knowledge to move outside of their ethnoreligious group.

Other women, specifically teachers, deaconesses, and missionaries, turned their talents and training to the work of their church. They took tasks done by wives and mothers and expanded their audience beyond their own families. Some did so for a limited duration; some took this ministry as their life's work without ever establishing a family. The women's individual adaptations to their era were closely knit with that of the church. It was the arena for their work and they gave it their loyalty and labor. Even as they recast conventional women's roles, these women advanced the ministry of the church and shaped its corporate identity.

This statement can be made more generally as well. For many women the Norwegian Lutheran church provided the community in which they became Americans and it continued to be a significant aspect of the lives of their daughters. It is, however, important to acknowledge that there are other stories to be told; the same institutions and same set of factors had different, sometimes negative, influence on other women.

Likely, the Norwegian-American Lutheran community was too small and too inbred to nourish all of its daughters. A significant number did not join Lutheran churches. Some became members of other Norwegian speaking churches such as the Unitarian congregations founded by Kristofer Janson; others joined "American" churches such as the Congregationalist or Christian Scientist. Certainly there were women who did not associate themselves with any church at all. The church was not the only institution that fostered ethnic identity.

And not all women developed their identity as Norwegian-Americans. Some found the transition to the New World to be too difficult and returned to Norway; some retreated into mental illness; others blended into American society. I am convinced that there are stories of remarkable conflict and intense pain to be told in addition to the relatively pleasant ones I have told here.

This study is limited not only by the specific women it includes but also by the activities it portrays. It would be false to suggest that the arenas of home and family, of congregation and women's societies, and of education and ministry exhaust all the settings in which Norwegian-American Lutheran women lived. Many were also vigorous participants in the larger secular world through their clubs and professions and, I suspect, through their social contacts. The opportunities for these activities were more abundant and more varied in large towns and cities than in the small, relatively homogeneous communities in which most of the women considered here lived.

A glance at a few women demonstrates that Norwegian-American women had many careers besides that of the proverbial Scandinavian domestic servant. Hannah Astrup Larsen, daughter of Luther College's first president, returned from the Zululand mission late in the final years of the nineteenth century. She worked for *Amerika, Pacific-Posten,* and the *San Francisco Chronicle* before becoming editor of the *Scandinavian-American Review.*[2] Henrietta Larson, a St. Olaf graduate and sister of St. Olaf professor Agnes Larson, was an economic historian at Harvard and contributed to a history of Standard Oil.[3] Citizens of Ottertail County sent Hannah Kempfer to the Minnesota legislature for the first time in 1922; she served eighteen years.[4] Residents of the Red River Valley bought Degree of Honor insurance from traveling saleswoman Hannah Harris from the time that her children were teenagers until 1954, when she retired at age eighty-three.[5] Olive Fremstad delighted audiences in Europe and North America with her larklike singing; her life story provided the basis for Willa Cather's *The Song of the Lark.*[6] Not all careers were equally admirable: Belle Gunness, "the Lady Bluebeard," allegedly murdered "at least one husband, several women and children, and numerous would-be suitors who had answered her matrimonial advertisements placed in Norwegian-language immigrant newspapers" between 1901 and 1908.[7] In the 1870s and 1880s Ulrikk Feldtman Bruun established a home for girls in Chicago and published a temperance paper, *Det Hvide Baand (The White Ribbon).*[8] Martha Ostenso was able to support herself as a writer of fiction.[9] The range of possible professions for a young Norwegian-American woman was wide.

Women without paying careers were also involved in a variety of activities. In addition to serving as the first president of the *Prestekoneforening,* Inanda Torrison Bredesen, Lydia B. Sundby's mother, was a member of the visiting board for Martin Luther Children's Home and Skaalen Old People's Home, president of the Stoughton City Benevolence Society, treasurer of the school board, and a member of the city library board.[10] A survey of the biographies the fifty "Prominent Norse American Women" who were included in the *Souvenir* volume produced for the centennial of Norwegian immigration also produces a extraordinary record, suggesting that Mrs. Bredesen was not unusual.[11] Political groups such as the League of Women Voters and Republican women's clubs were frequently mentioned. Mrs. Josephine Alma Fyhrie was the first female ward chairman in St. Paul. Several women were members of groups supporting Fairview Hospital, Lyngblomsen and Ebenezer Homes in the Twin Cities. The Women's Christian Temperance Union had Nellie Paulson and Alma Gutterson among its supporters. Gutterson also participated in the Red Cross, Eastern Star, and the Young Women's Christian Association. The Parent Teacher Association, Business and Professional Women, Ladies' Auxiliary of the Railway Conductors, and the Dome Club for wives of Minnesota state legislators had Norwegian-American women among their members.

My sources are primarily literary and personal and are not readily quantified, nor are they easily compared. Observations by Caja Munch about Wisconsin in the mid-1800s or by Gro Svendsen about Iowa and recollections by Bolette Stub Bergh about western Minnesota in the late 1800s or by Barbara Levorsen about the Dakotas illustrate the difficulty of comparison. The differences among them might be attributed to date and location, or to class, or to generation. Caja and Gro were both immigrants; Bolette and Barbara were American born. Caja and Bolette were pastors' wives; Gro was a farmer's wife and Barbara a farmer's daughter. Gro and Caja were writing letters to family in Norway; the others wrote for publication in the United States long after the events took place. These individual characteristics appear in many configurations.

Even simple information is sometimes difficult to gather and unreliable once obtained. Eventually nearly every congregation had at least one women's society, but there was no identifiable origin for the movement. The information about the beginnings of local groups is scattered. In some cases the *kvindeforening* was clearly the idea of the pastor, or his wife, or the schoolteacher. In others it seems to have sprung from a woman in the congregation. Most often the local historian makes no mention of the genesis of the idea. Many congregational anniversary histories noted the year the *kvindeforening* began, but not all do. Because some listed one date for the first meetings and another for the founding, any date becomes suspect. As the federations were formed after the local groups, the national organizations' information is as uneven as the locals'.

There are things I would like to know about the women I have included. While it is evident that women came to use English at their meetings, very few

203

groups noted when this transition took place. Was it before or after the congregation switched? Similarly, one wonders about the use of English in homes. Did it come sooner in the homes of women who had worked for Yankee families? Many local groups assumed that all female members of the congregation were also members of the women's society. How many really took part? What other ways did they participate in their congregations? When did women begin to vote in congregational meetings? The answers to these questions are not to be found in my sources.

What can be said it this: Although the formal structures of Norwegian-American Lutheran churches did not have a place for them as leaders, many women still found personal satisfaction in their participation in women's societies and personal meaning in their faith. The ways they came to be Americans were mediated through their churches as were the ways they came to be modern women. Their lives are well understood as manifestations of their prayer that God's will be done among them.

Notes

INTRODUCTION

1. While this oversight is expected in older works, the failure of the contributors to E. Clifford Nelson, ed., *The Lutherans in North America* (Philadelphia: Fortress, 1975), even to mention that women were first ordained in American Lutheran churches in 1970 is inexplicable. One step toward a fuller history of Lutheran women is L. DeAne Lagerquist, *From Our Mothers' Arms: A History of Women in the American Lutheran Church* (Minneapolis: Augusburg Publishing House, 1987).

2. There is some debate about the terms "women's historian" and "feminist historian." In my interpretation a women's historian is one whose subject is women; a feminist historian is one who has adopted a particular viewpoint about history and whose present subject may or may not be women. Feminist historians may be distinguished from women's historians by their positions on the two issues that are discussed in the text. This is similiar to the difference between an economic historian and a Marxist historian. Feminism is not easily defined, as the term is used to denote a wide range of ideological positions. I suggest that these are all linked by the following negative statement upon which all feminists would agree: Women are no less important than men. On the basis for this statement, the program it prompts, and the refinement of it, feminists disagree.

   An instructive treatment of the variety of views within contemporary American feminism can be found in Gayle Graham Yates, *What Women Want: The Ideas of the Movement* (Cambridge: Harvard University Press, 1975). Yates displays her typology in a table on page 21. As with all such imposed schemes, this one does not always fit; however, I have found it to be extremely useful and my understanding of feminism as been aided by Yates. The literature on these issues is expanding rapidly; the following represent only a sample. Carl N. Degler, "What the Women's Movement Has Done to American History," *Soundings* 62 (Winter 1981):403-21; Nancy Schrom Dye, "Clio's American Daughter: Male History, Female Reality," in *The Prism of Sex*, ed. Julia A. Sherman and Evelyn Torton Beck (Madison: University of Wisconsin Press, 1979), pp. 9-32; Joan Kelly, *Women, History & Theory: The Essays of Joan Kelly* (Chicago: The University of Chicago Press, 1984); Gerda Lerner, *The Majority Finds Its Past: Placing Women in History* (Oxford: Oxford University Press,

1979); and Anne Firor Scott, *Making the Invisible Woman Visible* (Urbana: University of Illinois Press, 1984).
3. One of the few considerations of women in American Lutheranism is based on the views of its patriarch. Barbara Cunningham, "An Eighteenth-Century View of Femininity as Seen Through the Journals of H. M. Muhlenberg," *Pennsylvania History* 43 (July 1976):197-212.
4. Caroline Dorthea Margrethe Keyser Preus, *Linka's Diary on Land and Sea, 1845-1864*, trans. and ed. Johan Carl Keyser Preus and Diderikke Margrethe Brandt Preus (Minneapolis: Augsburg Publishing House, 1952); Elisabeth Koren, *The Diary of Elisabeth Koren, 1853-1855*, trans. and ed. David T. Nelson (Northfield: Norwegian-American Historical Association, 1955). I have relied heavily on them both, along with similar materials.
5. Eugene L. Fevold and E. Clifford Nelson, *The Lutheran Church Among Norwegian-Americans: A History of the Evangelical Lutheran Church*, 2 vols. (Minneapolis: Augsburg Publishing House, 1960); Charles P. Lutz, ed., *Church Roots: Stories of Nine Immigrant Groups That Became The American Lutheran Church* (Minneapolis: Augsburg Publishing House, 1985).
6. This phrase was applied in this way by Kathleen Neils Conzen at "Scandinavians and Other Immigrants in Urban America," a conference held at St. Olaf College, Northfield, Minnesota, October 26-27, 1984.
7. See for example Mrs. R. O. Brandt, "Social Aspects of Prairie Pioneering: The Reminiscences of a Pioneer Pastor's Wife," *Norwegian-American Studies and Records* (hereafter *NASR*) 7 (1933):1-46; Clara Jacobson, "Memories from Perry Parsonage," *NASR* 14 (1944):139-58; and Barbara Levorsen, "Early Years in Dakota," *NASR* 21 (1962):158-97; Barbara Levorsen, "Our Bread and Meat," *NASR* 22 (1963):178-97.
8. See for example Hasia R. Diner, *Erin's Daughters in America: Irish Immigrant Women in the Nineteenth Century* (Baltimore: The Johns Hopkins University Press, 1984); or Micaela di Leonardo, *The Varieties of Ethnic Experience: Kinship, Class, and Gender Among California Italian-Americans* (Ithaca: Cornell University Press, 1984). General works on "Yankee" women include those by scholars such as Nancy Cott, Carroll Smith-Rosenberg, and Gerda Lerner. Also relevant are works that consider women on the frontier, such as those by Glenda Riley and Julie Roy Jeffery.
9. Janice Reiff has published an article on Scandinavian women in Seattle. At a conference at the University of Wisconsin in 1984, Monys Haugen gave a paper on Norwegian women of the Wisconsin frontier, which is based on her master's thesis. Papers by Susan Everson and Todd Walsh are unpublished. Gracia Grindal's paper from this conference has recently been published as "The Americanization of the Norwegian Pastors' Wives," *Norwegian American Studies and Records* 32 (1989): 199-207. For detailed references see bibliography.
10. During these three periods, with the exception of 1908 and 1912, the number of emigrants was over 10,000 per year. See chart, "The Course of Norwegian Emigration, 1836-1928," in Theodore Blegen, *Norwegian Migration to America*,

vol. 2 (Northfield: The Norwegian-American Historical Association, 1940), p. 18.

11. This is particularly so for women whose activities are primarily in the arena of home and family. "A women's life is transhistorical. It is cyclical and repetitive." June Sochen, "Frontier Women: A Model for all Women?" *South Dakota History* 7 (Winter 1976):36-56.

12. A crucial difference was immigrant women's loss of contact with their mothers; the second generation had their mothers nearer at hand. Helen M. Bannan, "Warrior Women: Immigrant Mothers in the Works of their Daughters," *Women's Studies* 6 (1979):165-78.

13. di Leonardo, *The Varieties of Ethnic Experience*, pp. 22-25.

14. Einar Haugen, *The Norwegian Language in America: A Study in Bilingual Behavior* (Bloomington: Indiana University Press, 1969).

15. Modernization is used here in a sense influenced by the work of Peter Berger as it is articulated in Peter Berger, Brigitte Berger, and Hansfried Kellner, *The Homeless Mind: Modernization and Consciousness* (New York: Random House, 1973). There modernization is discussed as "the institutional concomitants of technologically induced economic growth" (p. 9). Primary carriers of modernization are identified as the modern state and bureaucracy; secondary carriers include the contemporary city, mass education and communication, and sociocultural pluralism. Characteristic of the process are technological change, dichotomization of private and public spheres, and segmentation of social life. In *The Sacred Canopy: Elements of a Sociological Theory of Religion* (Garden City, N.Y.: Anchor Books, 1969) Berger notes, "While secularization [one component of modernization] may be viewed as a global phenomenon of modern societies, it is not uniformly distributed within them" (p. 108). It also may be said that the influence of modernization is not uniformly distributed. Proximity to the carriers is a crucial factor in this unevenness.

I am not suggesting that the experience of immigrants was the same as the experience of those who remained in Norway. My claim is far more modest. Immigrants' adaptation to America was significantly shaped by their shifted proximity to carriers of modernization. Further, it may be the case that their ease or dis-ease with the process was influenced by the degree to which their prior modernization corresponded to the stage of modernization in their new homes.

16. "Detachment seems to be a crucial and basic personality trait of the Norwegian modal personality. . . . Detachment is composed of many characteristic tendencies: the need for privacy, the need for isolation, withdrawal, emotional detachment, rationality, conformity, rigidity, uniqueness, independence, self-sufficiency, avoidance of competition, avoidance of obvious prestige and success, and yet the need for a certain kind of uniqueness and superiority." Christian T. Jonassen, *Value Systems and Personality in a Western Civilization: Norwegians in Europe and America* (Columbus: Ohio State University Press, 1983), p. 289.

CHAPTER ONE

1. The benefits of this approach were demonstrated masterfully and early in Oscar Handlin, *Boston's Immigrants: A Study in Acculturation* (Cambridge: Harvard University Press, 1941).
2. I make use of standard works on the history of Norway throughout this chapter and note these volumes at the beginning of my consideration of a particular figure or topic.
3. B[rynjolf] J[akob] Hovde, *The Scandinavian Countries, 1720-1865: The Rise of the Middle Class*, 2 vols. (Ithaca: Cornell University Press, 1948); Karen Larsen, *A History of Norway* (Princeton: Princeton University Press, 1948).
4. Peter A. Munch, "Authority and Freedom: Controversy in Norwegian-American Congregations" *NASR* 28 (1979):5; see also the work of Scandinavian ethnologists such as Øyvind Østerud, *Agrarian Structure and Peasant Politics in Scandinavia* (Oslo: Universtets forlaget, 1976) and Orvar Löfgren, "Historical Perspectives on Scandinavian Peasantries," *Annual Review of Anthropology* 9 (1980):187-215.
5. Brit Berggreen, course lecture, Norwegian Culture and Society, International Summer School, University of Oslo, Oslo, Norway, 1983.
6. Orvar Löfgren, "Family and Household among Scandinavian Peasants," *Ethnologia Scandinavica* (1974), pp. 20-21.
7. Ibid., p. 28.
8. It should be noted, however, that inheritance patterns varied by region. In sparsely settled areas and those with intricate systems of household production, inheritance tended to be partiable. "In agrarian districts where land was becoming a scarce resource and growing stratification made landowning peasants more anxious to preserve their farm property intact," inheritance was generally impartiable. Ibid., pp. 36-37.
9. Eilert Sundt, *On Marriage in Norway*, trans. Michael Drake (Cambridge: Cambridge University Press, 1980), p. 143.
10. Berggreen, course lecture.
11. Rigmor Frimannslund, "Farm Community and Neighborhood Community," *The Scandinavian Economic History Review* 4 (1956):65.
12. Berggreen, course lecture.
13. Brit Berggreen used the term *mangeysleri* (the multiple occupational system) in "The Female Peasant and the Male Peasant: Division of Labour in Traditional Norway," in *Scandinavian Peasant Ecotypes*, ed. Brit Berggreen (Oslo: University of Oslo International Summer School, 1983), p. 6.
14. Ibid., pp. 10-11.
15. Ibid., p. 12.
16. Frimannslund, "Farm Community and Neighborhood Community," p. 70.
17. Ibid., p. 73.

18. Jon Gjerde, "Peasants to Bourgeoisie: The Migration from Balestrand, Norway to the Upper Middle West" (Ph.D. dissertation, University of Minnesota, 1982), pp. 167, 174, 176-84.
19. Michael Drake, Introduction to Sundt, *On Marriage in Norway*, p. xvi.
20. Hovde, *The Scandinavian Countries*, 2:747.
21. Sundt, *On Marriage in Norway*, pp. 31-47.
22. Hovde, *The Scandinavian Countries*, 1:281, 296, provides figures on the increase of cultivated land.
23. Ibid., 1:289. Orvar Löfgren discusses this process among Swedish marginal peasant households in "Peasant Ecotypes: Problems in the Comparative Study of Ecological Adaptation," *Ethnologia Scandinavica* (1976), pp. 103-8.
24. Löfgren, "Family and Household," p. 26.
25. Ibid., pp. 47-49.
26. Berggreen, course lecture.
27. Karen Larsen, *A History of Norway* (Princeton: Princeton University Press, 1948), p. 432.
28. Karen Larsen, *Ingeborg Astrup Larsen: Her Family and Girlhood in Norway* (Northfield: privately printed, 1958).
29. Hovde, *The Scandinavian Countries*, 2:690.
30. Larsen, *History of Norway*, pp. 446-47.
31. Ibid., pp. 471-72.
32. Ibid., pp. 447-48.
33. Thomas B. Wilson, *History of the Church and State in Norway from the Tenth to the Sixteenth Century* (London: Archibald Constable, 1903), p. 68.
34. K. E. Christopherson, "Hallelujahs, Damnations, or Norway's Reformation as Lengthy Process," *Church History* 48 (September 1979):279-89.
35. Ibid., pp. 287-88.
36. Hovde, *The Scandinavian Countries*, 1:308.
37. Knut Gjerst, *History of the Norwegian People*, 2 vols. (New York: The Macmillian Company, 1915), 2:334.
38. Fevold and Nelson, *Lutheran Church*, 1:30.
39. Ibid., 1:11.
40. Grundtvig (1783-1872) was a Danish theologian who passed through several phases in his religious life and theological development. When Stenersen and Hersleb knew him in Copenhagen he was "on the road back to a Biblical, orthodox, Christianity and a Lutheran confessionalism" that opposed rationalism. The direction of his later development was set by *The Church's Reply* (1825). Grundtvig's "churchly" position asserted that the Apostle's Creed was directly from Jesus and used it as the standard of dogmatic orthodoxy. It highlighted the baptismal covenant rather than conversion. In Norway this position was opposed on the grounds its advocates underestimated the extent of human sinfulness as well as the historical fallacy of its claims for the origin of the Creed. Grundtvig was, however, influential in the folk high school movement in Norway and through his hymns. Einar Molland, *Church Life in*

Norway, 1880-1950, trans. Harris Kaasa (Minneapolis: Augsburg Publishing House, 1957), pp. 26-31, 59-65.
41. Hovde, *The Scandinavian Countries*, 1:306-7.
42. Molland, *Church Life in Norway*, p. 5.
43. Peter A. Munch, "Social Class and Acculturation," in *The Strange American Way: Letters of Caja Munch from Wiota, Wisconsin, 1855-1859*, trans. Helene Munch and Peter A. Munch (Carbondale: Southern Illinois University Press, 1970), p. 203.
44. Nelson, *The Lutherans in North America*, pp. 159-60.
45. Molland, *Church Life in Norway*, p. 39.
46. Fevold and Nelson, *Lutheran Church*, 1:38.
47. Larsen, *History of Norway*, p. 358.
48. Gjerst, *History of the Norwegian People*, 1:139.
49. Ibid., 1:334.
50. Hovde, *The Scandinavian Countries*, 1:311.
51. In the first two decades of the century, 1800-1820, 73% of ordinands were the sons of physicians, bureaucrats, pastors, military officers, or teachers; 3.1% were the sons of fishers or farmers, by far the largest occupational groups. By the end of the century, 1880-1900, the sons of fishers and farmers were 28% of the ordinands. Dagfinn Mannsaker, *Det Norske presteskapet i det 19. hundrearet* (Oslo: Det norske samlaget, 1954), pp. 21, 70, 143-44, cited by Frederick Hale, "The Impact of Kierkegaard's Anticlericalism in Norway," *Studia Theologica* 34 (1980):156.
52. Into the late twentieth century Norway continues to have several standards for its language. Larsen, *History of Norway*, pp. 442-43.

CHAPTER TWO

1. By 1975, after 150 years of immigration, the number of Norwegians who had moved to the United States (855,000) nearly equaled the 1820 population of their home country. Peter A. Munch, "Norwegians," in *Harvard Encyclopedia of American Ethnic Groups*, ed. Stephan Thernstrom (Cambridge: The Belknap Press of Harvard University Press, 1980), pp. 250-51; Carlton C. Qualey and Jon A. Gjerde, "The Norwegians," in *They Chose Minnesota: A Survey of the State's Ethnic Groups*, ed. June Drenning Holmquist (St. Paul: Minnesota Historical Society, 1981), pp. 220-21.
2. Semmingsen, Ingrid, "Norwegian Immigration to America during the Nineteenth Century," *NASR* 11 (1940):69.
3. Sundt, *On Marriage in Norway*, p. 39.
4. The number of persons aged twenty to thirty increased by one-third in the decade between 1835 and 1845, while the total population increased by one-tenth. Blegen, *Norwegian Migration to America*, p. 166.
5. Semmingsen, "Norwegian Immigration," p. 71.

6. Ibid., pp. 75-77.
7. Blegen, *Norwegian Migration to America*, pp. 98, 169.
8. Carleton C. Qualey, *Norwegian American Settlement* (Northfield: Norwegian-American Historical Association, 1938), p. 204.
9. Jacob Neumann, "A Word of Admonition to the Peasants," trans. and ed. Gunnar J. Malmin, *NASR* 1 (1926):108-9.
10. Qualey, *Norwegian Settlement*, pp. 209-212.
11. Both Reiersen and Waerenskjold were temperance advocates in Norway. Reiersen published a monthly paper, *Norge og Amerika*, promoting immigration. After he left for the United States, Tvede served as editor until she herself went to Texas, where she married William Waerenskjold. Her career is recorded in Elise Waerenskjold, *Lady with the Pen: Elise Waerenskjold in Texas*, ed. C. A. Clausen (Northfield: Norwegian-American Historical Association, 1961; reprint ed., New York: Arno Press, 1979).
12. Qualey, *Norwegian Settlement*, pp. 214-38.
13. Semmingsen, "Norwegian Immigration," p. 80.
14. Ingrid Semmingsen, *Norway to America: A History of the Migration*, trans. Einar Haugen (Minneapolis: University of Minnesota Press, 1978), p. 61.
15. A careful survey of the development of various settlements may be found in Qualey, *Norwegian Settlement*, pp. 14-15 and *passim*.
16. U.S., Congress, Senate. Report of the Immigration Commission, S. Doc. 338, 61st Cong., 2nd sess., 1911, Serial no. 5665, vol. 1, table 19, p. 145.
17. Qualey, *Norwegian Settlement*, p. 109.
18. Gjerde, "Peasants to Bourgeoisie"; Robert Ostergren, "A Community Transplanted: The Formative Experience of a Swedish Immigrant Community in the Upper Middle West," *Journal of Historical Geography* 5 (1979):189-212; and John G. Rice, *Patterns of Ethnicity in a Minnesota County, 1880-1905* (Umea, 1973).
19. Marjorie M. Kimmerle, "Norwegian-American Surnames," *NASR* 12 (1941):1-32.
20. Einar Haugen, "Language and Immigration," *NASR* 10 (1930):22-34 and *The Norwegian Language in America*.
21. Fevold and Nelson, *Lutheran Church*, 1: 242.
22. Eugene L. Fevold, "The Norwegian Immigrant and His Church," *NASR* 23 (1967):8.
23. Ibid., p. 12. The 1916 federal census shows the following premerger membership: Hauge Synod, 29,893; Eielsen, 1,206; Norwegian Synod, 112,673; Lutheran Free Church, 28,180; United Church, 176,084; Brethren, 892. If all of the members of the three merging groups had joined the new church, which they did not, it membership would have been 318,650 to a combined total of the others of 30,278. The respective percentages would have been 91.3 and 8.6.
24. Fevold and Nelson, *Lutheran Church*, 1:100.

25. The Four Points drawn up by Dietrichson and signed by the members of the East and West Koshkonong congregations were:

1. Do you desire to become a member of the Norwegian Lutheran congregation in this place?

2. Will you to that end subject yourself to the church order that the Ritual of the Church of Norway prescribes?

3. Will you promise that you shall not call or accept any other minister and pastor than such as can clearly establish according to the Norwegian Lutheran Church Order that he is a regularly called and rightly consecrated pastor? And will you show the pastor thus called by you and the congregation to spiritual leadership the attention and obedience that a member of a congregation owes to his pastor in all things that he requires and does according to the Ritual of the Church of Norway?

4. Will you, by signing your name or by permitting it to be signed, here make acknowledgment that you have joined the congregation on the above-named conditions?

Ibid., 1:105.

26. J[ohan] C[arl] K[eyser] Preus, "From Norwegian State Church to American Free Church," *NASR* 25 (1972):187.

27. Ibid., p. 215.

28. Ibid., pp. 190-91.

29. Dietrichson, September 25, 1844, cited by Theodore Blegen, *Land of Their Choice: The Immigrants Write Home* (Minneapolis: The University of Minnesota Press, 1955), p. 138.

30. Preus, "From Norwegian State Church to American Free Church," p. 211.

31. Jon N. Bjørndalen, 5 January 1844, cited by Blegen, *Land of Their Choice*, p. 185.

32. Fevold and Nelson, *Lutheran Church*, 2:95.

33. Koren, *Diary*, pp. 118-19.

34. Anniversary History, Bear Creek Lutheran, Grand Meadow, Minnesota, American Lutheran Church Archive (hereafter ALC Archive), St. Paul, Minnesota. This is now the archive for Region 3 of the Evangelical Lutheran Church in America.

35. Nina Draxten, *Kristofer Janson in America* (Boston: Twayne Publishers, 1976), pp. 187-88.

36. Fevold and Nelson, *Lutheran Church*, 2:95-96.

37. Fiftieth Anniversary History, Hawley Lutheran, Hawley, Minnesota, ALC Archive.

38. J. C. K. Preus, ed., *Norsemen Found a Church: An Old Heritage in a New Land* (Minneapolis: Augsburg Publishing House, 1953), pp. 298-304.

39. *Kirkelig maanedstidende* 9 (June and September 1864):191, cited by B. H. Narveson, "The Norwegian Lutheran Academies," *NASR* 14 (1944):191.

40. Preus, *Norsemen Found a Church*, p. 151.

41. I. F. Grosse, "The Beginnings of St. Olaf College," *NASR* 5 (1930):115.

42. Odd Lovell, *The Promise of America: A History of the Norwegian-American People* (Minneapolis: University of Minnesota Press, 1984), p. 67.
43. Frank S. Nelsen, "The School Controversy and Norwegian Immigrants," *NASR* 26 (1974):206-19; Laurence M. Larson, "Skandinaven, Professor Anderson, and the Yankee School," in *The Changing West* (Northfield: Norwegian-American Historical Association, 1937), pp. 116-20; Narveson, "The Norwegian Lutheran Academies."
44. Fevold and Nelson, *Lutheran Church*, 1:291.
45. Ibid., 2:109-12; Elizabeth Fedde, "Diary, 1883-38," trans. and ed. Beulah Folkedahl, *NASR* 20 (1959):170-96.
46. Fevold and Nelson, *Lutheran Church*, 2:103.

CHAPTER THREE

1. John Lindas, in Beulah Folkedahl, trans. and ed., "Norwegians Become American," *NASR* 21 (1962):131-32.
2. Søren Bache and Johannes Johansen, 1839, in Blegen, ed., *Land of Their Choice*, p. 69.
3. Anders Wiig, Brynnild Leqve, and Johannes Wiig, in Blegen, *Land of Their Choice*, p. 76.
4. Gro Svendsen, *Frontier Mother: The Letters of Gro Svendsen*, trans. and ed. Pauline Farseth and Theodore C. Blegen (Northfield: Norwegian-American Historical Association, 1950), p. 28.
5. Svend Svenssen and Grui Sanders-datter, February 1860, in Blegen, *Land of Their Choice*, p. 69.
6. J. R. Christianson, "Literary Traditions of Norwegian-American Women," in *Makers of an American Immigration Legacy*, ed. Odd S. Lovoll (Northfield: Norwegian-American Historical Association, 1980), pp. 92-110.
7. Svendsen, *Frontier Mother*, p. 8.
8. Elizabeth Hampsten, *Read this Only to Yourself: The Private Writings of Midwestern Women, 1880-1910* (Bloomington: Indiana University Press, 1982), p. 15. Hampsten also discusses the notion of writing at "close range" in which women's private writings appear to be detached from specific localities or regions. She contends that women's writings yield few clues to the place in which they were written, as they focus on the women's close range experiences.
9. Martha Reishus, *The Rag Rug* (New York: Vantage Press, Inc., 1955), p. 34.
10. Erna Oleson Xan, *Wisconsin, My Home: The Story of Thurine Oleson as Told to Her Daughter* (Madison: The University of Wisconsin Press, 1950), p. 23.
11. Ibid., p. 25.
12. Svendsen, *Frontier Mother*, pp. 13-14.
13. Ibid., p. 19.
14. Preus, *Linka's Diary*, p. 183.
15. Koren, *Diary*, p. 38.

16. Many of Linka Koren's sketches are housed in the Luther College Library in Decorah, Iowa. Gracia Grindal, "An Immigrant Woman Views Niagara" and "The Americanization of Norwegian Pastors' Wives," papers, Decorah, Iowa, n.d.
17. Preus, *Linka's Diary*, p. 151.
18. Ibid., p. 175.
19. Munch, *The Strange American Way*, p. 7.
20. Preus, *Linka's Diary*, p. 183.
21. Blegen, *Land of their Choice*, pp. 390-91.
22. Endre Endresen Eidsvaage in Folkedahl, "Norwegians Become American," *NASR* 21 (1962): 107.
23. Olaf Morgan Norlie, *Ho Ga Te Me: A Centennial Sketch of Martha Karolina (Juel) Norlie, 1846-1918, a Norwegian-American Pioneer* (Northfield: Eilron Mimeopress, 1946), p. 25.
24. Munch, *Strange American Way*, p. 13.
25. Gunhild Andrine Jacobsdatter, Papers 210, Norwegian American Historical Association Archive (hereafter NAHA Archive), Northfield, Minnesota.
26. Svendsen, *Frontier Mother*, p. 24.
27. Erling Ylvisaker, *Eminent Pioneers: Norwegian-American Pioneer Sketches* (Minneapolis: Augsburg Publishing House, 1934; reprint ed. Freeport, N.Y.: Books for Libraries Press, 1970), pp. 1-2 and Joseph Dorfman, *Thorstein Veblen and His America* (New York: The Viking Press, 1934).
28. L. DeAne Lagerquist, "Grace Abbott and the Secularization of Social Wefare," University of Chicago, 1982, p. 6.
29. Personal conversation with Judith Nord.
30. Guri Oldsdatter (Endreson) and Henrietta Jessen in Theodore Blegen, ed., "Immigrant Women and the American Frontier: Three Early 'America Letters,' " *NASR* 4 (1929):23, 29.
31. Svendsen, *Frontier Mother*, pp. 85-86.
32. Xan, *Wisconsin*, p. 30.
33. Koren, *Diary*, p. 107.
34. Mrs. Assur H. Groth cited in Knut Gjerset and Ludvig Hektoen, "Health Conditions and the Practice of Medicine Among the Early Norwegian Settlers, 1825-1865," *NASR* 1 (1926): 11.
35. Brandt, "Social Aspects of Prairie Pioneering," p. 15.
36. Svendsen, *Frontier Mother*, p. 72.
37. Mary Syverson Torbenson, Papers 389, NAHA Archive.
38. Ole S. Johnson, *Nybyggerhistorie fra Spring Grove og omegn* (Minneapolis: n.p., 1920), pp. 103-5, cited in Carleton C. Qualey, "A Typical Norwegian Settlement: Spring Grove, Minnesota," *NASR* 9 (1936):60-61.
39. For an extensive discussion of immigrant furnishings see Marion J. Nelson, "The Material Culture and Folk Arts of the Norwegians in America," in *Perspectives on American Folk Art*, ed. Ian M. G. Quimby and Scott T. Swank (n.p.: Winterthur Museum, 1980), pp. 79-133.

40. Svendsen, *Frontier Mother*, p. 39.
41. Mathilde Berg Grevstad, Papers 746, NAHA Archive.
42. Reishus, *Rag Rug*, p. 121.
43. Xan, *Wisconsin*, pp. 102-3.
44. Svendsen, *Frontier Mother*, pp. 53-54.
45. Aagot Raaen, *Grass of the Earth: Immigrant Life in the Dakota Country* (Northfield: Norwegian-American Historical Association, 1950), pp. 10-11.
46. Eva Thortvedt, Oral History, No. S707, Northwest Minnesota Historical Center, Moorhead State University, Moorhead, Minnesota.
47. Levorsen, "Our Bread and Meat," p. 196.
48. Barbara Levorsen, *The Quiet Conquest* (Hawley, Minnesota: The Hawley Herald, 1974), p. 75.
49. Preus, *Linka's Diary*, p. 262.
50. Works Project Administration (hereafter WPA), Manuscripts, box 171, Minnesota Historical Society, St. Paul, Minnesota.
51. Ylvisaker, *Eminent Pioneers*, pp. 43-44.
52. Hannah Harris, Oral History, No. S770, Northwest Minnesota Historical Center.
53. Guri Olsdatter (Endreson Rosseland) in Blegen, "Immigrant Women," pp. 26-29; Lovoll, *The Promise of America*, pp. 86-91.
54. Mathilde Berg Grevstad, Papers 746, NAHA Archive.
55. Martha Hove Hougstad, Papers 174, NAHA Archive.
56. Henrietta Jessen in Blegen, "Immigrant Women and the American Frontier," pp. 14-29.
57. Reishus, *Rag Rug*, p. 66.
58. Mrs. Assur H. Groth, cited in Gjerset and Hektoen, "Health Conditions," p. 11.
59. Mary Syverson Torbenson, Papers 389, NAHA Archive.
60. Bolette Marie Stub Bergh, Papers 38, NAHA Archive.
61. Svendsen, *Frontier Mother*, August 1, 1869, p. 98.
62. Ibid., p. 136.
63. Monys Ann Hagen, "Norwegian Pioneer Women: Ethnicity on the Wisconsin Agricultural Frontier" (M.A. thesis, University of Wisconsin, Madision, 1984), p. 53.
64. See similar photographs in Michael Lesy, *Wisconsin Death Trip* (New York: Pantheon Books, 1973).
65. Julie Roy Jeffrey, *Frontier Women: The Trans-Mississippi West, 1840-1880* (New York: Hill and Wang, 1979), p. xv.
66. Martha Hove Hougstad, Papers 174, NAHA Archive.
67. Women's Missionary Federation of the Evangelical Lutheran Church, *Some Marthas and Marys of the N.L.C.A.: Life Sketches of Pioneer Lutheran Women First in their Field*, Ser. 1 (Minneapolis: Augsburg, n.d.), p. 26.
68. Preus, *Linka's Diary*, April 1, 1850, pp. 83-84.
69. Ibid., April 11, 1850, pp. 84-85.
70. Ibid., September 15, 1850, p. 105.
71. Ibid., September 24, 1850, p. 107.

72. Ibid., p. 194.
73. Anniversary History, Cross of Christ Lutheran, Houston, Minnesota, ALC Archive.
74. Dr. G. H. Stub, *"Fra fars og mors liv,"* (1907), p. 27.
75. Ibid.
76. Blegen, *Land of their Choice*, January 8, 1856, p. 376.
77. "Pioneer Pastors' Wives Scrapbook," 2 vols., Women's Missionary Federation Papers (hereafter WMF), ALC Archive.
78. Preus, *Norsemen Found a Church*, pp. 73-74.
79. Munch, *Strange American Way*, December 21, 1856, p. 55.
80. Ibid., February 13, 1857, p. 71.
81. Ibid., p. 49.
82. Clara Jacobson, "Memories from Perry Parsonage" *NASR* 14 (1944):142.
83. Karen Larsen, *Laur. Larsen: Pioneer College President* (Northfield: Norwegian-American Historical Association, 1936), p. 82.
84. Koren, *Diary*, January 28, 1855, p. 354.
85. Ibid., p. 143.
86. Ibid., p. 174.
87. Fredrika Bremer, *The Homes of the New World: Impressions of America*, 2 vols., trans. Mary Howitt (New York: Harper and Brothers, Publishers, 1853), 2:632-33.
88. Koren, *Diary*, June 16, 1854, p. 240.
89. "Scrapbook," WMF, ALC Archive.
90. Mrs. Gisle Bothne in "Scrapbook," WMF, ALC Archive.
91. Marie Lee, "Memories of Koshkonong Parsonage," "Scrapbook," WMF, ALC Archive.
92. A partial list of interrelationships includes the following: A. C. Preus and H. A. Preus were cousins; G. F. Dietrichson was a cousin of J. W. C. Dietrichson's father and his wife Pauline was A. C. Preus's sister; Nils Brandt married into the Otteson family, as did Lauritz Larsen in his second marriage. Brandt's sister, Elizabeth Lomen, was a part of the Luther College community, where she served as the first housekeeper. Caja Munch and Elisabeth Koren had known each other as young girls near Larvik, Norway. Karen Larsen's sister, Henriette Neuberg, became a beloved friend and companion to Linka Preus and was often resident in the Spring Prairie parsonage. The Neuberg sisters—Karen, Henriette, and Karine—were favorites of Rev. J. A. Otteson, who valued their sensitiveness to the graces of life and Karen's "fresh, unconventional approach even to serious matters and a whimsical mode of expression." Larsen, *Laur. Larsen*, p. 105.
93. This drawing is printed in Leigh D. Jordahl, "The Gentry Tradition—Men and Women of a Leadership Class," in Lutz, *Church Roots*, p. 113.
94. Blegen, *Land of Their Choice*, p. 384.
95. Caroline Mathilde Koren Naeseth, "Memories from Little Iowa Parsonage," trans. Henriette Caroline Koren Naeseth, *NASR* 13 (1943):72.
96. Stub, *"Fra fars og mors liv,"* p. 36.

97. J. Magnus Rohne, *Norwegian Lutheranism up to 1872* (New York: The Macmillian Company, 1926), p. 74.
98. Munch, *Strange American Way*, pp. 29-30.
99. Alfred Erickson, "Scandinavia, Wisconsin," *NASR* 15 (1949):194-96.
100. Stub, *"Fra fars og mors liv,"* pp. 31-32.
101. Koren, *Diary*, p. 103.
102. Ibid., pp. 121-22.
103. Mrs. L. Larsen pamphlet (1927), in "Scrapbook," WMF, ALC Archive.
104. Preus, *Norsemen Found a Church*, p. 373.
105. Based on her study of prescriptive literature, Barbara Welter identified the cult of true womanhood, a set of ideals for nineteenth-century American women. The four cardinal virtues were piety, purity, submissiveness, and domesticity. With these characteristics a woman was equipped to fullfil her primary responsibilities as wife and mother, which included providing a safe home and teaching her children her values. Barbara Welter, "The Cult of True Womanhood, 1820-1860," in *Dimity Convictions* (Athens: Ohio University Press, 1976), pp. 83-102.

Sherry Ortner makes a similar point from an anthropological perspective in "Is Female to Male as Nature is to Culture?" in Michelle Zimbalist Rosaldo and Louise Lamphere, eds. *Women, Culture and Society* (Stanford: Stanford University Press, 1974), pp. 67-88. Ortner argues that women are the mediators of culture whose task it is to socialize the young into their culture.

Although it appears some decades after Brandt's career, a newspaper summary of Miss Norma Thronson's address, "Woman and Her Sphere," given in 1911 at her commencement from Lutheran Ladies' Seminary, suggested this ideal: "The speaker recognized the claims and demands that were being made upon woman's time and energies in these strenuous times when her power and influence were obtaining larger appreciation than the world had heretofore given them. . . . Notwithstanding all these, Miss Thronson insisted that woman's greatest, noblest and most natural sphere was as a homekeeper and character builder. She emphasized the value of the newer educational ideas which would fit the girl more definitely for the arduous duties of a common but devoted domestic life. Cooking, housekeeping, dressmaking, and kindred training had the possibilities of culture in them as well as languages. She closed with a eulogy of home and woman as its queen, inspiring the husband as the breadwinner and caring for and training the children who bless it." Lutheran Ladies' Seminary, Goodhue County Historical Society, Red Wing, Minnesota.
106. Mrs. L. Larsen pamphlet (1927).
107. This notion is also discussed briefly in Jordahl, "The Gentry Tradition," pp. 108-14.
108. Among these women was Anna Reque Böe, born in Wisconsin in 1849, educated at Albion Academy, and married to Rev. N. E. Böe in 1870; Marie Olson Anderson (b. 1854, m. 1874), wife of Rasmus B. Anderson's clergyman brother Abel and sister of Ramus's wife; Inanda Amalie Torrison Bredesen (b. 1857, m. 1878), first president of *Prestekoneforening* (Pastors' Wives' Society);

Mary Francis Lehman Rasmussen (b. 1858, m. 1883), daughter of the president of the Ohio Synod and Capital University and of German descent; and Indianna Olsin Hjetaas (b. 1858, m. 1885), who had been baptized by Pastor Stub in Muskego.

109. Some of the marriages contracted in the second generation were as follows: Louise Augusta (Lulla) Hjort married Christian Keyser Preus; Maren Pauline Ovidia (Linka) Hjort married Johan William Preus; Didrikka Otteson married H. G. Stub; Mathilde Stub married Hans B. Thorgrimsen; Bolette Stub married J. E. Bergh; Elisabeth C. H. Stub married Knut Seehus; Agnes Preus married Daniel Kvasse; Pauline (Sina) Preus married J. Nordby; Caroline M. Koren married C. A. T. Naeseth; Elisabeth Koren married I. B. Torrison, whose sister, Inanda A. Torrison Bredesen was married to a clergyman; Rolf O. Brandt married Thalette Galby; Olaf Brandt married Emma Louise Galby. In the third generation the connections were again reinforced.

110. The activites of pastors' wives in congregational women's societies is further considered in Chapter Four.

111. Bolette Marie Stub Bergh, "Memoirs," trans. O. O. Enestvedt, *Sacred Heart News*, 1, 8, 15 June, 1944, Papers 38, NAHA Archive.

112. Brandt, "Social Aspects of Prairie Pioneering," p. 23.

113. Lydia Bredesen Sundby, "Parsonage Memories—Stoughton, Wisconsin," 1959, WMF, ALC Archive.

114. Svendsen, *Frontier Mother*, p. 56.

115. Nellie S. Johnson Houkom, Papers 173, NAHA Archive; Qualey, *Norwegian American Settlement*, pp. 72-73.

116. *St. Paul Daily Pioneer*, 3 July 1866, WPA Manuscripts, box 171.

117. How long this practice continued in the Midwest is not clear. Other options such as teaching school may have been more attractive to American-born women. In the Pacific Northwest second-generation Norwegian-American women were less likely to work as domestic servants than were their mothers. Janice Reiff Webster, "Domestication and Americanization: Scandinavian Women in Seattle, 1888-1900," *Journal of Urban History* 4 (1975):275-90.

118. Lovoll, *The Promise of America*, p. 167.

119. Anniversary History, Round Prarie Lutheran, Glenville, Minnesota, ALC Archive.

120. *Fergus Falls Journal*, 15 October, 19 and 26 November 1880, Otter Tail County Historical Society.

121. *Minnesota*, 17 January 1872, trans. Alvar Norbeck, WPA Manuscripts, box 171.

122. WPA Manuscripts, box 171.

123. Lovoll, *The Promise of America*, p. 88.

124. Mrs. Ella Lindhjem, "Homesteading in North Dakota," *Souvenir: Norse-American Women, 1825-1925* (Minneapolis: The Lutheran Free Church Publishing Co., 1926), p. 424.

125. Ibid., pp. 425-26.

126. Joan N. Buckely, "Martha Ostenso: A Norwegian-American Immigrant Novelist," *NASR* 28 (1979):69-81.

127. Svendsen, *Frontier Mother*, p. 27.
128. Ibid., p. 134.
129. Personal conversation with Dagney Nord Larson.
130. Larsen, *Laur. Larsen*, p. 287.
131. Ibid., pp. 114-55.
132. Ibid., p. 150.
133. Ibid., p. 120.
134. A large collection of glass slides of pastors' families taken in this period are housed in the ALC Archive.
135. Svendsen, *Frontier Mother*, p. 10.
136. Ibid., p. 9.
137. Aagot Raaen, *Grass of the Earth*, p. 126.
138. Brandt, "Social Aspects of Prairie Pioneering," pp. 25-26.
139. *Fergus Falls Journal*, 3 March 1910, Otter Tail County Historical Society.
140. Xan, *Wisconsin*, p. 128.
141. Ibid., p. 130.
142. Ibid., pp. 188-90.
143. Draxten, *Kristofer Jansen in America*, p. 360.
144. Gracia Grindal, "Three Vignettes and an Idea," Paper, Decorah, Iowa, n.d., pp. 28-30.
145. Eva Lund Haugen and Einar Haugen, eds. and trans., *Land of the Free: Bjørnstjerne Bjørnson's America Letters, 1880-1881* (Northfield: Norwegian-American Historical Association, 1978), p. 269.
146. *Amerika*, n.d. [1902-22?], trans. C. Jacobsen, St. Olaf College Archive, Northfield, Minnesota.
147. Draxten, *Kristofer Jansen in America*, p. 269.
148. J. C. K. Preus to E. W. Sihler, 1965, typescript of conversation in ALC Archive.
149. Gjerde, "Peasants to Bourgeoisie."
150. Ibid., pp. 329-39.
151. Löfgren, "Family and Household."
152. Robert Ostergren, "A Community Transplanted: The Formative Experience of a Swedish Immigrant Community in the Upper Middle West," *Journal of Historical Geography* 5 (1979):189-212; John G. Rice, *Patterns of Ethnicity in a Minnesota County, 1880-1905* (Umea, 1973).
153. Gjerde, "Peasants to Bourgeoisie," pp. 240-49.
154. Richard M. Bernard, *The Melting Pot and the Altar* (Minneapolis: University of Minnesota Press, 1980), p. 117.
155. Douglas Marshal, "Nationality and Emerging Culture," *Rural Sociology* 13 (March 1948):40-47; Evon Z. Vogt, "Social Stratification in the Rural Midwest: A Structural Analysis," *Rural Sociology* 12 (December 1947):364-75.
156. Marshal, "Nationality and Emerging Culture," p. 43.
157. Kimmerle, "Norwegian-American Surnames," p. 20 and *passim*.
158. Gjerde, "Peasants to Bourgeoisie," p. 351.
159. Ibid., pp. 361-74.

160. Ibid., pp. 375-76.

CHAPTER FOUR

1. Within the study of American women and religion these foci are evident along with a concern for reform movements. See for example Barbara Leslie Epstein, *The Politics of Domesticity: Women, Evangelism, and Temperance in Nineteenth Century America* (Middletown: Wesleyan University Press, 1981); Mary Farrell Bednarowski, "Outside the Mainstream: Women's Religion and Women Religious Leaders in Nineteenth-Century America," *Journal of the American Academy of Religion* 48 (1979):207-31; Lawrence Foster, *Religion and Sexuality: The Shakers, the Mormons, and the Oneida Community* (Urbana: University of Illinois Press, 1984); Janet Wilson James, ed., *Women in American Religion* (Philadelphia: University of Pennsylvania Press, 1980); Amanda Porterfield, *Feminine Spirituality in America: From Sarah Edwards to Martha Graham* (Philadelphia: Temple University Press, 1980); and Rosemary Radford Ruether and Rosemary Skinner Keller, eds., *Women and Religion in America*, 2 vols. (San Francisco: Harper and Row, 1981 and 1983).
2. Edna Hong, *The Book of a Century: The Centennial History of St. John's Lutheran Church, Northfield, Minnesota* (n.p., [1969]), p. 9.
3. Martha Hove Hougstad, papers 174, NAHA Archive.
4. Mathilde Berg Grevstad, papers 746, NAHA Archive.
5. *The Book of Concord*, trans. and ed. Theodore G. Tappert (Philadelphia: Fortress Press, 1959), p. 362.
6. Johan Carl Keyser Preus, *Herman Amberg Preus: A Family History* (n. p.: The Preus Family Book Club, 1966), p. 122.
7. Munch, *The Strange American Way*, p. 91.
8. Svendsen, *Frontier Mother*, p. 33.
9. Preus, *Linka's Diary*, pp. 184-85.
10. Mary Godley Starr Cheston, "Seedtime at Ullman," 1902, Northwest Minnesota History Center, Moorhead, Minnesota. Cheston recorded Pastor Kvitrud's words as they were related to her by one of the Norwegians: "Behold the winter is past, the rain is over and gone. The fruit tree puts forth her green leaves and the vines with the young grapes give a good smell. You have honored your Heavenly Father and obeyed His commandment, and have come up into the house of the Lord. You have shown that you have not forgotten Him. Neither will He forget you. Go now, my people, and work in your fields. Put in your seed today as fast as you can, for the ground is ready at last. Seed wheat today, and pray the Lord of the harvest to grant increase, that rain may be withheld until all the seed is underground. Work speedily, and with thankfulness in your hearts, and in due season ye shall reap if ye faint not."
11. Mathilde Berg Grevstad, papers 746, NAHA Archive.
12. Preus, *Linka's Diary*, p. 217.

13. Koren, *Diary*, pp. 119, 360-61.
14. Munch, *Strange American Way*, p. 23.
15. Svendsen, *Frontier Mother*, p. 34.
16. Anniversary History, Central Freeborn Lutheran Church, Clark's Grove, Minnesota, ALC Archive.
17. Abraham Brandt, "A Pioneer Pastor's Journey to Dakota in 1861," *NASR* 6 (1931), p. 58.
18. Reishus, *Rag Rug*, pp. 108-9.
19. Mrs. Rueben Tollefson, WMF, ALC Archive.
20. Svendsen, *Frontier Mother*, p. 33.
21. Anniversary History, Salem Lutheran Church, Hitterdahl, Minnesota, ALC Archive.
22. Anniversary Histories, Good Shepherd Lutheran Church, Appleton, Minnesota, and Hegland Lutheran Church, Hawley, Minnesota, ALC Archive.
23. Anniversary History, Tonseth Lutheran Church, Erhard, Minnesota, ALC Archive.
24. Anniversary History, Lime Creek Lutheran Church, Emmons, Minnesota, ALC Archive.
25. In 1897 the women of Jackson Lake Lutheran purchased a painting of the Last Supper by Sarah Rougland, a Norwegian-American artist, for $50.00. Rougland's work was found in other congregations as well. Anniversary History, Jackson Lake Lutheran, Amboy, Minnesota, ALC Archive.
26. Svendsen, *Frontier Mother*, pp. 73, 120.
27. Preus, *Linka's Diary*, p. 216.
28. Editor Wheaton, *Rice County Journal*, 17 November 1881, cited by Hong, *The Book of a Century*, pp. 26-28.
29. Ylvisaker, *Eminent Pioneers*, p. 19.
30. This is based on a survey of the records of the following Lutheran congregations: Norway Grove in DeForest; Sun Prairie in rural Madison; Marshall, Primrose, Christ, and First in Stoughton; First in Whitewater and Wiota, Wisconsin; Trinity and Our Savior's in Benson; Trinity in Minneapolis; Sverdrup in Underwood, Minnesota.
31. Anniversary History, Greenfield Lutheran Church, Harmony, Minnesota, ALC Archive.
32. Xan, *Wisconsin, My Home*, pp. 66-69.
33. Munch, *Strange American Way*, p. 27.
34. Koren, *Diary*, p. 356.
35. Anniversary History, Grace Lutheran Church, Ada, Minnesota, ALC Archive.
36. Preus, *Linka's Diary*, pp. 274-75.
37. Henry Holloway, *The Norwegian Rite: Translated into English* (London: Arthur H. Stockwell, Ltd., 1934), pp. 155-57.
38. Anniversary History, Salem Lutheran Church, Hitterdahl, Minnesota, ALC Archive.
39. Anniversary History, Grace Lutheran Church.

40. *The Hauge Movement in America* (Minneapolis: The Lutheran Free Church Publishing Company, 1941), pp. 81-82.
41. Ibid., pp. 96-97. Ingerid Meningen's experience in moving from the Haugean pietists of Norway to the more staid Norwegian Synod is illuminated by Ruether and McLaughlin's thesis that religious groups that confer authority on the basis of spiritual gifts rather than official office are more likely to allow women positions of influence. Rosemary Radford Ruether and Eleanor McLaughlin, *Women of Spirit: Female Leadership in the Jewish and Christian Traditions* (New York: Simon and Schuster, 1979), pp. 19-20.
42. Raaen, *Grass of the Earth*, pp. 160-65.
43. Anniversary History, Waterloo Ridge Lutheran Church, Dorchester, Minnesota, ALC Archive.
44. Unmarried, confirmed persons were likely to have been hired out to work on farms or in the homes of local Yankee families. The differences in suggested contributions undoubtedly reflect the differences in earning power. Anniversary History, Round Prairie Lutheran Church, Glenville, Minnesota, ALC Archive.
45. Svendsen, *Frontier Mother*, p. 51.
46. Ibid., pp. 148-49.
47. Koren, *Diary*, p. 192.
48. Anniversary History, Solem Lutheran, Hawley, Minnesota, ALC Archive.
49. Based on survey of the records of several congregations. See note 30.
50. Xan, *Wisconsin*, pp. 94, 96-97.
51. Mrs. Emman Bonhus, "Our Churches of Yesterday," 1943, WMF, box 11, ALC Archive.
52. Levorsen, *The Quiet Conquest*, pp. 13-14.
53. Bolette Marie Stub Bergh, "Memoirs," translated by O. O. Enestvedt in *Sacred Heart News*, Sacred Heart, Minnesota, 8 June 1944, papers 38, NAHA Archive.
54. See photograh in Lovoll, *The Promise of America*, p. 64.
55. Holloway, *The Norwegian Rite*, p. 61.
56. Marie Lee, "Memories of Koshkonong Parsonage," "Pioneer Pastors' Wives Scrapbook," 2 vols., WMF, ALC Archive.
57. Anniversary History, East and West Zion Lutheran Church, Hancock, Minnesota, ALC Archive.
58. Jennie Vennerström Cannon, *Watershed Drama: Battle Lake, Minnesota* (Berkeley: privately printed, 1943), p. 37.
59. Raaen, *Grass of the Earth*, p. 238.
60. Preus, *Linka's Diary*, p. 113.
61. Ibid.
62. Ibid., p. 231.
63. Ibid., p. 255.
64. Ibid., pp. 258, 269.
65. Ibid., p. 252.
66. Ibid., p. 267.
67. Ibid., p. 149.
68. Ibid., pp. 224-26.

69. Ibid., pp. 271-72.
70. Ibid., p. 274.
71. Ibid., p. 267.
72. E. Koren to L. Preus, March 16, 1856, trans. Gracia Grindal.
73. Preus, *Linka's Diary*, p. 27.
74. Ibid., p. 266.
75. Ibid., p. 211.
76. Ibid., pp. 231-32.
77. Ibid., p. 215.
78. Svendsen, *Frontier Mother*, p. 123.
79. Ibid., p. 116.
80. Ibid., p. 130.
81. Ibid., p. 121.
82. Ibid., p. 42.
83. Ibid., pp. 31, 33.
84. Ibid., p. 120.
85. Ibid., p. 129.
86. This discussion of Karine Neuburg draws upon Gracia Grindal, "The Americanization of Norwegian Pastors' Wives," paper, Decorah, Iowa, n.d. and an unpublished opera libretto based on Karine Neuburg's life, also by Grindal.
87. Elizabeth to Rasmus Anderson, December 27, 1862 cited by Lloyd Hustvedt, *Rasmus Bjørn Anderson: Pioneer Scholar* (Northfield: Norwegian-American Historical Association, 1966), pp. 25-26.
88. Mrs. Harry Ranger, no. OH 69, Otter Tail County Historical Society.
89. Draxten, *Kristofer Janson in America*, pp. 283-84.
90. Ibid., p. 55.
91. James Gustafson, *Theocentric Ethics* (Chicago: The University of Chicago Press, 1981), 1:201; Martin Luther, "Preface to The Small Catechism" in *The Book of Concord*, ed. and trans. Theodore G. Tappert (Philadelphia: Fortress Press, 1959), p. 338.
92. For an account of the ongoing work of these groups see Lagerquist, *From Our Mothers' Arms*.
93. Anniversary History, Vang Lutheran Church, Dennison, Minnesota, ALC Archive.
94. Nellie S. Johnson Houkom, Papers 173, NAHA Archive.
95. Louise Torgerson, 1941, Bethel Lutheran Church, Madison, Wisconsin, WMF, box 22, ALC Archive.
96. Mrs. C. A. Ericson, "The Spring Prairie Ladies Aid," WMF, box 22, ALC Archive.
97. Mrs. M. O. Wee, "Reminiscences," WMF, box 11, ALC Archive.
98. Anniversary History, Red Oak Grove Lutheran Church, Austin, Minnesota, ALC Archive.
99. Levorsen, *The Quiet Conquest*, p. 111.
100. Anniversary History, First (Ness) Lutheran Church, Elbow Lake, Minnesota, ALC Archive.

101. Christie Monson, "Interview with charter member of Ladies' Aid (Mrs. Belle Nelson)," n.d., WMF, ALC Archive.
102. Lois Paulson Moe (Mrs. Engolf M.), Madison Circuit Historian, WMF, box 22, ALC Archive.
103. Nellie S. Johnson, papers 173, NAHA Archive.
104. Lydia Bredson, "Forty Years as a W.M.F.," *Women's Missionary Messenger* 23 (July-August 1957):4-5.
105. Mrs. K. J. Hanson, "Beginnings," 1947, WMF, box 2, ALC Archive.
106. Anniversary History, Hawley Lutheran Church, Hawley, Minnesota, ALC Archive.
107. *Marshall A.L.C.W. History and Cookbook* (Little Cedar Lutheran Church), Adams, Minnesota, ALC Archive.
108. Mrs. Emil Thorstad, Deerfield Ladies' Aid, WMF, box 22, ALC Archive.
109. Anniversary History, St. Paul's English Lutheran Church, Preston, Minnesota, ALC Archive.
110. Mrs. Lorraine B. Carlson, Anniversary History, St. John's Lutheran Church, Northfield, Minnesota, ALC Archive.
111. WMF, box 22, ALC Archive.
112. Anniversary History, Red Oak Grove Lutheran Church, Austin, Minnesota, ALC Archive.
113. Fergus Falls Circuit, WMF, box 31, ALC Archive.
114. *Marshall ALCW History and Cookbook.*
115. *Fifty-fifth Anniversary West Crow River Ladies' Aid*, Belgrade, Minnesota, ALC Archive.
116. Anniversary History, Red Oak Grove Lutheran Church, Austin, Minnesota, ALC Archive.
117. Anniversary History, St. Paul's English Lutheran Church, Preston, Minnesota, ALC Archive.
118. Anniversary History, Comstock Norwegian Evangelical Lutheran Church, Comstock, Minnesota, ALC Archive.
119. *Fiftieth Anniversary Rock Valle Ladies' Aid*, ALC Archive.
120. *Fergus Falls Journal*, 2/3/1910, Otter Tail County Historical Society.
121. Hong, *The Book of a Century*, p. 20.
122. Mrs. R. O. Brandt, "Social Aspects of Prairie Pioneering," *NASR* 7 (1933):16-17 and Anniversary History, Reque Lutheran Church, Scott Township, Minnesota, ALC Archive.
123. The women's group of Jackson Lake Lutheran in Amboy, Minnesota was able both to enhance their own congregation and support a female Norwegian-American artist, Sarah Rougland. They purchased her altar painting, "The Last Supper," for $50.00 in 1897.
124. Anniversary History, Salem Lutheran Church, Hitterdahl, Minnesota, ALC Archive.
125. A partial list of those projects includes: Wild Rice Orphans' Home, blankets; church in Math, N.D., building fund; Glenwood Old Peoples' Home; new church at Big Grove; girls' homes at Entumini and in China; women

missionaries; Minnie Saboe in China; Fairview and Thomas Hospitals, Minneapolis; St. Olaf College building fund and Pacific Lutheran College; clothing to needy in Canada, the Dakotas, and Montana; sewing kits were made and sent to Norway; old and new Christmas cards and soap sent to China; birthday gift sent to Mrs. Helen Nelson. *West Crow Ladies Aid History*, Belgrade, Minnesota, ALC Archive.

126. Anniversary History, Bear Creek Lutheran Church, Grand Meadow, Minnesota, ALC Archive.
127. Mrs. Rueben Tollefson, Central Lutheran Church, Edgerton, Wisconsin, WMF, box 22, ALC Archive.
128. Anniversary History, Waterloo Ridge Lutheran Church, Dorchester, Minnesota, ALC Archive.
129. Anniversary History, Rothsay Lutheran Church, Rothsay, Minnesota, ALC Archive.
130. Anniversary History, Bethlehem Lutheran Church, Fergus Falls, Minnesota, ALC Archive.
131. Mrs. Moe, WMF, box 22, ALC Archive.
132. Mrs. M. O. Wee, "Mrs. Hannah Rønning," n.d., WMF, ALC Archive.
133. Mrs. K. J. Hansen, "Beginnings," 1947, WMF, box 2, ALC Archive.
134. Lydia Bredesen Sundby, "The Touch of the Handmaid," in Preus, *Norsemen Found a Church*, pp. 365-78.
135. Mrs. Th. Eggen, "Mrs. T. H. Dahl," in Women's Missionary Federation of the Evangelical Lutheran Church, *Some Marthas and Marys*, p. 19.
136. Mrs. Th. Eggen, "The Women's Missionary Federation of the United Church Previous to the Union in 1917," October 17, 1917, WMF, box 2, ALC Archive.
137. Mrs. M. O. Wee, "Reminiscences," n.d., WMF, box 11, ALC Archive.
138. Fergus Falls Circuit, WMF, box 31, ALC Archive.
139. Katharina Blilie, "Historical Script, 1952," WMF, box 2, ALC Archive.
140. Among the officers and committeewomen were Anna Skabo Stub (Mrs. H. G.), first vice president, 1917-20, and treasurer, 1920-23; Delia Davidson Ylvisaker (Mrs. I. D.), recording secretary, 1917-20, and general president, 1920-28; Emma Galby Brandt (Mrs. O.E.), board member at large, 1920-23; and Inga Holby Bøckman (Mrs. M. O.), treasurer, 1917-20. There appears to have been an effort to represent all the merging organizations in the leaderhip of the WMF.
141. Clara Rygh, "A Look Back Through the Years," n. d., WMF, box 2, ALC Archive.
142. Mathilde Rasmussen, "The First Decade of the WMF," n.d., WMF, box 2, ALC Archive.
143. Mrs. Amanda Ekem, n. d., WMF, box 11, ALC Archive.
144. Lydia Bredesen Sundby, WMF, box 23, ALC Archive.
145. Lena Dahl, "WMF," 1919, WMF, ALC Archive.
146. WMF Board Minutes, vol. 1, pp. 0028, 0068, WMF, ALC Archive.
147. Ibid., p. 0097.

148. Ibid., 9/1/19, p. 0011.
149. Ibid., 9/17/17, p. 0015.
150. The Minutes of the Board of Trustees, 1917-1924, 9/3/19, pp. 172-73, Norwegian Lutheran Church in America, ALC Archive.
151. Ibid., 3/5/18.
152. Ibid., 3/19/18.
153. Ibid., vol. 1, p. 0042.
154. Ibid., 6/9/20, p. 0083.
155. Ibid.
156. Robert Pierce Beaver, *All Loves Excelling* (Grand Rapids: Eerdmans, 1968); Elizabeth Howell Verdesi, *In But Still Out: Women in the Church* (Philadelphia: The Westminister Press, 1973).
157. Although this motivation was not explicitly expressed by those involved, the validity of this interpretation is supported by the centrality of the *Catechism* in the religious life of their communities and the conviction that there is continuity between the articulated doctrine of a group and the lived faith of its members.

CHAPTER FIVE

1. Virginia Lieson Breteson and Christa Ressmeyer Klein, "American Women in Ministry: A History of Protestant Beginning Points," in Ruether and McLaughlin, *Women of Spirit*, pp. 302, 320-21; Gracia Grindal, "Thea Rønning: First Hauge Synod Woman Missionary to China," paper, Decorah, Iowa, n.d., p. 4.
2. Breteson and Klein, "American Women in Ministry," pp. 303 and *passim*.
3. "Memories of Nils Brandt," *Decorah Journal*, July 23, 1970.
4. Lulla Hjort Preus, *Symra*, 1911, p. 148.
5. *Kirkelig maanedstidende*, 1 July 1867, cited by Narveson, "The Norwegian Lutheran Academies," p. 207.
6. Narveson, "The Norwegian Lutheran Academies," pp. 184-226.
7. Augsburg, founded by the Conference in 1869, combined prep school, college department, and seminary. Augsburg became coed in 1921; Luther did so in 1936.
8. *Kirelig maanedstidende*, 1 April 1869, cited in Narveson, "The Norwegian Lutheran Academies," pp. 193-94.
9. St. Olaf College Archive, Northfield, Minnesota.
10. Questionnaires used in Julie Peterson, " 'Pluck and Perseverance': The History of Women at St. Olaf College, 1874-1914." (M.A. thesis, Skidmore College, 1975.) The history of St. Olaf College has been well preserved in a fine and admirably organized archive and recorded in several books. On the occasions of its seventy-fifth and one hundredth anniversaries, large volumes were published: William C. Benson, *High on Manitou: A History of St. Olaf College* (Northfield: The St. Olaf College Press, 1949); Joseph M. Shaw, *History of St. Olaf College*,

1874-1974 (Northfield: The St. Olaf College Press, 1974). Shaw identifies two foci of St. Olaf education: worldly knowledge and Lutheran religious training. These are parallel to the first two characteristics noted here.

11. Peterson, "Pluck and Perseverance," p. 39.
12. An excellent account of this struggle and a fine interpretation of its significance related to coeducation and the role of women is found in Janice L. Shook, "Old Mohn Hall: Symbol of St. Olaf's Coeducation Struggle," St. Olaf College, n.d.
13. *Viking*, 1905, p. 29.
14. *Manitou Messenger*, February 1907.
15. Shaw, *A History of St. Olaf College*, p. 14.
16. Ida Rogne Farseth, "Diary," St. Olaf College Archive.
17. *Manitou Messenger*, December 1892.
18. Petra Hagen Diary, NAHA Archive.
19. *Manitou Messenger*, December 1892.
20. Petra Hagen Diary.
21. *Viking*, 1904, p. 155.
22. Ibid.
23. Ibid., p. 149.
24. Peterson, "Pluck and Perseverance," p. 16.
25. Georgina Dieson Hegland, *As It Was in the Beginning* (Northfield: The St. Olaf College Press, 1950), pp. 22-23, cited by Peterson, "Pluck and Perseverance."
26. *Manitou Messenger*, January 1981.
27. Peterson, "Pluck and Perseverance," pp. 49-50.
28. Emma Quie Bonhus, "We Live in Deeds, Not Years," *The Friend* 16 (July 1939): 14.
29. Women's Social League, "Minutes book," St. Olaf College Archive.
30. *Viking*, 1904, p. 35.
31. Peterson, "Pluck and Perseverance," p. 57.
32. Agnes Mellby to President Kildahl, 1903, cited in ibid., p. 54.
33. Peterson, "Pluck and Perseverance," p. 56.
34. Henrietta, class of 1918, was the first female graduate of St. Olaf to earn a Ph.D. when she received hers in 1926; she was a professor of economic history at Harvard. Nora was a bacteriologist who worked for Hormel and later taught at St. Olaf. Henrietta and Nora were both active in the American Association of University Women and their local Lutheran congregations. Carol Jenson, "The Larson Sisters: Three Careers in Contrast," in *Women of Minnesota: Selected Biographical Essays*, ed. Barbara Stuhler and Gretchen Kreuter (St. Paul: Minnesota Historical Society, 1977), pp. 301-24.
35. Agnes Larson to Clemens M. Granskou, May 10, 1960, cited by Jenson, "The Larson Sisters," p. 308.
36. Agnes Larson to Clemens M. Granskou, March 21, 1942, ibid.
37. *Catalogue for 1894 and Announcements for 1895 and 1896: The Lutheran Ladies' Seminary*, Lutheran Ladies' Seminary, ALC Archive.
38. Todd Walsh, "The Lutheran Ladies' Seminary of Red Wing, Minnesota (1894-1920)," Macalaster College, 1982, pp. 11-14.

39. *Twenty-fifth Annual Catalogue of the Lutheran Ladies' Seminary and School of Music*, 1919-1920, p. 8.
40. Rev. J. R. Baumann, "Baccalaureate Sermon, 1908," Lutheran Ladies' Seminary (hereafter LLS), Goodhue County Historical Society, Red Wing, Minnesota.
41. Norma Thronson Kammen, "Personal History," LLS, box 5.
42. *1884 Catalogue*, pp. 14-15. A double-length postcard was issued with a panoramic view of the ladies marching two-by-two to Sunday morning worship.
43. Walsh makes much of the German influence on LLS, "The Lutheran Ladies' Seminary," pp. 44-45, 47-48, 49-50, first as it contributed to the school's growth, and then as a factor in its decline between 1914 and 1919.
44. "Class Day at Ladies' Sem.," unidentified newspaper clipping, LLS.
45. Martha Reishus Langemo, "A History of the LLS, Red Wing, Minnesota, 1967," LLS.
46. *1919 Catalogue*, p. 10.
47. Langemo, "A History of the Lutheran Ladies' Seminary," pp. 4-5.
48. *Twenty-fifth Annual Catalogue*, p. 9.
49. Langemo, "A History of the Lutheran Ladies' Seminary," p. 10.
50. Ibid., p. 11.
51. Lillian Seebach, "School-Girl Days: A Memory Book, 1910," LLS; Jo Riveland, "My Commencement, 1911," LLS.
52. Walsh, "The Lutheran Ladies' Seminary," p. 25.
53. Josephine Riveland, "Presentation of the Peace Pipe at L.L.S., n.d." Goodhue County Historical Society, cited ibid., pp. 25-26.
54. Jo Riveland, "My Commencement, 1911," LLS.
55. *Twenty-fifth Annual Catalogue*, p. 9.
56. For example: Lydia Bredesen Sundby was a grandniece of Elisabeth and Vihlhelm Koren and a district and general president of the Women's Missionary Federation; Laura Forde was a daughter of Rev. Nils and Nora Otilia Erickson Forde and a teacher at LLS; Bessie Fries Gullixson was the wife of Luther Seminary president; Valborg Hjort was a granddaughter of Rev. Ove J. and Christine Hjort; Emma Brandt Naeseth was a daughter of Rev. R. O. and Thallette Brandt and a granddaughter of Rev. Nils and Diderikke Otteson Brandt; Henrietta Preus was a daughter of Rev. C. K. and Lulla Hjort Preus; Idella Haugen Preus was the wife of the governor of Minnesota; and Sibyl and Slema Ylvisaker were daughters of Rev. I. D. Ylvisaker, president of the North Dakota Synod, and Delia Davidson Ylvisaker, the second general president of the Women's Missionary Federation.
57. Walsh, "The Lutheran Ladies' Seminary," pp. 51-52.
58. It is generally believed that the second fire was a result of arson. For the details of the argument see ibid., pp. 63-66.
59. Richard W. Solberg, *Lutheran Higher Education in North America* (Minneapolis: Augsburg Publishing House, 1985).
60. Ibid., pp. 102, 107-8, 276.
61. Rev. H. O. Hendrikson, *In Retrospect: A History of the Lutheran Normal School* (n.p.: A Committee of Alumni, 1958), p. 197.

62. Ibid., p. 15.
63. Ibid., p. 205.
64. Ibid., pp. 123-79.
65. Ibid., p. 23.
66. Ibid., pp. 32-36.
67. Ibid., pp. 37-39.
68. Ibid., p. 26.
69. Ibid., pp. 210-11.
70. Ibid., pp. 213-14.
71. Ibid., p. 46.
72. Ibid., p. 198.
73. A survey of the birth date and place of the 308 teachers whose last names begin with *A*, *B*, or *C* listed in Olaf Morgan Norlie, compiler and ed., *School Calendar, 1824-1924: A Who's Who among Teachers in the Norwegian Lutheran Synods of America* (Minneapolis: Augsburg Publishing House, 1924) shows that of the 88 female teachers none was born prior to 1870, 14.7% were born prior to 1880, and 90.9% (eighty women) were born in the United States. In contrast, of the 220 male teachers 56% were born prior to 1870 and less than 40% were born in the United States. While women were only 28.5% of the total; they were 39.2% of those born in the United States and 60% of those born after 1880 and 66.3% of those who were born after 1880 in the U.S. My assertation that American-born women were providing more of the teaching in the early 1900s is based on the fact that in the decade of 1880-1890 there were thirty-three future female teachers were born and thirty-four future male teachers; in the following decade the number of women increased to thirty-four while the number of men decreased to fifteen. If these teachers began their careers between ages fifteen and twenty, an equal number of women and men commenced teaching in the years 1895-1905 and twice as many women as men did so in the years 1905-1915.
74. Of the sixty-five female teachers from Norlie whose careers I analyzed, fourteen attended or graduated from St. Olaf, twenty-four from the Lutheran Normal School in Madison, and twelve from Lutheran Ladies' Seminary. There were a few cases in which one women attended two of these institutions and many in which a woman was a student at several different schools. In addition to public high schools and other Lutheran schools the places at which these teachers studied included Chicago Music College, Milwaukee-Downer College, University of Minnesota, Northwestern School of Music, Drake University, Moorhead State Teachers' College, the University of Chicago, and Oxford University. Not quite three-quarters (forty-eight of the sixty-five, or 73.8%) reported receiving at least a portion of their education at a Lutheran school.
75. Because some women reported teaching in more than one sort of school, the total number of the sample (sixty-five) is exceeded by the number of responses. Twenty-nine taught in parochial schools; twenty-eight in common schools; eight in high schools; four in academies; three in normal schools; seven in seminaries; sixteen in colleges; nine in other sorts of institutions.

76. Norlie, *School Calendar*, p. 27.
77. In this sample of sixty-five only twenty-one women were married. This figure is, however, misleading, as Norlie's information was gathered in the early 1920s; as nearly half of the women were born after 1900 they were less than thirty years old at that time. Given that none of the women who married did so before age twenty-one and sixteen did so after age twenty-five, it seems safe to assume that others married in subsequent years.
78. Norlie, *School Calendar*, p. 73.
79. Only eight of the sixty-five teachers were identified as from clergy families. Fifty were not. Seven could not be identified.
80. One third of the married women in this sample were married to clergymen. Two of those seven came from clerical families.
81. Norlie, *School Calendar*, p. 69.
82. Ibid., p. 84.
83. Raaen, *Measure My Days*, pp. 19-20.
84. Ibid., p. 119.
85. Eva Thortvedt, S707, Northwest Minnesota Historical Center, Moorhead State University, Moorhead, Minnesota.
86. Ingeborg Sponland, *My Reasonable Service* (Minneapolis: Augsburg Publishing House, 1938), pp. 66-67.
87. *Oxford Dictionary of the Christian Church*, second edition, s.v. "Deaconess."
88. The *Oxford Dictionary of the Christian Church* attributed the cause of this disappearance to a decline in adult baptisms and abuses by deaconesses: they "arrogated to themselves ministerial functions . . . they administered Holy Communion women, read the Scriptures in public . . ." (p. 381). The recent work of scholars such as Elizabeth Schüssler Fiorenza and Suzanne F. Wemple concerning the loss of female leadership in the early church and the misogyny of the hierarchy in the early Middle Ages suggests that the evidence might bear reinterpretation.
89. For a discussion of opposition to the Beguines in the thirteenth century see Brenda M. Bolton, "Mulieres Sanctae," in *Women in Medieval Society*, ed. Susan Mosher Stuard (Philadelphia: University of Pennsylvania Press, 1976), pp. 141-58.
90. Susan Corey Everson, "The Demise of a Movement: A Study of Norwegian Lutheran Deaconesses in America," paper, University of Minnesota, May 1979, p. 4 and *Oxford Dictionary of the Christian Church*, s.v. "Kaiserswerth."
91. Sponland, *My Reasonable Service*, p. 28.
92. Women's Missionary Federation of the Evangelical Lutheran Church. *Some Marthas and Marys*, p. 31.
93. Sponland, *My Reasonable Service*, pp. 20-21.
94. Ibid., p. 41.
95. Ibid., pp. 44, 61.
96. This decline and its sources are well analyzed in Everson, "The Demise of a Movement."
97. Ibid., pp. 7-8.

98. Ibid., pp. 6-7.
99. Ibid., p. 16.
100. Sponland, *My Reasonable Service*, p. 61.
101. Ibid., p. 147.
102. *Some Marthas and Marys*, p. 59,
103. This "new and unfamiliar venture" lasted through only one contract due to Sister Laura Eng's illness and the congregation's lack of funds. Katherine Blilie, "50th Anniversary, First Parish Worker," WMF, box 11, ALC Archive.
104. Sponland, *My Reasonable Service*, pp. 70-71.
105. Ibid., p. 67.
106. Everson, "The Demise of a Movement," p. 10.
107. *The Norwegian Lutheran Deaconesses' Home and Hospital: A Brief History* (n.p., 1923), p. 12.
108. Sponland, *My Reasonable Service*, p. 69.
109. Indeed, there were teachers who lived their entire lives and pursued their careers without marrying, but it was not assumed that a woman's choice of teaching as career was a choice against marriage and motherhood.
110. "A Word About Missions: By Women, For Women," WMF, box 2, ALC Archive.
111. Grindal, "Thea R∅nning," p. 4.
112. For a detailed study of female involvement in missions see Beaver, *All Loves Excelling*. Beaver's volume was written prior to recent feminist work in women's history. Some of the interpretations that perspective suggests may be found in Barbara Welter, "She Hath Done What She Could: Protestant Women's Missionary Careers in Nineteenth-Century America," in *Women in American Religion*, ed. Janet Wilson James (Philadelphia: University of Pennsylvania Press, 1978), pp. 111-26; and in Joan Jacobs Brumberg, *Mission for Life: The Story of the Family of Adoniram Judson* (New York: The Free Press, 1980).
113. This gathering of pennies began as early as 1800 with the organization of the Boston Female Society for Missionary Purposes. Beaver, *All Loves Excelling*, pp. 14, 17-19.
114. Ibid., pp. 85-114.
115. According to Beaver, this process took place in the half century following 1910.
116. Nelson, *The Lutherans in North America*, p. 280.
117. Ibid.
118. Ibid., p. 279.
119. Henderikson, *In Retrospect*, pp. 83-84.
120. Ibid.
121. Alma A. Guttersen and Regina Hilleboe Christensen, eds., *Souvenir "Norse-American Women" 1825-1925* (Minneapolis: The Lutheran Free Church Publishing Co., 1926), p. 344.
122. *Lysets Seier: Skisser og fortaellinger fra missionsmarken* (Minneapolis: Augsburg Publishing House, 1910), p. 9.
123. Guttersen and Christensen, *Souvenir*, p. 344.

124. Martha Stolee, WMF, ALC Archive.
125. Guttersen and Christensen, *Souvenir*, pp. 348-49.
126. Nelson, *Lutherans in North America*, p. 280.
127. Grindal, "Thea Rønning," p. 23. In this section I have relied heavily on the important work done by Grindal.
128. Ibid., pp. 18-19.
129. Ibid., pp. 27-28.
130. *Budbearen*, 23 March 1895, p. 184, ibid., "Thea Rønning," p. 35.
131. Grindal, "Thea Rønning," pp. 31-32.
132. *Some Marthas and Marys*, p. 79.
133. The Rev. Joseph Titlie, "Agnes Margaret Kittelsby," in *Some Marthas and Marys*, pp. 67-74.
134. Ibid., p. 73.
135. Sponland, *My Reasonable Service*, p. 110.
136. Ibid.

CHAPTER SIX

1. Mrs. M. O. Wee, "Reminiscences," n.d., "Pioneer Pastors' Scrapbook," WMF, ALC Archive.
2. Larsen, *Laur. Larsen*, p. 336.
3. Henrietta Melia Larson and Kenneth Wiggins Porter, *History of Humble Oil and Refining Company* (New York: Harpers, 1959); Jensen, "The Larson Sisters," pp. 311-19.
4. "Hannah Jensen Kempfer," Biography Files, Ottertail County Historical Society.
5. Hannah Harris, Oral History, No. S770, Northwest Minnesota Historical Center.
6. Cecyle S. Neidle, *America's Immigrant Women* (New York: Hippocrene Books, Inc., 1975), p. 223.
7. Janet L. Langlois, "Belle Gunness, the Lady Bluebeard: Narrative Use of a Deviant Woman," in *Women's Folklore, Women's Culture*, Rosan A. Jordan and Susan J. Kalcik, eds. (Philadelphia: University of Pennsylvania Press, 1985), pp. 109-24.
8. Lovoll, *The Promise of America*, p. 143.
9. Buckely, "Martha Ostenso."
10. "Pioneer Pastors' Wives Scrapbook," WMF, ALC Archives.
11. Guttersen and Hilleboe, *Souvenir*.

Bibliography

Primary and Contemporary Materials

Blegen, Theodore C., ed. and trans. "Immigrant Women and the American Frontier: Three Early 'America Letters.' " *Norwegian American Studies and Records* 4 (1929):14-29.

Brandt, Mrs. R. O. "Social Aspects of Prairie Pioneering: The Reminiscences of a Pioneer Pastor's Wife." *Norwegian American Studies and Records* 7 (1933):1-46.

Bredesen, Adolph. "Pastor Nils Brandt's *rerindringer fra aarene 1851 til 1855.*" *Symra: en aarbog for norske paa begge sider af havet* (1907), pp. 97-122.

Bremer, Fredrika. *The Homes of the New World: Impressions of America.* 2 vols. Translated by Mary Howitt. New York: Harper and Brothers, Publishers, 1853.

Cannon, Jennie Vennerström. *Watershed Drama: Battle Lake, Minnesota.* Berkeley: privately printed, 1943.

Erickson, Alfred O. "Scandinavia, Wisconsin." *Norwegian American Studies and Records* 15 (1949):185-209.

Estness, Borghild T. *Josie Rykken's Family.* Gardena, California: Xenos Books, 1983.

Fedde, Elizabeth, "Diary, 1883-38," Translated and edited by Beulah Folkedahl. *Norwegian American Studies and Records* 20 (1959):170-96.

Folkedahl, Beulah, ed. and trans. "Norwegians Become American." *Norwegian American Studies and Records* 21 (1962):95-135.

Guttersen, Alma A., and Regina Hilleboe Christensen, eds. *Souvenir "Norse-American Women" 1825-1925.* Minneapolis: The Lutheran Free Church Publishing Co., 1926.

Henderikson, H. O., ed., *In Retrospect: A History of the Lutheran Normal School, Madison, Minnesota, 1892-1932.* n.p.: Published by a Committee of Alumni, 1958.

Jacobson, Abraham. "A Pioneer Pastor's Journey to Dakota in 1861." Translated by J. N. Jacobson. *Norwegian American Studies and Records* 6 (1931):53-65.

Jacobson, Clara. "Memories from Perry Parsonage." *Norwegian American Studies and Records* 14 (1944):139-58.

Koren, Elisabeth. *The Diary of Elisabeth Koren, 1853-1855*. Translated and edited by David T. Nelson. Northfield: Norwegian-American Historical Association, 1955.

Langemo, Martha Reishus. "A History of the Lutheran Ladies Seminary, Red Wing, Minnesota, 1967." Goodhue County Historical Society, Red Wing, Minnesota.

Levorsen, Barbara. "Early Years in Dakota." *Norwegian American Studies and Records* 21 (1962):158-97.

_____. "Our Bread and Meat." *Norwegian American Studies and Records* 22 (1963):178-97.

_____. *The Quiet Conquest*. Hawley, Minnesota: The Hawley Herald, 1974.

Lysets Seier: Skisser og fortaellinger fra missionsmarken. Minneapolis: Augsburg Publishing House, 1910.

Moorhead, Minnesota. Northwest Minnesota History Center. Moorhead State University. Cheston, Mary Godley Starr. "Seedtime at Ullman," 1902.

_____. Oral History S747, Johanna Aune.

_____. Oral History S768, Mabel Enger.

_____. Oral History S769, Mabel Fynskov.

_____. Oral History S770, Hannah Harris.

_____. Oral History S707, Eva Thortvedt.

Munch, Caja. *The Strange American Way: Letters of Caja Munch from Wiota, Wisconsin, 1855-1859*. Translated by Helene Munch and Peter A. Munch. Carbondale: Southern Illinois Univeristy Press, 1970.

Naeseth, Caroline Mathilde Koren. "Memories from Little Iowa Parsonage." Translated by Henriette C. K. Naeseth. *Norwegian American Studies and Records* 13 (1943):66-74.

Norlie, Olaf Morgan. *Ho Ga Te Me (She Gave to Me): A Centennial Sketch of Martha Karolina (Juel) Norlie, 1846-1918, a Norwegian-American Pioneer*. Northfield: Eilron Mimeopress, 1946.

Northfield, Minnesota. Norwegian American Historical Association. Papers 38, Bolette Marie Stub Bergh.

_____. Papers 746, Mathilde Berg Grevstad.

_____. Papers 174, Martha Hove Hougstad.

_____. Papers 173, Nellie S. Johnson Houkom.

_____. Papers 672, Clara Jacobson.

_____. Papers 210, Gunhild Andrine Jacobsdatter Larsen.

_____. Papers 389, Mary Syverson Torbenson.

Preus, Caroline Dorothea Margrethe Keyser. *Linka's Diary on Land and Sea, 1845-1864.* Translated and edited by Johan Carl Keyser Preus and Diderikke Margrethe Brandt Preus. Minneapolis: Augsburg Publishing House, 1952.

Raaen, Aagot. *Grass of the Earth: Immigrant Life in the Dakota Country.* Northfield: Norwegian-American Historical Association, 1950.

_____. *Measure of My Days.* Fargo: North Dakota Institute for Regional Studies, 1953.

Red Wing Minnesota, Goodhue County Historical Society, Lutheran Ladies Seminary, Box 4, Clara Allen (Mrs. Aikan Brooks Sheldon), "The Girl Graduate: Her Own Book."

_____. Edith Quarve, "School-Girl Days: A Memory Book."

_____. Josephine Riveland, "My Commencement."

_____. Lillian Seebach, "School-Girl Days: A Memory Book."

Reiersen, Johan R. "Norwegians in the West in 1844: A Contemporary Account." Translated and edited by Theodore C. Blegen. *Norwegian American Studies and Records* 1 (1926):110-25.

Reishus, Martha. *The Rag Rug.* New York: Vantage Press, Inc., 1955.

St. Paul, Minnesota. American Lutheran Church Archive. Biography files. Larsen, Karen. *Ingeborg Astrup Larsen: Her Family and Girlhood in Norway.* Northfield: privately printed, 1958.

_____. Sonnack, *Paul G. Thorvald Olsen Burntvedt (May 29, 1888—May 12, 1960): An Oral History Project.*

_____. Sundby, Mrs. G. A. (Lydia Bredesen). "Parsonage Memories—Stoughton, WI, 1881-1902."

Sponland, Ingeborg. *My Reasonable Service.* Minneapolis: Augsburg Publishing House, 1938.

Stub, Dr. H. G. *"Fra fars og mors liv."* Symra: en aarbog for norske paa begge sider af havet (1907), pp. 14-42.

Sundby, Lydia Bredesen. "Forty Years as a W.M.F." *Women's Missionary Messenger* 23 (July-August 1957):4-5.

Svendsen, Gro Nilsdatter. *Frontier Mother: The Letters of Gro Svendsen.* Translated and edited by Pauline Farseth and Theodore C. Blegen. Northfield: Norwegian-American Historical Association, 1950.

Women's Missionary Federation of the Evangelical Lutheran Church. *Some Marthas and Marys of the N.L.C.A.: Life Sketches of Pioneer Women First in Their Field*. Series One. Minneapolis: Augsburg Publishing House, n.d.

Xan, Erna Oleson. *Wisconsin, My Home: The Story of Thurine Oleson as Told to Her Daughter*. Madison: University of Wisconsin Press, 1950.

Interpretive and Secondary Materials

Aarflot, Andreas. *Hans Nielsen Hauge: His Life and Message*. Translated by Joseph M. Shaw. Minneapolis: Augsburg Publishing House, 1979.

Bannan, Helen M. "Warrior Women: Immigrant Mothers in the Works of their Daughters," *Women's Studies* 6 (1979):165-78.

Barstow, Anne Llewellyn. "The First Generation of Anglican Clergy Wives: Heroines or Whores?" *Historical Magazine of the Protestant Episcopal Church* 52 (March 1983):3-16.

Barton, H. Arnold. "Scandinavian Immigrant Women's Encounter with America," *Swedish Pioneer Historical Quarterly* 25 (1974):37-42.

Benson, William C. *High on Manitou: A History of St. Olaf College, 1874-1949*. Northfield: The St. Olaf College Press, 1949.

Berggreen, Brit, ed., *Scandinavian Peasant Ecotypes*. Oslo: University of Oslo, International Summer School, 1983.

Bernard, Richard M. *The Melting Pot and the Altar: Marital Assimilations in Early Twentieth-Century Wisconsin*. Minneapolis: University of Minnesota Press, 1980.

Blegen, Theodore C. *Norwegian Migration to America*. Northfield: The Norwegian-American Historical Association, 1940. Vol. 2: *The American Transition*.

Boyd, Lois A. "Presbyterian Ministers' Wives—A Nineteenth-Century Portrait," *Journal of Presbyterian History* 59 (Spring 1981):3-17.

Bringeus, Nils-Arvid. "The Communicative Aspect in Ethnology and Folklore," *Ethnologia Scandinavica* (1979), pp. 5-17.

Buckely, Joan Naglestad. "Martha Ostenso: A Critical Study of Her Novels." Ph.D. Dissertation. The University of Iowa, 1976.

_____. "Martha Ostenso: A Norwegian-American Immigrant Novelist," *Norwegian American Studies and Records* 28 (1979):69-81.

Chrislock, Carl H. *Ethnicity Challenged: The Upper Midwest Norwegian-American Experience in World War I*. Topical Studies, vol. 3. Northfield: The Norwegian-American Historical Association, 1981.

Christiansen, Palle Ove. "Peasant Adaptation to Bourgeois Culture? Class Formation and Cultural Redefinition in the Danish Countryside," *Ethnologia Scandinavica* (1978), pp. 98-152.

Christianson, J. R. "Literary Traditions of Norwegian-American Women." In *Makers of An American Immigrant Legacy*, pp. 92-110. Edited by Odd S. Lovoll. Northfield: Norwegian-American Historical Association, 1980.

Christopherson, K. E. "Hallelujahs, Damnations, or Norway's Reformation as Lengthy Process," *Church History* 48 (September 1979):279-89.

Conzen, Kathleen Neils. "Peasants Into Pioneers: Patterns of Intra-Family Land Transmission Among German Immigrants in Rural Minnesota, 1856-1905." Paper, University of Chicago, March 1983.

Cunningham, Barbara. "An Eighteenth-Century View of Femininity as Seen Through the Journals of H. M. Muhlenberg," *Pennsylvania History* 43 (July 1976):197-212.

di Leonardo, Micaela. *The Varieties of Ethnic Experience: Kinship, Class, and Gender Among California Italian-Americans*. Ithaca: Cornell University Press, 1984.

Dorfman, Joseph. *Thorstein Veblen and His America*. New York: The Viking Press, 1934.

Draxten, Nina. *Kristofer Janson in America*. Boston: Twayne Publishers, 1976.

Dye, Nancy Schrom. "Clio's American Daughter: Male History, Female Reality." In *The Prism of Sex*, pp. 9-32. Edited by Julia A. Sherman and Evelyn Torton Beck. Madison: University of Wisconsin Press, 1979.

Everson, Susan Corey. "The Demise of a Movement: A Study of Norwegian Lutheran Deaconesses in America." Paper, University of Minnesota, May 1979.

Fairbanks, Carol, and Sara Brooks Sundberg. *Farm Women on the Prairie Frontier: A Sourcebook for Canada and the United States*. Metuchen: The Scarecrow Press, Inc., 1983.

Fevold, Eugene L. "The Norwegian Immigrant and His Church," *Norwegian American Studies and Records* 23 (1967):3-16.

Fevold, Eugene L., and E. Clifford Nelson. *The Lutheran Church Among Norwegian-Americans: A History of the Evangelical Lutheran Church*. 2 vols. Minneapolis: Augsburg Publishing House, 1960.

Flint, John T. "Historical Role Analysis in the Study of Secularization: The Laity/Clergy Ratio in Norway, 1800-1950," *Journal for the Scientific Study of Religion* 7 (Fall 1968):272-79.

_____. "The Secularization of Norwegian Society," *Comparative Studies in Society and History* 6 (1964):325-44.

Frimannslund, Rigmor. "Farm Community and Neighborhood Community," *The Scandinavian Economic History Review* 4 (1956):62-81.

Frykman, Jonas. "Ritual as Communication," *Ethnologia Scandinavica* (1979), pp. 54-63.

Gjerde, Jon Alan. "Peasants to Bourgeoisie: The Migration from Balestrand, Norway to the Upper Middle West." Ph.D. dissertaion, University of Minnesota, 1982.

Gjerest, Knut. *History of the Norwegian People.* 2 vols. New York: The Macmillan Company, 1915.

Gjerset, Knut, and Ludvig Hektoen. "Health Conditions and the Practice of Medicine Among the Early Norwegian Settlers, 1825-1865," *Norwegian American Studies and Review* 1 (1926):1-59.

Gordon, Milton. *Assimilation in American Life: The Role of Race, Religion, and National Origins.* New York: Oxford University Press, 1964.

Grindal, Gracia. "An Immigrant Woman Views Niagara: The Sketches of Linka Preus." Paper, Decorah, Iowa, n.d.

_____. "The Americanization of Norwegian Pastors' Wives," *Norwegian American Studies and Records* 32 (1989): 199-207.

_____. "Thea Rønning: First Hauge Synod Woman Missionary to China," Paper, Decorah, IA, n.d.

_____. "Three Vignettes and an Idea," Paper, Decorah, Iowa, n.d.

Grosse, I. F. "The Beginnings of St. Olaf College," *Norwegian American Studies and Records* 5 (1930):110-21.

Hagen, Monys Ann. "Norwegian Pioneer Women: Ethnicity on the Wisconsin Agricultural Frontier." M. A. thesis, University of Wisconsin, Madison, 1984.

Hale, Frederick. "The Impact of Kierkegaard's Anticlericalism in Norway," *Studia Theologica* 34 (1980):153-71.

Hampsten, Elizabeth. *Read this Only to Yourself: The Private Writings of Midwestern Women, 1880-1910.* Bloomington: Indiana University Press, 1982.

Hansen, Marcus L. "Immigration and Puritanism," *Norwegian American Studies and Review* 9 (1936):1-28.

Hanssen, Börje. "Common folk and gentlefolk," *Ethnologia Scandinavia* (1973):67-100.

Hareven, Tamara K. "The Family Process: The Historical Study of the Family Cycle," *Journal of Social History* 7 (Spring 1974):322-29.

Hauge Inner Mission Federation. *The Hauge Movement in America.* Minneapolis: The Lutheran Free Church Publishing Company, 1941.

Haugen, Einar. "Language and Immigration," *Norwegian American Studies and Review* 10 (1930):1-43.

_____. *The Norwegian Language in America: A Study in Bilingual Behavior.* Bloomington: Indiana University Press, 1969.

Haugen, Eva Lund, and Einar Haugen, eds. and trans. *Land of the Free: Bjørnstjerne Bjørnson's America Letters, 1880-1881.* Author Series, vol. 5. Northfield: The Norwegian-American Historical Association, 1978.

Hong, Edna. *The Book of a Century: The Centennial History of St. John's Lutheran Church, Northfield, Minnesota.* n.p., [1969].

Hovde, B. J. *The Scandinavian Countries, 1720-1865: The Rise of the Middle Class.* 2 vols. Ithaca: Cornell University Press, 1948.

Hustvedt, Lloyd. *Rasmus Bjørn Anderson: Pioneer Scholar.* Author Series, vol. 2. Northfield: The Norwegian-American Historical Association, 1966.

Jenson, Carol. "The Larson Sisters: Three Careers in Contrast," in *Women of Minnesota: Selected Biographical Essays,* pp. 301-24. Edited by Barbara Stuhler and Gretchen Kreuter. St. Paul: Minnesota Historical Society, 1977.

Jonassen, Christian T. *Value Systems and Personality in a Western Civilization: Norwegians in Europe and America.* Columbus: Ohio State University Press, 1983.

Kimmerle, Marjorie M. "Norwegian-American Surnames," *Norwegian American Studies and Records* 12 (1941):1-32.

Krontoft, Torben. "Factors in Assimilation: A Comparative Study," *Norwegian American Studies and Records* 26 (1974):184-205.

Larsen, Karen. "A Contribution to the Study of the Adjustment of a Pioneer Pastor to American Conditions: Laur. Larsen, 1857-1880," *Norwegian American Studies and Records* 4 (1929):1-14.

_____. *A History of Norway.* Princeton: Princeton University Press, 1948.

_____. *Laur. Larsen: Pioneer College President.* Northfield: Norwegian-American Historical Association, 1936.

Löfgren, Orvar. "Family and Household among Scandinavian Peasants: An Exploratory Essay," *Ethnologia Scandinavica* (1974), pp. 17-52.

Lönnqvist, Bo. "Symbolic Values in Clothing," *Ethnologia Scandinavica* (1979), pp. 92-105.

Lovoll, Odd S. *The Promise of America: A History of the Norwegian-American People*. Minneapolis: University of Minnesota Press, 1984.

Lutz, Charles P., editor. *Church Roots: Stories of Nine Immigrant Groups That Became The American Lutheran Church*. Minneapolis: Augsburg Publishing House, 1985.

Mann, Arthur. *The One and the Many: Relfections on the American Identity*. (Chicago: The University of Chicago Press, 1979).

Molland, Einar. *Church Life in Norway, 1800-1950*. Translated by Harris Kaasa. Minneapolis: Augsburg Publishing House, 1957.

Munch, Peter A. "Authority and Freedom: Controversy in Norwegian-American Congregations," *Norwegian American Studies and Records* 28 (1979):3-34.

_____. "Social Class and Acculturation," in Caja Munch, *The Strange American Way*, pp. 193-248.

Naess, Harald S., ed. *Norwegian Influence on the Upper Midwest: Proceedings of an International Conference*. Duluth: Continuing Education and Extension, University of Minnesota, 1976.

Narveson, B. H. "The Norwegian Lutheran Academies," *Norwegian American Studies and Records* 14 (1944):184-226.

Neidle, Cecyle. *America's Immigrant Women*. New York: Hippocrene Books, Inc., 1975.

Nelson, E. Clifford, ed. *The Lutherans in North America*. Philadelphia: Fortress Press, 1975.

Nelsen, Frank S. "The School Controversy and Norwegian Immigrants," *Norwegian American Studies and Records* 26 (1974):206-19.

Nelson, Marion J. "The Material Culture and Folk Arts of the Norwegians in America," in *Perspectives on American Folk Art*, pp. 79-133. Edited by Ian M. G. Quimby and Scott T. Swank. n.p.: Winterthur Museum, 1980.

Norlie, Olaf Morgan, comp. and ed. *Norsk lutherske prester i Amerika, 1843-1913*. Minneapolis: Augsburg Publishing House, 1914.

_____. *School Calendar, 1824-1924: A Who's Who among Teachers in the Norwegian Lutheran Synods of America*. Minneapolis: Augsburg Publishing House, 1924.

Nydahl, Theodore L. "Social and Economic Aspects of Pioneering as Illustrated in Goodhue County, Minnesota," *Norwegian American Studies and Records* 5 (1930):50-59.

Odland, Martin W. *The Life of Knute Nelson*. Minneapolis: The Lund Press, 1926.

Peterson, Julie " 'Pluck and Perseverence': The History of Women at St. Olaf College, 1874-1914." M.A. thesis, Skidmore College, 1975.

Preus, J[ohan] C[arl] K[eyser]. "From Norwegian State Church to American Free Church," *Norwegian American Studies and Records* 25 (1972):186-224.

_____. *Herman Amberg Preus: A Family History*. n.p.: Preus Family Book Club, 1966.

_____, ed. *Norsemen Found a Church: An Old Heritage in a New Land*. Minneapolis: Augsburg Publishing House, 1953.

Qualey, Carleton C. *Norwegian American Settlement*. Northfield: Norwegian American Historical Association, 1938.

_____. "A Typical Norwegian Settlement: Spring Grove, Minnesota," *Norwegian American Studies and Records* 9 (1936):54-66.

Riley, Glenda. *Frontierswoman: The Iowa Experience*. Ames: The Iowa State University Press, 1981.

Rohne, J. Magnus. *Norwegian Lutheranism up to 1872*. New York: The Macmillian Company, 1926.

Schlissel, L. "Women's Diaries on the Western Frontier," *American Studies* (University of Kansas) 18 (Spring 1977):87-100.

Seller, Maxine S. "Beyond the Stereotype: A New Look at the Immigrant Woman, 1800-1924," *Journal of Ethnic Studies* 3 (Spring 1975):59-70.

_____. "The Education of the Immigrant Woman, 1900-1935," *Journal of Urban History* 4 (1975):307-30.

Semmingsen, Ingrid. "Emigration from Scandinavia," *The Scandinavian Economic History Review* 20 (1972):45-60.

_____. *Norway to America: A History of the Migration*. Translated by Einar Haugen. Minneapolis: University of Minnesota Press, 1978.

_____. "Norwegian Immigration to America during the Nineteenth Century," *Norwegian American Studies and Records* 11 (1940):66-81.

_____. "A Pioneer: Agnes Mathilde Wergeland, 1857-1914." In *Makers of An American Immigrant Legacy*, pp. 111-30. Edited by Odd S. Lovoll. Northfield: Norwegian-American Historical Association, 1980.

Shaw, Joseph M. *History of St. Olaf College, 1874-1974*. Northfield: The St. Olaf Press, 1974.

Shook, Janice L. "Old Mohn Hall: Symbol of St. Olaf's Coeducation Struggle." Paper, St. Olaf College, n.d.

241

Sochen, June. "Frontier Women: A Model for all Women?" *South Dakota History* 7 (Winter 1976):36-56.

Solberg, Richard W. *Lutheran Higher Education in North America.* Minneapolis: Augsurg Publishing House, 1985.

Stratton, Joanna. *Pioneer Women: Voices from the Kansas Frontier.* New York: Simon and Schuster, 1981.

Sundt, Eilert. *On Marriage in Norway.* Translated and with introduction by Michael Drake. Cambridge University Press, 1980.

Sweet, Leonard I. *The Minister's Wife: Her Role in Nineteenth-Century American Evangelicalism.* Philadelphia: Temple University Press, 1983.

Swanson, H. F. "A Pioneer Church Library," *Norwegian American Studies and Records* 11 (1940):57-65.

Verdesi, Elizabeth Howell. *In But Still Out: Women in the Church.* Philadelphia: The Westminster Press, 1973.

Walsh, Todd M. "The Lutheran Ladies' Seminary of Red Wing, Minnesota (1894-1920)." Paper, Macalester College, 1982.

Webster, Janice Reiff. "Domestication and Americanization: Scandinavian Women in Seattle, 1888-1900," *Journal of Urban History* 4 (1975):275-90.

Willson, Thomas B. *History of the Church and State in Norway from the Tenth to the Sixteenth Century.* London: Archibald Constable and Co., Ltd., 1903.

Index

Aadne, Eli, 98
Aaker, Marie, 157
Aarhus, Karen O., 99
Aarthun, Knud, 69
Aasen, Ivar, 31
Addams, Jane, 164, 169
Adolphus, Gustavus, 172
Agneberg, Matilda
  See Johnson, Matilda Agneberg
Ahlstrom, Sydney, ix
Alfsen, Karen, 135
Allen, Clara, 169
Allen, Margaret, 36
Allen, Pres., 164
Americanization
  church's role in, 201
  and education, 170, 175, 179, 194
  of immigrants, 55, 57-58, 102-5, 197-98
  of women, 102-5, 201, 204
  women's societies and, 149-50
"The Americanization of Norwegian Pastors'
  Wives" (Gracia Grindal), 223n
Amtmandens Døtre (*The Governor's
  Daughters*) (Camilla Collett), 20-21
Amundson, Johanna Cornelia
  See Krogness, Johanna Cornelia Amund-
  son
Anderson, Abel, 131, 217n-18n
Anderson, Elizabeth, 131
Anderson, Marie Olson, 123, 217n-18n
Anderson, Martha, 131
Anderson, Rasmus B., 131, 155, 156,
  217n-18n
Ansgar, Archbishop, 21
Arentz, Ingeborg

  See Stub, Ingeborg Arentz
Arndt, Ernst, 25
Arndt, Johann, 45
Arnegaard, Margit, 98
Asbjørnsen, Peter Christen, 19, 31
Assimilation, 8-10
Astrup, Hannah
  See Larsen, Hannah Astrup
Astrup, Hans, 54
Astrup, Nils, 54
Augsburg College, 226n
Awes, Astrid Pernilla Dahl, 189-90

Bache, Søren, 45-46
Backer, Harriet, 1-2
Bakke, Martha, 184
Baptism, 117-18, 121, 124
Baptists, 48, 50
Bartke, Emma, 169
Baumann, J. R., 165
Benson, William C., 226n-27n
Bentsen, Louise, 131
Berg, Mathilde
  See Grevstad, Mathilde Berg
Bergan, Clara
  See Fatland, Clara Bergan
Berger, Brigitte, 207n
Berger, Peter, 207n
Berggreen, Brit, 16, 208n
Bergh, Bolette Stub, 76, 90-91, 103, 123,
  203, 218n
Bergh, J. E., 218n
Bergh, Reverend, 76, 123
Bergh, Sophie

243

Kalhein, Agnes, 169
Kalmar Union, 6, 14, 27
Kellner, Hansfried, 207n
Kempfer, Hannah, 202
Keyser, Caroline (Linka) Dorothea
  Margrethe
  See Preus, Caroline (Linka) Dorothea
  Margrethe
Kielland, Mrs. Gustava, 132
Kierkegaard, Søren, 128
Kildahl, H. B., 182
Kildahl, J. K., 144
Kildahl, J. N., 142
Kildahl, Johan, 158
Kildahl, Nikoline, 158
Kildahl, Pres., 163
Kirelig Maanedstidende, 156
Kittelsby, Agnes Margaret, 162, 164, 192
Kjeldergaard, Ole, 173
Kjosness, Gunder P., 171
Kluver, Birgitte Muus, 53
Knutson, Sønnøva, 76
Koefod, Dorothea
  See Norman, Dorothea Koefod
Koren, Caroline, 87
  See also Naeseth, Caroline M. Koren
Koren, Elisabeth, 49, 50-51, 60, 63, 67, 68,
  69, 73, 76, 81-82, 84, 85, 88-89, 111-12,
  117, 121, 122, 127-28, 199, 216n
  See also Torrison, Elisabeth Koren
Koren, Henriette, 117
Koren, Lina, 158
Koren, Linka, 214n
Koren, Vilhelm, 48, 49, 51, 67, 68, 81-82,
  84, 117, 121, 192
Koshkonong, Wis., 40, 41, 47-48, 52
Krause, L. F. E., 46
Krog, Gina, 21
Krogness, Johanna Cornelia Amundson, 82
Krogness, S. M., 82
Kvasse, Agnes Preus, 218n
Kvasse, Daniel, 218n
Kvindeforening
  See Women's Societies
Kvitrud, Pastor, 220n

Labor
  Norwegian division of, 16-17, 18

and women, 72-74, 82-84
Ladies' Aid
  See Women's Societies
Lady with a Pen: Elise Waerenskjold in Texas
  (Elise Waerenskjold), 211n
Lagerquist, L. DeAne, xiii, xiv
Laity
  in Norwegian Lutheran Church of
  America, 117-18
Landahl, C. W., 191
Landahl, Thea Rønning, 190
  See also Rønning, Thea
Langemo, Martha Reishus, 169
  See also Reishus, Martha
Large Catechism (Martin Luther), 110, 121
Larsen, Gunhild, 66
Larsen, Hannah Astrup, 202
Larsen, Ingeborg, 90
Larsen, Karen Neuberg, 84, 89, 97-98, 130,
  164, 216n
Larsen, Lars (Geilane), 36
Larsen, Lauritz, 48, 84, 97-98, 130, 216n
Larson, Agnes, 163-64
Larson, Henrietta, 163, 202, 227n
Larson, Nora, 163, 227n
Larvik, J. R., 176
Larvik, Sophie Bergh, 176, 177, 179
Laukandt, Bernard F., 166
Lee, Marie, 86-87
Lee, O. H., 86-87
Lehman, Mary Francis
  See Rasmussen, Mary Francis Lehman
Lehne, Anne, 113
Levorsen, Barbara, 72, 73, 78, 123, 203
Lie, Jonas, 21
Lien, Esther, 166
Lindhjem, Ella, 95-96
"Little Lutheran Biographies" (Women's
  Missionary Federation), 60
LLS
  See Lutheran Ladies' Seminary
Lokensgaard, Ole, 173
Lomen, Elizabeth Brandt, 216n
Lovoll, Odd, 95
Lunden, Hage, 93
Luther, Martin, 11, 24, 26, 29, 30, 46, 53,
  110, 115, 128, 131, 132, 141, 150, 157,
  172
Lutheraneren, 147

Lutheran Higher Education in North America (Richard Solberg), 170
Lutheran Ladies' Seminary, 164-70, 200, 228n, 229n
Lutheran Normal School, 170-75, 200, 229n
Lutherans, Norwegian
    compared to Norwegian-American Lutherans, 47
    and women, 4-5
Lutherans, Norwegian-American
    and assimilation, 9
    characteristics of, 107-8, 130
    charity work of, 54-55
    and church contributions, 112-14
    community activities of, 52
    compared to Norwegian Lutherans, 47
    compared to other religions, 107-8
    congregational life of, 109-20
    and deaconesses, 179-85
    development of church, 2
    divisions among, 44-45, 47, 199, 211n
    and doctrinal purity, 44-45
    and education, 52-54, 119-20
    and ethnicity, 6
    and Grundtvigianism, 28, 47
    importance of women's societies to, 200
    and missionaries, 54, 187-88
    and music, 118-19
    personal religion of, 120-32
    practices of, 212n
    religious alternatives for, 130-32
    women in, 4
    women's activities with, 108
    and women's societies, 54
    See also Norwegian Lutheran Church of America (NLCA)
The Lutherans in North America (E. Clifford Nelson), 205n
Luther College, 154, 226n
Lylegrav, Turid, 93

McLaughlin, Eleanor, 222n
Magdalene, Marie, 189
Magelsen, Dr., 130
Magelsen, Karine Neuberg, 130
    See also Neuberg, Karine
Mann, Arthur, xi
Margenbladet, 38

Marion College for Women, 170
Marriage
    age of women at, 230n
    among missionaries, 191, 193
    among second-generation Norwegian-Americans, 218n
    as spur to immigration, 94-95
    and careers, 231n
    celebration of anniversaries, 124
    and community acceptance, 130
    description of weddings, 122-23
    relationships in, 96-101
Marty, Martin E., ix, 1
Matters, Anna, 113
Mead, Sidney E., ix
Measure of My Days (Aagot Raaen), 177
Medicine, 75-76
Mellby, Agnes, 161-63, 164, 192
"Memories of Koshkonong Parsonage" (Marie Lee), 86
Meningen, Ingerid, 118, 222n
Messenger, 189
Methodists, 48, 50, 107-8, 131
Midboe, Thea
    See Felland, Thea Midboe
Mikkel, Gamle, 117
Minerva, 160
Missionaries
    marriage among, 191, 193
    in Norway, 29
    and Norwegian-American Lutherans, 54
    in United States, 51
    women as, 185-93, 194-95, 201
    women's societies and, 142-45
Mission Bladet, 136
Mjøvik, Jørgine, 189
Moe, Mrs., 136
Moe, Flora, 184
Moë, Jørgen, 31
Møen, Lars, 80
Møen, Thorbjør, 117
Mohn, Mrs. Thorbjørn, 162
Mohn, Thorbjørn N., 156, 157, 159
Molland, Einar, 26
Mormons
    See Church of Jesus Christ of the Latter-day Saints
Mueller, Charlotte
    See Dietrichson, Charlotte Mueller

Torbenson, Mary Syverson, 70
Torgerson, Dina, 131
Torgerson, T. A., 131
Torrison, Elisabeth Koren, 218n
  See also Koren, Elisabeth
Torrison, I. B., 218n
Torrison, Inanda Amalie
  See Bredesen, Inanda Amalie Torrison
Torsen, Gunda, 181
Tou, E. H., 54
Trovatten, Ole Knudsen, 47-48
*True Account of America for the Information
  and Help of Peasant and Commoner* (Ole
  Rynning), 37
True Christianity (Ernst Arndt), 25
Truth Unto Godliness (Erik Pontoppidan),
  24, 25, 46
Tryggvessön, Olaf, 22
Tvede, Elise Amalie
  See Waerenskjold, Elise Amalie Tvede
Tverberg, Elise Holland, 188-89

Unitarians, 51, 131
United Church, 45, 211n
Utile Dulci, 160

"The Value of Domestic Education" (Esther
  Lien), 166
Veblen, John, 67
Veblen, Kari Bunde, 72
  See also Bunde, Kari
Vie, Mrs., 76
The Viking, 161, 162
Vossing Correspondence Society of Chicago,
  38

Waerenskjold, Elise Amalie Tvede, 38, 211n
Waerenskjold, William, 211n
Waldeland, Caia Holmboe, 82
Waldeland, O., 82
Walsh, Todd, 164
Weddings
  See Marriage
Wee, Mary Nelson, 141, 143, 147
  See also Nelson, Mary
Wee, M. O., 133, 199

Wee, Mrs. M. O., 133
Welter, Barbara, 217n
Wemple, Suzanne F., 230n
Wergeland, Henrik, 31, 37
Wesley, John, 26
Wexels, W. A., 29, 30
*What Women Want: The Ideas of the
  Movement* (Gayle Graham Yates), 205n
Wheaton, Editor, 115
The White Ribbon (Ulrikk Feldtman Bruun),
  202
Widows
  See Women, unmarried
Winchester, Wis., 116
Winsnes, Hanna, 21
Wisconsin, My Home (Thurine Oleson), 62
Wisløff, Carl, 24
"Wives Submit Yourselves to Your Husbands"
  (Kristofer Janson), 96
"Woman and Her Sphere" (Norma Thron-
  son), 217n
Women
  activities of, 59, 202-3, 207n
  age of at marriage, 230n
  Americanization of, 102-5, 201, 204
  assimilation of, 9-10
  careers of, 175-93, 202, 218n, 222n, 227n
  and churches, 2-3, 4, 108, 117-20, 147-48
  clerical duties of, 109-11
  comparison of Norwegian-American and
    Norwegian, 58-59
  and congregational life, 109-20
  as culture carriers, 89-90, 217n
  as deaconesses, 179-85, 194-95, 201,
    230n
  and doctrinal disputes, 199
  and education, 119-20, 154-75, 200-201
  education of, 193-94
  as homesteaders, 95-96
  and immigration, 1, 62-64, 65, 207n
  labor of, 16-17, 18, 20, 58-60, 72-74,
    82-84
  and marriage, 94-95, 96-101
  and medicine, 75-76
  ministerial roles of, 179, 185, 193, 194-95
  as missionaries, 185-93, 194-95, 201
  ordination of, 205n
  problems of, 67-68

(continued, over)